What people are  saying about

CIRCUMCISION: THE HIDDEN TRAUMA

"I hope *Circumcision: The Hidden Trauma* will be read by men and women because it will force us to confront the unrecognized personal and social harm that results from this practice."
—Sam Keen, Ph.D.,
author of *Fire in the Belly*

"A revealing explanation of the misunderstanding in the medical community about this practice." —Leonard Marino, M.D.,
pediatrician, Plainview, N.Y.

"Goldman's book, though long-overdue, is timely."
—Penelope Leach, Ph.D.,
child development educator,
author of *Your Baby & Child*

"I am very impressed with the depth of Goldman's research and his willingness to deal so thoroughly with the most important question of the possible effect of circumcision on boys."
—Warren Farrell, Ph.D.,
author of *Why Men Are the Way They Are*

"This is an important book, not just for expectant parents, but for the rest of society as well. It contains thought-provoking new information available nowhere else."
—Constance Bean, M.P.H.,
author of *Methods of Childbirth*

"A summons to examine some of our cultural values and rethink how we view and treat children."
—Paul Fleiss, M.D., M.P.H.,
pediatrician, Los Angeles

"This book is required reading for all prospective parents."
—Charles Konia, M.D.,
psychiatrist, Easton, Pa.

CIRCUMCISION
THE HIDDEN TRAUMA

ALSO BY RONALD GOLDMAN

Questioning Circumcision: A Jewish Perspective

The Circumcision Resource Center is a nonprofit educational organization with the purpose of providing information and support to the
public and professionals concerning the practice of circumcision.
The Center offers publications, consultation, telephone counseling,
lectures, and seminars. For more information contact

Circumcision Resource Center
P.O. Box 232
Boston, MA 02133
(617) 523-0088
www.circumcision.org
crc@circumcision.org

CIRCUMCISION
The Hidden Trauma

How an American Cultural Practice Affects Infants
and Ultimately Us All

Ronald Goldman, Ph.D.

Foreword by
Ashley Montagu, Ph.D.

VANGUARD PUBLICATIONS
Boston

Vanguard Publications
P.O. Box 8055
Boston, MA 02114

01 00 99 98 97   5 4 3 2 1

Photographs used with permission of The Saturday Evening Post © 1981
Line drawings used with permission of Edward Wallerstein © 1980

Cataloging-in-Publication Data

Goldman, Ronald.
    Circumcision, the hidden trauma : how an American cultural practice affects infants and ultimately us all / Ronald Goldman.
    p. cm.
    Includes bibliographical references and index.
    ISBN 0-9644895-3-8

    1. Circumcision—Psychological aspects. 2. Circumcision—Social aspects.
    3. Psychic trauma in children. I. Title.

RD590.G65 1997   617.463'059
        96-20217

UNIVERSITIES AND PROFESSIONAL ORGANIZATIONS
Discounts are available on bulk purchases of this book. Excerpts can also be created to fit your specific needs. Contact the publisher for more information.

To the children of the future

Our very life depends on everything's recurring till we answer from within.

—Robert Frost

Contents

Foreword

As an anthropologist, I have been interested for many years in the rituals, practices, and myths adopted by different societies. One of the most enduring of these practices is circumcision, which has been practiced by various cultures for thousands of years. It is typically a rite of passage marking a transition from one status to another. Such rites of passage, celebrated at birth, puberty, marriage, and death, are frequently associated with certain procedures entailing bodily mutilation. This removal of a part of the body, however, is not regarded in most societies as a mutilation. More often than not, it is seen as a religious consecration that makes the individual holy and invested with a special status.

In the United States we have invented "reasons" to replace religion in justifying circumcision. Myths associated with circumcision have become an accepted part of our society. Thus far the power of precedent and social custom has resisted the force of knowledge, reason, and logic.

The perpetuation of myths about circumcision in this country is not unlike the persistence of myths in other, divergent societies. Those in so-called civilized societies may believe that they are too "advanced" to believe in myths, but that, too, is a cultural myth. We are all subject to believing in myths. At this juncture in our history we should remember that civilization is not a gift, but an achievement, and that civilization is a race between education and catastrophe.

One outstanding characteristic that marks us as human beings is our educability. We have had to learn almost everything we know and do from other human beings, beginning with our principal caregivers, our parents, and then our teachers and others. Consequently, to be human is to be in danger, for we are capable of being taught unsound things as well as sound ones. Therefore, we need good teachers who will challenge entrenched beliefs and practices by setting out the facts that need to be considered in arriving at a just decision.

This is why I welcome, as I am sure the reader will, Ronald Goldman's beautiful and powerful book on circumcision. It is the most enlightening and dependable examination of a most important aspect of human life. It is a book that is designed to be helpful to both the curious and the perplexed. In this Ronald Goldman succeeds admirably, for he writes clearly and simply from a wide background of knowledge, and is a sympathetic guide through the labyrinth of controversy to the truths that he so ably makes available. It is an illuminating book, and I hope it will be widely read.

Ashley Montagu, Ph.D.

Note: Dr. Montagu's distinguished career as an anthropologist has spanned six decades. He has taught at several universities and has received many honorary degrees and awards for his outstanding work on human nature and development. Dr. Montagu has authored over fifty books, including *On Being Human, The Natural Superiority of Women, The American Way of Life, The Nature of Human Aggression, The Peace of the World, Life Before Birth, Living and Loving, The World of Humanity,* and *Sex, Man, and Society.*

Preface

I have been curious about circumcision since I was about eleven years old. I was reading a book on sex and saw a diagrammatic illustration of a penis with a foreskin. Having never before seen a foreskin in a locker room or elsewhere, I could make no sense of the drawing. Noticing the foreskin in an illustration or in a locker room is a common male experience that is not often talked about.

Over the years and in the course of writing this book, I have had lots of questions about circumcision. I have discovered that many others have questions, too. The perspectives of both traditional and more recent, innovative psychological theories have been helpful in addressing some of these. To investigate other issues, I have generally relied on the existing medical, psychological, and sociological literature and research conducted by the Circumcision Resource Center, a nonprofit educational organization that I founded. This work has consisted of hundreds of contacts with men, parents, and mental health and medical professionals. Small group meetings with circumcised men, clinical experience, and independent surveys of attitudes toward circumcision also contributed to a greater understanding of the deep feelings some people have about circumcision.

Since the medical arguments concerning circumcision have been discussed at length elsewhere, I have included only a short summary here. The Resources section contains recommended books

xvi   *Preface*

for those who seek a more detailed medical critique. Those interested in a discussion from a Jewish viewpoint are referred to my book *Questioning Circumcision: A Jewish Perspective.*

My main purpose is to increase awareness by bringing together, for general readers and professionals, much of what is known that relates to circumcision and evaluating its meaning. In areas where no studies exist, I examine the possibilities. A secondary purpose is to encourage research into the many unanswered questions. However, my position is that there is already enough information available to challenge prevailing assumptions and practice.

I gratefully acknowledge those people who made helpful comments on the manuscript. They include Jean Alonso, Barbara Brandt, Lance Carden, Gena Corea, Chris Farrow, Michael Kristan, Hilda Scott, Steven Styos, and Suzanne Wymelenberg. I especially want to thank Myron Sharaf, Barbara Nash, Richard Schwartzman, Maggie Carr, and David Chamberlain for their assistance, and Jack Engler for his guidance and encouragement. Others who have offered valuable help were Marilyn Milos, Hanny Lightfoot-Klein, Tim Hammond, and Rosemary Romberg. I am also thankful to Michael Brooks, Donald Bryant, Susan Dart, George Denniston, Larry Gilligan, Christian Green, Scott Kremer, Melova, Rick Reinhert, Jr., and Laurance Rockefeller for their support.

Finally, I sincerely wish to thank those who trusted me with intimate details of their experiences and feelings. By revealing what generations before have hidden, they have made the most significant contribution.

Introduction
Controversial Questions

Mankind has always been ready to discuss matters in the inverse
ratio to their importance, so that the more closely a question is felt
to touch the heart of all of us, the more incumbent it is considered
upon prudent people to profess that it does not exist.
                                                        —Samuel Butler

The American public generally assumes that our cultural practice
of circumcision is a trivial and benign procedure, hardly worthy of
serious consideration and discussion. We believe that such a
widespread practice must be grounded in a consensus that it is
safe and effective, that it benefits the child or at least does no harm.

   In fact, there is considerable disagreement about the advisability of circumcision. According to one national survey, 33 percent
of American obstetricians and pediatricians are personally opposed to circumcision, though some of them may not disclose this
to their patients.[1] Some doctors and nurses have refused to participate in circumcisions. In addition, some circumcised men are
revealing long-standing opposition to circumcision or are adopting
such a stance after learning more about the practice. Parents'
views and choices are changing, too. According to the National
Center for Health Statistics, the circumcision rate has dropped from
a peak of about 85 percent to about 60 percent nationally and to
only about 35 percent in some areas of the country (see Fig. 1).[2]

   What do these people know? What motivates their opposition?
Is it wise to continue subjecting our children to a practice that has
provoked growing criticism and questioning? Does it matter that
about 3,500 circumcisions are still performed every day, one every
twenty-five seconds?

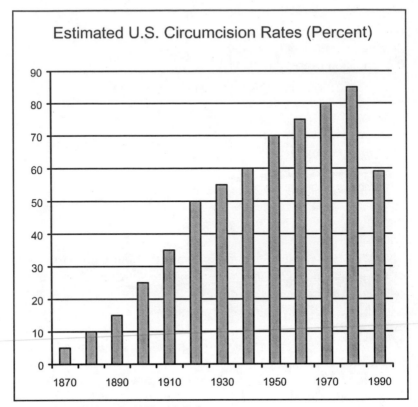

Estimated U.S. Circumcision Rates (Percent)

Adapted from Wallerstein 1980, table B-2

Fig. 1

From a global perspective, most of the world rejects circumcision: over 80 percent of the world's males are intact (not circumcised).[3] Most circumcised men are Muslim or Jewish. The United States is the only country in the world that circumcises most of its male infants for nonreligious reasons.

The public perception is that there are valid health reasons to circumcise associated with cleanliness and protection from various diseases. However, the American Academy of Pediatrics, the country's largest organization of physicians who care for infants, has not found any proven medical benefit from circumcision. In fact, no national medical organization in the world recommends routine circumcision of male infants. Furthermore, the results of the latest research are arousing some concern about this often misunderstood surgical procedure, and critics are charging that circumcision causes serious harm.

How can a common, routine procedure cause harm? How could this alleged harm have escaped the notice of doctors, parents, men—the whole society—for so long? How would people react, and what would it say about us if circumcision were found to have a negative impact?

The public is generally unaware of the controversy about circumcision, because circumcision has never had the full and open debate that many believe it deserves. However, that is changing. Increasingly, newspaper and magazine articles, radio and television shows, and a growing network of committed people are focusing attention on the subject. Some media stories on circumcision have elicited a surprising amount of mail and comment requesting better and more extensive reporting on this issue.

New information about circumcision often conflicts with previous teachings and long-held beliefs. Many people, including doctors, are confused by what they learn. If our world makes sense, then there must be a coherent explanation for all the apparently contradictory information. The conflicting conclusions, beliefs, and opinions surrounding circumcision, together with the tenacity with which advocates and opponents of circumcision hold on to their viewpoints, suggest that deep psychological factors are involved. I believe that the heart of the circumcision issue lies beyond the field of medicine.

This book addresses two main questions: (a) Why are circumcisions really being done? and (b) What effect does circumcision have on us? More specific questions include

1. What motivates doctors and parents to circumcise? Is this a rational or an emotional decision?

2. Why is the United States the only country in the world that circumcises most of its male infants for nonreligious reasons? Do we know something other countries don't, or do they know something we don't want to know?

3. What, exactly, happens during a circumcision? Is it "just a little snip" or much more, as some claim?
4. Does the infant feel "discomfort" or extreme pain and possibly trauma? If circumcision is traumatic, psychological effects could be long-term.
5. Can infants remember their experience? Any evidence that a male retains such memories would support possible long-term effects.
6. What are the possible long-term psychological effects of circumcision? Could something that happened that long ago make any difference now?
7. What is the sexual impact of circumcision? Does sex feel the same without a foreskin as with one?
8. How does circumcision affect the mother-child relationship? Any negative effect that results from the procedure could also have long-term implications.
9. Does circumcision affect the male-female relationship? If there are effects, women cannot avoid them.
10. How does circumcision affect our society? Is there any possible connection to either common or extreme forms of social behavior?

Amazingly, some of these questions have never been studied, perhaps because they are too disturbing. Close examination could threaten personal and cultural beliefs and challenge current mainstream assumptions about medical and mental health practice. Despite our possible discomfort, we need to know if we are harming ourselves and our children.

Since circumcision touches on so many aspects of life—physical, sexual, psychological, social, historical, and religious, to name a few—many find learning about the practice both engaging and challenging. Indeed, examining the subject of circumcision is a surprisingly rewarding path to learning more about ourselves. I would like to learn more. If you have had a memorable experience related to circumcision, I would like you to write it down and send it to me.

If this book challenges any of your most firmly held assumptions and beliefs about circumcision and society, I urge you to allow yourself to question them. Perhaps it would be even more valuable to allow yourself to notice and experience any feelings that may be stimulated by what you read.

It is not so important that all agree about the ideas presented in this book, but it is critical that an open discussion take place. I hope this work serves to stimulate and expand the dialogue. Whatever you think and feel about what you read, I would welcome your response.

1

Infant Development and

Response to Circumcision

To protect newborn children from fear, we must unveil the
world to them infinitely slowly, in an endless sequence of
severely limited revelations. And not overwhelm them with
more new sensations than they can support and integrate.

—Frederick Leboyer,
obstetrician and author

Imagine that you are resting comfortably, perhaps with a dearly
loved person you enjoy being physically close to, when a few
strange people enter the room and proceed to pick you up to carry
you away. You ask what this is about, and get no answer. You
protest and struggle, but they are stronger than you are. They take
you to another room where they remove your clothes and strap
you down on your back on a table. You try to free yourself, but
the only part of your body that you can move is your head. All this
time they continue to disregard your protest. Then a man enters,
and after seeing that you are secure, he picks up a knife and starts
to cut off a piece of skin from your genitals. The procedure lasts
for about fifteen minutes. Your screams of pain are ignored. How
do you feel?

There is no question that for an adult such an experience
would be intolerable. It is likely that it would result in trauma.
Psychologists have long known that trauma has long-term effects
on one's inner life and on social behavior and functioning. One

important characteristic of trauma is that the precipitating event, along with connections to current symptoms and behaviors, is often hidden from awareness. This book looks at circumcision as a possible traumatic event that could have a wide-ranging impact on individuals and society. Subsequent chapters will explore hidden facts and ramifications of this practice and expose them to light for others to examine.

Before we proceed with this psychological and social excavation, it is necessary to ask how much the above imagined scene is like an infant's circumcision. How does being circumcised feel to the infant? Does it matter how it feels to the infant? To answer these questions, it is important to learn about infants.

Since the turn of the century, infants have not generally been regarded as fully human persons by the American public and professionals. For example, some researchers have believed that infants' brains are insufficiently developed for emotion, learning, and memory. Doctors and parents have not typically considered the effect of their practices and attitudes on infants. They assume that if infants cannot perceive or remember experiences, then it will not matter much how they are treated.

This cultural view of infants is generally based on beliefs of the medical profession that were prevalent when it took over the domain of childbirth practice. In 1895, a renowned infant specialist at the University of Pennsylvania wrote, "When the baby is just born . . . it is . . . very little more intelligent than a vegetable. . . . It is, in fact, not directly conscious of anything."[1]

Fifty years later, newborn infants were believed to be incapable of anything except eating, moving, crying, and sleeping. In 1946 pediatrician Benjamin Spock reported the following developmental ages for various abilities and behaviors:

> By the time he's 2 to 3 months old, he recognizes a human face and responds to it. By 3 months he looks around in all directions. . . . A newborn baby seems to be deaf the first day or two. . . . Somewhere around two months of age your baby will smile. . . . He knows little at this age, he can't use his hands, or even turn his head from side to side. . . . Around the middle of the first year, he learns how to reach something that's brought within arms' reach.[2]

The limited ability of the newborn infant was and still is partly a result of the standard obstetrical practice of administering drugs to the mother. The drugs reach the fetus in nearly the same concentration as in the mother. Consequently, the newborn baby is born drugged and is less responsive to the environment. Infrequent smiling, irritability, and difficulty in feeding may result.[3] (Studies have found that effects can interfere with early adjustment and mother-infant interaction and last at least a year. Long-term effects in adults have also been noted.[4])

CHANGING VIEWS OF INFANTS

The failure to appreciate the aptitude of infants may also be connected with a cultural and professional bias toward believing in less capability of the infant rather than more. Research in infant development requires a proper attitude toward infants, careful selection of test subjects, and appropriate testing methods. Pioneer infant researcher T. G. R. Bower concludes that without these, "anyone can fail to replicate any claim that young infants can do anything."[5] He reports that it is possible to work with infants for years and not notice particular behaviors and talents if one is convinced that they do not exist. To assess the abilities of infants accurately, the observer must be open-minded, and all subjects should be born drug free. Since this type of birth is the exception to the rule, much research still tends to conclusions that diminish infant capability.

Those who investigate infant behavior are vulnerable to cultural beliefs about infants. They also have additional beliefs based on what they have learned from authorities in their field going back decades. Infant behavior that does not conform to these theories may then be ignored. Perceptions are limited by beliefs. Because researchers are not aware of many of their beliefs about infants, they do not think to examine them. Americans are not the only ones with cultural beliefs about infants. In Russia, swaddling was defended as a means to prevent the infant from "destroying itself," such as tearing off an ear or breaking a leg.[6]

One basic question about infants is how their world or subjective experience of the world compares to ours. There is a need to make this comparison so that findings can be communicated in terms that adults can understand. However, experimenters are also likely to believe that their view of the world is superior to that of the infant and fail to appreciate the differences. One difference is that stimuli or events that seem inconsequential to adults may be much more significant to the infant. In addition, the researcher's view of the world is essentially a mental one, limited and in conflict with the general way the infant experiences and responds to the world, through feelings.

Infant research psychiatrist and theorist Daniel Stern believes that the resistance among some researchers to accepting the existence of feelings in infants may be due to an "overemphasis" on the connection between mental and emotional development. He observes, "The realization is now occurring that . . . infants' feelings, especially in the beginning, can and must be considered irrespective of what they know."[7]

Infants function on a level that most adults have long ago left behind. It is a very deep feeling-experiential-body level that relies on its own kind of knowing. No intellectual abilities are required. Infants have no need to channel experiences and responses through the usual adult routing of a conceptual or linguistic pathway. Researchers, on the other hand, tend to focus strongly on the intellectual sector of experience. This inclination may allow observation of an infant's response without fully feeling and understanding the infant's experience. If this happens, part of the meaning of the infant's communication is lost.

Despite cultural beliefs and the adverse effects of drugs on infants, in the last twenty years we have been recognizing increased abilities in newborn infants. This is partly due to improved testing methods. Ways that infants can respond to their environment include turning their heads, sucking, and looking. Researchers have reevaluated their view of the infant using these three responses and other approaches, such as the preference method. In this case, the infant is presented with two or more stimuli, and investigators observe which stimulus the infant prefers. As a result of these methods, abilities that were once thought to be learned weeks or months after birth are now understood to be innate.

An overview of the research on newborn infants confirms these abilities and can help provide a better understanding of the impact of circumcision on infants. While reading about this research in the following pages, one can marvel at what infants can do, and imagine experiencing the world from their perspective. The references to circumcision ending each discussion are included to make a connection between infants' abilities and the circumcision experience.

SENSORY RESPONSE

Touch

Newborn infants need and enjoy touch. They are comforted by skin to skin contact. The infant's deeper breathing in response to touch provides more oxygen to tissues. Stroking has been shown to result in greater alertness and faster weight gain. More generally, increased tactile stimulation results in improved physical and emotional well-being and is required for proper growth and development.[8] At the end of his book on the importance of touch, Ashley Montagu concludes, "The newborn should, whenever possible, be placed in his mother's arms."[9]

Newborn infants' skin sensitivity is also demonstrated by their response to changes in texture, moisture, and pressure. They can also detect slight temperature changes on their skin.[10] These changes are sensed during circumcision, when an infant is often removed from the warmth of his mother's body and placed on a hard board of molded plastic.

Hearing

Hearing in the infant is well developed. Newborns can distinguish between familiar and unfamiliar sounds, loudness, pitch, and types of sounds. They can also determine the direction from which sound is coming.[11]

Newborns can recognize different crying sounds. They respond differently to cries of older infants, electronically simulated cries, and cries of younger infants. They even appear to recognize their own cry, because they will almost completely stop crying when they hear a recording of it.[12]

Infants like to hear human speech. Their heart rate increases when talk is directed to them rather than elsewhere. They can tell the difference between the vowels *a* and *i* on the second day after birth.[13] They can also distinguish their mother's voice. In one study, researchers wired a pacifier to allow an infant to control what was heard through headphones. By varying the rate of sucking, an infant could choose to hear the mother's voice or that of a stranger. Eight out of ten infants chose to listen to their mothers.[14] Newborns showed no preference for the father's voice. That preference appears later. However, there are reports of infants who did recognize the father's voice shortly after birth. These fathers had talked to the child prior to birth, using a calm voice and simple words.[15]

During circumcision an infant hears either no voice or a strange voice, rather than the preferred voice of the mother.

Sight

Babies one day old will look at things put in front of them, sometimes staring for minutes. Their vision is binocular. The typical one-week-old baby can see black and white stripes one-tenth of an inch wide one foot away.[16] This is thirty times wider than stripes that can be seen by an adult. The limited vision of an infant serves the purpose of helping to avoid excessive visual stimulation. The vision then improves rapidly during the first few months.

The eyes of a newborn infant focus best in the range of about eight to twelve inches. Not coincidentally, this is about the distance between an infant's face and the mother's face during nursing.[17] Newborn infants look and act differently when looking at faces than at inanimate patterns. Their arms and legs move more smoothly, and they make more vocal sounds.

Newborn infants have strong natural visual preferences. Patterns are preferred over plain surfaces, face-like images over random arrangements. They prefer complex patterns over simpler patterns, and curves to straight lines. Objects are preferred over photographs of objects.[18] This is determined by simply exposing an infant to different visual stimuli and observing where the infant looks. The image of what the infant sees is reflected in the pupil. A visual stimulus can change an infant's mood from crying to quiet if it is sufficiently interesting.

Newborns can distinguish some colors—yellow, orange, red, green, and turquoise—from gray. They do not respond to blue, purple, or chartreuse.[19] Other research has shown that newborns will follow a moving object with their eyes and turn their heads toward it. Sight and hearing are coordinated, and having a visual stimulus helps the infant locate the source of a sound.[20]

During circumcision an infant's eyes are tightly closed, possibly indicating that he does not want to see what is happening to him.

Smell

Studies of newborn infants indicate that their responses to smell are similar to adult responses. For example, babies were averse to the smell of rotten eggs and smiled when presented with the smell of honey. Responses to odors include changes in facial expression, heart and respiration rate, and movement of arms and legs.[21]

In a test of newborn infants to determine whether they could recognize the smell of their mother and her milk, breast pads moistened with mother's milk were placed on one side of a baby's face. Another mother's pad was placed on the other side. Infants turned toward their mother's pad three-quarters of the time.[22]

An infant being circumcised smells the strange hospital odors and not the familiar preferred smell of mother.

Taste

At birth, infants made facial expressions after drops of various substances were placed on their tongues.[23] The expressions of the babies resembled those of adults. Sugar water elicited a slight smile; citric acid, a pursing of the lips; and quinine, a grimace.

The newborn's sensation of saltiness is different from that of an adult because the fluid environment in the womb contains a lot of sodium, the active ingredient in salt. When the mouth of the fetus is open, it is soaked in a sodium solution. This exposure accounts for a level of sodium in the saliva of a newborn infant that is two or three times that in an adult. As a result, the infant's response to salt is different. Slightly salted water tastes sweet, and plain water tastes sour or bitter.[24]

An infant's sense of taste is not stimulated during circumcision unless he vomits. To prevent this possibility, feeding is not permitted before the procedure.

OTHER ABILITIES AND QUALITIES

States of Consciousness

Researchers have classified behavioral states of newborns into six different categories. The three awake states include quiet alert, active alert, and crying. Drowsiness is a transition between wakefulness and sleep. The two sleep states are quiet sleep and active sleep. Each state of consciousness has its own specific set of behaviors.[25]

In the quiet alert state, infants are attentive and receptive. There is little movement, and they generally focus on seeing and hearing. The infant is usually in this state within the first hour after birth. Many studies are best conducted when infants are in the quiet alert state. Therefore, researchers have to wait until an infant is in this state before they can do their experiments.

The active alert state involves more energy. The baby may make sounds and move the arms, legs, body, or face about every minute, suggesting a certain rhythm. The eyes are unfocused. Breathing is fast and irregular from the physical exertion.

Crying, of course, is an important way that the infant communicates with others. Studies have shown that the cry varies depending on how the infant feels and what the infant wants (see "Expression"). The limbs move actively, and the face becomes distorted.

In drowsiness, the eyelids partially close, the eyes are unfocused, and movements sometimes occur. In quiet sleep the infant is very relaxed, with deep, regular breathing and virtually no movement of the body or eyes. Active sleep includes periods of rapid eye movements and body movements, somewhat irregular and shallow breathing, and facial expressions. The slightest disturbance may cause waking. The two sleep states alternate about every thirty minutes.

Infants are typically in a crying state during circumcision.

Movement

A newborn infant might reach out for an interesting item with open hand. Babies born without medication provided to the mother before birth had a better chance of exhibiting reaching motions. Hand-to-mouth coordination has also been observed.[26] Grasping and holding onto an adult finger or making a fist signals distress. Head movement supplements eye movement by the fourth day. If a newborn infant is supported, stepping movements simulate walking.[27]

Studies have demonstrated purpose in the movements of newborn infants. If the infant is placed on the mother's abdomen after birth, the infant will crawl to the breast and nurse.[28] Special photographic techniques have established that babies' movements in the active alert state form a definite pattern. Movement and still periods alternate in about one- to two-minute intervals. The amount of activity varies widely among newborn infants and also varies with the cultural group.[29]

The connection between adult speech and infant body movements was shown by filming infants while they were being spoken to. An analysis of the film indicated that the infants moved in synchrony with the speech. As spoken sound changed, so did the infants' movement. This response was consistent with speech, whether the language was English or Chinese. Spoken sounds that were not in verbal form did not elicit a response. This change demonstrated infants' ability to distinguish language patterns from random vocal sounds.[30]

Infants' movements are also related to what they see. Babies moved differently when looking at a toy than when they were looking at parents. The difference could be detected by observing movement of a toe or finger.[31]

An infant ten days old exhibited a defensive reaction to an approaching object. The reaction included head retraction and placing the hands between the object and the face.[32] This type of reaction was thought to be learned when it was observed in older infants. However, because the younger infant had no prior similar experience, the defensive reaction may be innate behavior.

Infants being circumcised cannot move to defend themselves when they are placed on their backs with their arms and legs secured by straps. The restraint also prevents active limb movements that would normally accompany crying.

Expression

At birth, infants are capable of nearly all of the same facial expressions as adults. Many researchers have observed newborn infants smiling at birth, while dreaming, and while urinating or defecating. In the first week, mothers have reported observing interest, joy, distress, anger, disgust, surprise, sadness, and fear. Various expressions have been confirmed by videotape analysis.[33] Emotional expression often involves movement of the whole body, particularly expression of anger. The whole body may also quiver with pleasure when the baby smiles. Hand positions may indicate distress or state of waking or sleeping.[34]

The newborn's cry may vary in pitch, duration, and loudness. Graphic analysis of these characteristics with special equipment has confirmed what mothers have always known: babies have

different cries to express different feelings. The subjective evaluation of cries by trained observers yields similar conclusions. Even
different segments of the same cry can convey different mes-
sages.[35] This realization by researchers demonstrates that infant
communication is meaningful and that we are born with the ability
to express specific feelings and needs. An infant's cry may be a
request for nourishment, contact, relief from discomfort or pain,
or a sign of other distress. A variety of other vocalizations also
convey meaningful communication.

The infant's cry during circumcision is a sign of distress.

Learning

Newborn infants are enthusiastic learners. They seek out and
engage in learning opportunities. In many cases, they find learning
particularly pleasurable and respond with smiles when they learn
how to control something in their environment, such as kicking to
move a mobile tied to their leg with a string. They also learn
which way to turn their heads to receive a reward. During an
eighteen-minute session, two-day-old infants learned to differentiate between speech sounds to obtain a reward.[36]

The connection between learned behavior and reward is strong.
Researchers found that after infants learned a behavior to get a
reward, the infants were upset when the reward was received
without being contingent on the behavior. Other infants who
received the reward first without it being contingent on behavior
could not learn the contingent behavior.[37]

Investigators have also demonstrated infants' listening preferences and learning capability operating together. They set up
headphones and an electrically wired nipple for one- and two-day-
old infants. The voices heard by the infant through the headphones depended on the rate of sucking on the nipple. Almost all
infants easily learned this relationship. Infants tended to suck at a
rate that would result in a woman's voice being heard through the
headphones rather than a male voice.[38] They also preferred their
mother's voice to that of other women (see "Hearing").

Newborn infants learn their mother's face within a few minutes after birth and will respond differently to the mother if she wears a mask and is silent during feeding.[39] They not only recognize and differentiate facial expressions of adults, but are capable of imitating them, including sticking out their tongue, opening their mouth, and pursing their lips. A study of infants thirty-six hours old showed that they could imitate happy, sad, and surprised facial expressions.[40] In one case, an eight-hour-old Chinese baby imitated the facial expression made earlier by an adult when she was presented to the adult at a later time. The memory of the initial expression made by the adult had apparently lasted at least several minutes.[41]

Newborns have also exhibited classical conditioning. After receiving repeated forehead stroking immediately followed by tasting a sweet solution, infants exhibited sucking responses and head-turning during the stroking alone.[42]

Researcher T. G. R. Bower concludes that "infants are rational."[43] They behave logically. Bower describes a striking example from his personal experience. He was contacted by a couple whose infant took hours to consume a bottle. Bower then discovered that the only time they held the baby was during bottle feeding. His conclusion was that the baby learned this connection and used it to be held. When the parents were made aware of this, they changed their behavior toward the infant, and the infant no longer extended feeding time in order to be held.

Bower believes that infants have a "sense of personal efficacy."[44] This is the relationship between the infant's actions and how well and how often the infant's needs are met. The response the infant gets teaches the infant to either act or do nothing. For example, if the infant cries for the mother and the mother does not come, the infant may withdraw and stop crying.

Infants being circumcised experience that their expression of distress is not heeded. Because of the lack of response, some infants may learn that they are not safe and withdraw. (This behavior is discussed later in this chapter under "Behavioral Response Following Circumcision.")

Memory

Since memory is a prerequisite for learning, the studies under "Learning" also serve to demonstrate infants' memory. The infant's response to the smell of mother's milk described earlier also signifies memory.

Studies indicate that the fetus can be given a stimulus while in the womb, and after birth, the infant demonstrates familiarity with the stimulus through marked behavioral and physiological response. For example, in one experiment mothers read a story twice a day during the last six weeks of their pregnancy. After birth, the infants were able to select which story they wanted to hear by sucking on a nipple that was wired to recordings of stories and headphones. The rate of sucking determined which story the infants would hear through the headphones. Ten out of twelve infants sucked at the rate required to hear the familiar story. In another study, fetuses were exposed to a television theme song during pregnancy. After birth, they responded to the same song with changes in heart rate, behavioral state, and degree of movement.[45]

If infants are presented with an object to observe, their interest will wane over time, indicating a type of memory. This effect, called habituation, suggests that infants become bored, and it demonstrates an ability to remember the object. Tests of visual memory indicate a preference for looking at new colors and shapes. In one auditory memory study, three-day-old infants remembered two-syllable words by showing decreasing interest. They then demonstrated increased interest in listening to new words by turning their heads toward the sounds.[46]

In another experiment, four-week-old infants were allowed to suck on either of two types of pacifiers: one was a smooth ball, the other a nubby ball. In each case the infant was not shown the pacifier. Then, when the infants were shown pictures of each pacifier, they tended to look at the type that they had just sucked. This showed they were able to associate information from what they felt in the mouth to what they saw.[47]

Behavior changes after circumcision demonstrate memory of the event. This will be discussed in detail following the section on pain response to circumcision.

Pain Response

In a comprehensive review of recent medical literature on newborn pain, investigators at Children's Hospital in Boston looked at anatomical, neurological, and neurochemical systems; cardiorespiratory, hormonal, and metabolic changes; body movement; facial expressions; crying; and complex behavioral responses such as temperament and sleep states. They concluded in an article published in the *New England Journal of Medicine* that newborn responses to pain are "similar to but greater than those observed in adult subjects."[48] This work is often cited in the medical literature whenever there is a discussion of infant pain, and the conclusions are now generally accepted by medical authorities.

As indicated earlier, the effect of anesthetics given to the mother prior to birth may reduce infant responses. It takes no less than a week for these anesthetics to leave the infant's body. Until that occurs, the newborn infant's vocal behavior is affected by them.[49] Therefore, absence of crying does not preclude the possibility that the infant feels pain. There will be more about this point later in this chapter.

Heart rate and blood pressure of newborn infants increase following a heel stick (a puncture to obtain a blood sample). Even infants born three months prematurely had physiological responses to the procedure.[50] Facial expressions of newborns while responding to painful stimuli are similar to the facial expressions of adults. Facial activity and cry pitch, intensity, and duration increase if procedures are more invasive.[51]

When a heel stick is done to a newborn infant, the behavioral response is to withdraw the foot and cry. This response to pain is biological, not learned. The infant will even use the free foot to kick the doctor's hand away from the other foot. In a study using small electric shocks and pin pricks, some infants tried to use their hands to protect the area where they felt the pain.[52] In summary, the literature consistently supports the conclusion that infants feel, locate, and respond to painful stimuli. Of course, this conclusion has a direct bearing on their reaction to circumcision.

PAIN RESPONSE DURING CIRCUMCISION

To help in determining the degree of pain and stress caused by circumcision, infant response was compared to that resulting from other procedures. Levels of cortisol (a hormone released into the blood in response to stress) and behavioral responses were recorded for newborns undergoing circumcision, heel-stick blood sampling, weighing and measuring, and discharge examination. Circumcision resulted in significantly higher levels of behavioral distress and blood cortisol levels than did the other procedures. Since the infant is restrained during circumcision, the response to the use of restraint was similarly tested and was not found to be measurably distressing to newborns.[53]

Circumcision is a surgical procedure that involves forcefully separating the foreskin from the glans and then cutting it off. It is typically accomplished with a special clamp device (see Fig. 2). Over a dozen studies confirm the extreme pain of circumcision. It has been described as "among the most painful [procedures] performed in neonatal medicine."[54] In one study, researchers concluded that the pain was "severe and persistent."[55] Increases in heart rate of 55 beats per minute have been recorded, about a 50 percent increase over the baseline.[56] After circumcision, the level of blood cortisol increased by a factor of three to four times the level prior to circumcision.[57] Investigators reported, "This level of pain would not be tolerated by older patients."[58]

Circumcision pain is described in this research study by Howard Stang and his colleagues from the Department of Pediatrics, Group Health Inc., and the University of Minnesota Institute of Child Development: "There is no doubt that circumcisions are painful for the baby. Indeed, circumcision has become a model for the

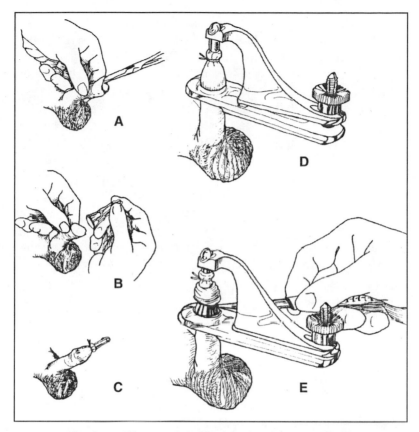

Fig. 2   Circumcision with the Gomco Clamp

The Gomco clamp is commonly used to perform circumcisions. It consists of three parts: a metal plate with a hole at one end, a round metal cap, and a screw device. The foreskin is first separated from the glans and cut lengthwise to expose the glans (A). Then the cap is placed over the glans (B). The foreskin is stretched up over the cap and tied securely to the cap handle (C). The hole at the end of the plate is placed over the cap and foreskin, and the flange on the handle is fitted into a groove in the screw device (D). Turning the screw device forces the cap against the hole and squeezes the foreskin. This squeezing prevents bleeding. Then the foreskin is cut off (E). The clamp remains in place at least five minutes to allow for clotting before it is removed.

analysis of pain and stress responses in the newborn" (see Figs. 3 and 4).They report that the infant will "cry vigorously, tremble, and in some cases become mildly cyanotic [having blueness or lividness of the skin, caused by a deficiency of oxygen] because of prolonged crying."[59]

According to adult listeners in one study, the infant's response during circumcision included a cry that changed with the level of pain being experienced. The most invasive part of the procedure caused the longest crying. These cries were high pitched and were judged most urgent.[60] A subsequent study confirmed that cries with higher pitch were perceived to be more distressing and urgent.[61] Excessive crying can itself cause harm. In a rare case, an infant cried vehemently for about ninety minutes and ruptured his stomach.[62] Using a pacifier during circumcision reduced crying but did not affect hormonal pain response.[63] Therefore, while crying may be absent, other body signals demonstrate that pain is always present during circumcision.

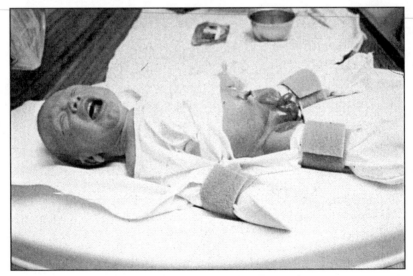

Reprinted by permission from The Saturday Evening Post

Fig. 3

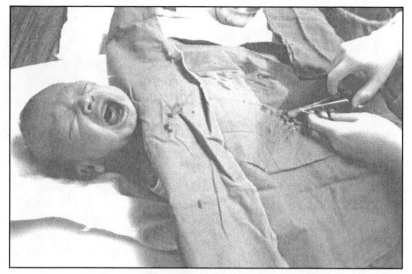

Reprinted by permission from The Saturday Evening Post

Fig. 4

Another perspective on the infant's response to circumcision pain is provided by Marilyn Milos, who witnessed a circumcision during her training in nursing school:

> We students filed into the newborn nursery to find a baby strapped spread-eagle to a plastic board on a counter top across the room. He was struggling against his restraints—tugging, whimpering, and then crying helplessly. . . . I stroked his little head and spoke softly to him. He began to relax and was momentarily quiet. The silence was soon broken by a piercing scream—the baby's reaction to having his foreskin pinched and crushed as the doctor attached the clamp to his penis. The shriek intensified when the doctor inserted an instrument between the foreskin and the glans (head of the penis), tearing the two structures apart. The baby started shaking his head back and forth—the only part of his body free to move—as the doctor used another clamp to crush the foreskin lengthwise, which he then cut. This made the opening of the foreskin large enough to insert a circumcision instrument, the device used to protect the glans from being severed during the surgery. The baby began to gasp and choke,

severed during the surgery. The baby began to gasp and choke, breathless from his shrill continuous screams. . . . During the next stage of the surgery, the doctor crushed the foreskin against the circumcision instrument and then, finally, amputated it. The baby was limp, exhausted, spent.[64]

There is disagreement among physicians about using anesthesia during circumcisions. Prior to the mid-1980s, anesthesia was not used because infant pain was denied by the medical community (see Chapter 2). That belief has changed among many physicians, but an anesthetic (local injection, the best option tested) still is not typically administered due to a lack of familiarity with its use, as well as the belief that it introduces additional risk.[65] Although there is indication that the risk is minimal, most physicians who perform circumcisions do not use anesthetics even after they are taught how. When an anesthetic is used, it relieves only some but not all of the pain, and its effect wanes before the postoperative pain does.[66] Because no experimental anesthetic has been found to be safe and effective in preventing circumcision pain, research in this area continues. Meanwhile, some physicians' views about the use of anesthesia during circumcision grow more intense. In a recent medical article on the subject, the writers described circumcision without pain relief as "barbaric."[67] Another physician wrote that subjecting an adult to the same practice would be "unfathomable."[68]

BEHAVIORAL RESPONSE FOLLOWING CIRCUMCISION

Beginning in the 1970s, some studies investigated the effect of circumcision on infant behavior. Researchers found differences in sleep patterns and more irritability among circumcised infants.[69] In addition, changes in infant-maternal interaction were observed during the first twenty-four hours after circumcision.[70] For example, breast- and bottle-fed infants' feeding behavior has been shown to deteriorate after circumcision.[71] Other behavior differences have been noted on the day following the procedure.[72] The American Academy of Pediatrics (AAP) Task Force on Circumcision noted these various behavioral changes resulting from circumcision in their report.[73]

Researchers found that European reports of newborn infant responses to hearing and taste stimulation showed little difference in responses between males and females, while related tests on American infants showed significant gender differences.[74] Investigators suggested that these differences could be the result of circumcision and not gender.

In one of the most important studies, the behavior of nearly 90 percent of circumcised infants significantly changed after the circumcision.[75] Some became more active, and some became less active. The quality of the change generally was associated with whether they were crying or quiet respectively at the start of the circumcision. This suggests the use of different coping styles by infants when they are subjected to extreme pain. In addition, the researchers observed that circumcised infants had lessened ability to comfort themselves or to be comforted by others.

Some mothers and nurses who contacted the Circumcision Resource Center also noted behavior changes. Sally Hughes, an obstetrical nurse who has seen many circumcised infants before they go home, reported,

> When you lay them on their stomachs they scream. When their diaper is wet they scream. Normally, they don't scream if their diaper is wet. Baby boys who are not circumcised do not scream like that. The circumcised babies are more irritable, and they nurse poorly.[76]

Mothers reported that their infants changed temperament after the circumcision, cried for extended periods at home, and seemed inconsolable.

Researchers at Children's Hospital in Boston noted changes in sleep patterns, activity level, irritability, and mother-infant interaction. They concluded,

> The persistence of specific behavioral changes after circumcision in neonates implies the presence of memory. In the short term, these behavioral changes may disrupt the adaptation of newborn infants to

their postnatal environment, the development of parent-infant bonding, and feeding schedules.[77]

There is one study of the impact of circumcision several months after the event. A group of investigators at the Hospital for Sick Children in Toronto reported that male infants aged four to six months had a stronger response than females to pain during vaccinations. They wondered whether circumcision was a factor and reviewed the data to test that hypothesis. Researchers found that the circumcised boys had increased behavioral pain response and cried for significantly longer periods than the genitally intact boys.[78]

Based on the latest research, infants' abilities and responses can be summarized as follows:

INFANT DEVELOPMENT AND RESPONSE TO CIRCUMCISION

1. Newborn infants are aware, perceptive, sensitive, and responsive. All senses are working, and infants seek sensory stimulation.
2. Purposeful movement has been observed within minutes of birth.
3. Facial expressions are similar to those of adults. Smiling has been observed at birth. Cries are meaningful and can express specific feelings and needs.
4. The behavior of infants is rational, and they are enthusiastic learners. They have specific preferences, and they can even evaluate their experience.
5. Memory has been demonstrated from behavior and physiological response. Mental activity can be inferred from their learning ability and behavioral response.
6. Newborn infants can feel, locate, and respond to painful stimuli. Their pain responses are similar to those of adults or even greater.
7. During circumcision, which is typically performed without anesthesia, infants display significantly more distress than

during other procedures. Physiological and behavioral changes are abnormal and extreme. The latest research studies all support the conclusion that circumcision is overwhelmingly painful for infants.

8. Changes in behavioral responses following circumcision indicate that the experience is remembered. A study of infants' later responses to vaccination suggests that the effects of circumcision can last at least several months.

COMMENTS FROM PROFESSIONALS

Some physicians who perform circumcisions describe it as "temporary discomfort" for the infant or comparable to an injection. Others take a much stronger view.

David Chamberlain, psychologist and president of the Association for Pre- and Perinatal Psychology and Health, states, "I can only assume that parents have tolerated this [circumcision] in the mistaken belief that the baby will not know he is being tortured. He will."[79] (The term "tortured" refers to the infant's experience, not adult intentions.)

Howard Marchbanks, family medical practitioner, says, "My feeling is that it is a traumatic experience, and I am opposed to traumatizing the baby."[80]

Benjamin Spock writes that circumcision "is at least mildly dangerous. I also believe that there is potential danger of emotional harm resulting from the operation."[81]

Justin Call, infant psychologist and professor-in-chief of child and adolescent psychology at the University of California, describes the baby's response to circumcision:

> The helpless, panicky cry of an infant when circumcised is an abnormal kind of cry. It is a breathless, high-pitched cry that is never heard in other normally occurring circumstances. Then sometimes babies who are being circumcised do exactly the opposite. They lapse into a semi-coma. Both of these states, helpless crying and semi-coma are abnormal states in the newborn.[82]

Frederick Leboyer, obstetrician and author of a book that revolutionized childbirth, *Birth Without Violence*, observes of circumcision, "The torture is experienced in a state of total helplessness which makes it even more frightening and unbearable."[83]

Tonya Brooks, midwife and president of the International Association for Childbirth at Home, recalls, "In four of the nine circumcisions that I have seen, the baby didn't cry. He just seemed to be suddenly in a state of shock!"[84] Since the infant cannot escape physically, he attempts to escape psychologically.

Despite the fact that the latest research studies on circumcision pain all support the conclusion that circumcision is overwhelmingly painful for the infant, professional opinion differs widely about the infant's experience. Why is this? And why do parents agree to circumcise their newborn sons? A close examination of the circumcision decision reveals surprising answers.

2

Why Parents and Physicians Choose

to Circumcise Infants

Nothing is so firmly believed as what we least know.
—Michel de Montaigne

In 1965 Dr. William Morgan wrote an article critical of circumcision in a major medical journal. In the course of refuting the popular reasons to circumcise, Morgan arrived at the core question, which he then answered with apparent exasperation: "Why is circumcision practiced? One might as well attempt to explain the rites of voodoo!"[1]

Actually, there are sound, predictable psychological reasons that account for the practice of circumcision in America. Because many parents and physicians often overlook psychological factors connected with the circumcision decision, they have the impression that such reasons do not exist or are unimportant. However, the following psychological factors strongly affect the circumcision decision. They are generally connected with what we perceive, understand, believe, and feel about circumcision.

MENTAL FACTORS

Knowledge and Health Claims

Many parents make the circumcision decision without knowing what circumcision really is. They fail to appreciate that circumcision is surgery. In one study, 34 percent of men incorrectly identified their own circumcision status.[2] In another study, half of the mothers questioned did not know if the father of their child was circumcised.[3] A survey of 73 boys aged eleven to fourteen indicated that 32 percent did not correctly identify their circumcision status.[4] My own research survey of 60 adult graduate students revealed that 38 percent of the women and 45 percent of the men were not sure of the difference between a circumcised and an intact penis. The lack of parental knowledge about circumcision certainly contributes to acceptance of the procedure.

Furthermore, in the last fifty years, circumcision advocates in the medical profession have promoted various claims. (See Appendix A for a sample hospital circumcision information sheet with arguments for and against circumcision.) The most widely used current medical claim for circumcision is that it decreases the incidence of urinary tract infection (UTI) in the first year of life.[5] However, the UTI studies this position is based on have been criticized by other physicians, most notably by the American Academy of Pediatrics (AAP). They concluded that the test designs and methods of these studies may have "flaws."[6] A similar study found no confirmed cases of UTI in intact male infants without urinary birth defects.[7] Furthermore, the UTI defense of circumcision is weak, not just because the methods are flawed, but because the logic and reasoning leading to the conclusion are flawed.

The UTI studies do not justify routine infant circumcision for the following reasons:

1. Even according to the questionable studies, the overwhelming majority (96-99 percent) of intact male infants do not get UTIs in the first year.[8] It is not reasonable to subject them to circumcision and the associated pain without demonstrable benefit.
2. The studies do not consider the potential harm caused by circumcision. The rate of surgical complications is reported to be from 0.2 to 38 percent.[9] (The higher rate included complications reported during the infants' first year.) There are at least twenty different complications

including hemorrhage, infection, surgical injury, and in rare cases, death.[10] Other harm includes loss of the foreskin and behavioral consequences.[11]

3. Circumcision involves cutting off normal, healthy, functioning tissue to prevent potential UTI problems in the future. There is no disease or infection present at the time of surgery. If we were to apply this principle in trying to prevent other potential problems, then we would be pulling healthy teeth to prevent cavities. Clearly, this principle is irrational.

4. UTI is treatable with antibiotics.[12] If good medical practice requires the least intrusive form of effective treatment, then circumcision is not justified. Circumcision is a radical surgical treatment.

5. Females have a higher UTI rate than males,[13] yet no doctor advocates genital surgery to reduce female UTI.

Most of these arguments would be applicable to *any* claimed medical benefit. In addition, the AAP reports no proven benefit after reviewing other medical claims. Regarding circumcision and penile cancer, they state, "Factors other than circumcision are important in the etiology of penile cancer. The incidence of penile cancer is related to hygiene."[14] To support this conclusion, the AAP reports that the incidence of penile cancer among intact males in developed countries is only about 1 in 100,000. Developing nations with lower standards of hygiene have an incidence of from 3 to 6 per 100,000.

The AAP also states, "Evidence regarding the relationship of circumcision to sexually transmitted diseases is conflicting. . . . Evidence linking uncircumcised men to cervical carcinoma is inconclusive." Regarding the cleanliness issue, the AAP reports: "The uncircumcised penis is easy to keep clean; no special care is required."[15] Normal bathing is sufficient. Since the incidence of the medical need for circumcision in adults is as low as 6 in 100,000, circumcising an infant to prevent a later circumcision is unwarranted.[16]

Edward Wallerstein, who researched circumcision for twelve years, addressed the health issue in convincing detail in his book *Circumcision: An American Health Fallacy*. With approximately a thousand references to medical and associated literature around the world, Wallerstein found no health justification for routine circumcision. Rosemary Romberg reached a similar conclusion after a thorough review in *Circumcision: The Painful Dilemma*. (See books listed in "Resources" for more information.) Pediatrician Benjamin Spock reversed his original position in favor of circumcision and now writes: "I feel that there's no solid medical evidence at this time to support routine circumcision. . . . I recommend leaving the foreskin the way Nature meant it to be."[17]

Circumcision advocates, on the other hand, can only make the dubious claim that an unlikely or rare condition will be less likely to occur in the circumcised male. This benefit is sufficient justification to many people partly because circumcision is a surgical procedure that is done on *someone else*. It is pertinent to ask: Would you voluntarily submit to an unanesthetized surgical procedure on your healthy genitals for this "benefit"? The answer is also evident from the fact that intact male adults are not generally seeking to have themselves circumcised. While some circumcision advocates struggle to support their case with statistics, the factor which they typically and conveniently ignore is that *all medical claims used to defend routine circumcision are based on flawed reasoning.*

Beliefs about Infant Pain

In addition to questionable health claims, mistaken beliefs are used by many doctors to justify circumcision to themselves and others. One such common belief has been that newborn infants do not feel pain.[18] Nance Butler, a consultant in the health care field, inquired about the reason for this belief. "People in medicine and nursing reply, 'because the babies can't talk.'"[19] Because medical people have difficulty assessing nonverbal communication, they often do not respond to it.[20] Instead, some doctors believe that the newborn nervous system is not sufficiently developed to register or transmit pain impulses.[21] (See Chapter 1 for results of the latest research.) According to an article by pediatrician Neil Schechter, titled "The Undertreatment of Pain in Children: An Overview," this belief is "the major myth" of physicians regarding infant pain.[22] The fact that babies can't physically resist and stop the procedure also makes it easier to dismiss their pain.[23] Even if doctors accept that infants feel pain, many believe that infants do not remember it.

False beliefs about pain have been used to defend and justify performing various medical procedures on infants without anesthesia. As recently as 1986, infants as old as fifteen months were subjected to major surgery without pain relief.[24] An editorial in the *New England Journal of Medicine* attributed this practice to a "lack of awareness."[25] Public disclosure of these facts resulted in protest, a major review of medical literature on pain, and a reevaluation of practices. Though this review concluded that newborn infants do feel pain, decades of outdated medical beliefs and practices die hard. Circumcision without anesthesia is an established routine. Some doctors have done thousands of circumcisions without using anesthetics, and they would find changing their methods difficult.

Even today, some doctors still minimize circumcision pain by calling it "discomfort" or comparing it to the pain of an injection, although these opinions have been refuted by research studies.[26] Perhaps they do not read the current medical literature. Dr. K. J. S. Anand, co-author of the 1987 comprehensive study on infant pain that challenged medical thinking on this topic, has another view. He reported that in his meetings with hospital administrators, the evidence of pain in the newborn was still "denied," and the medical community was "uncomfortable" with findings about memory of infant pain. Anand speculated that this response may be due to guilt about inflicting pain on infants.[27]

Beliefs about the Foreskin

Probably the most common belief about circumcision is that the foreskin has no purpose. A current pediatric urology textbook states that the foreskin "probably has no major function."[28] A reputable urologist referred to it as "extra skin" that doesn't make "a whole lot of difference."[29] Thomas Wiswell, primary author of the UTI studies, said, "I believe the foreskin is a mistake of nature."[30] Doctors never explicitly state this kind of belief to parents. It is implied in other statements. For example, it is common for doctors to frame the circumcision decision for parents as a "win-win" situation. Pediatrician Jennifer Heath tells parents they "really can't go wrong," whatever choice they make, implying that no harm can be done.[31] Pediatrician T. Berry Brazelton states, "Particular studies can be used to prove that either alternative is safe for the baby. . . . I think the father should make the choice for his son."[32]

Despite the assurances given by some doctors, circumcising and not circumcising cannot have an equivalent impact on the child because cutting off a part of the penis diminishes it in form and function. The AAP acknowledged in a 1984 pamphlet called *Newborns: Care of the Uncircumcised Penis* that the functions of the foreskin include protecting the glans and urinary opening from irritation and infection.

In order to appreciate the sexual functions of the foreskin, refer to Figures 5–9, which clarify what the foreskin is and how it works. Figures 5 and 6 show the difference between a circumcised and a natural penis in the relaxed or flaccid state. Note that the foreskin serves to cover the glans or head of the penis. Figure 7 shows this diagrammatically. Figure 8 shows the circumcised penis in the erect state. The shaft skin is taut. Figure 9 shows the natural penis before, during, and after erection. Note that the inner foreskin layer becomes exposed and the entire foreskin moves to loosely cover the penile shaft.

Taylor, Lockwood, and Taylor studied the foreskin tissue at the Department of Pathology, Health Sciences Centre, University of Manitoba, Canada. They reported their results in the *British Journal of Urology* in an article titled "The Prepuce: Specialized Mucosa of the Penis and Its Loss to Circumcision." Based on the examination of 22 adult foreskins obtained at autopsy, they found that the outer foreskin's concentration of nerves is "impressive"

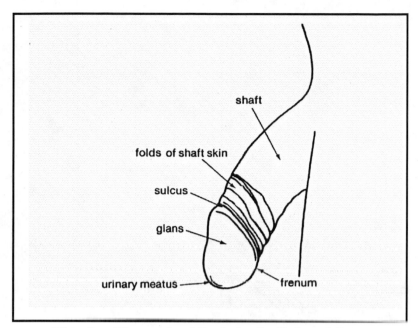

Fig. 5   Circumcised Penis in the Relaxed State

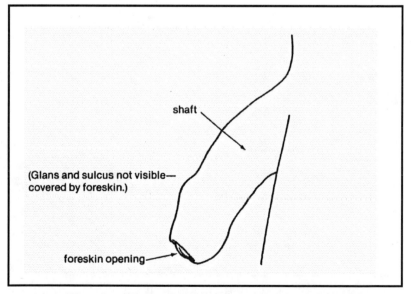

Fig. 6   Natural Penis in the Relaxed State

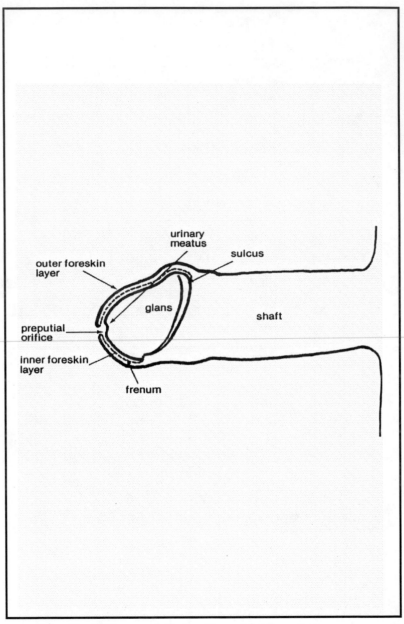

Fig. 7   Inner and Outer Foreskin Layers

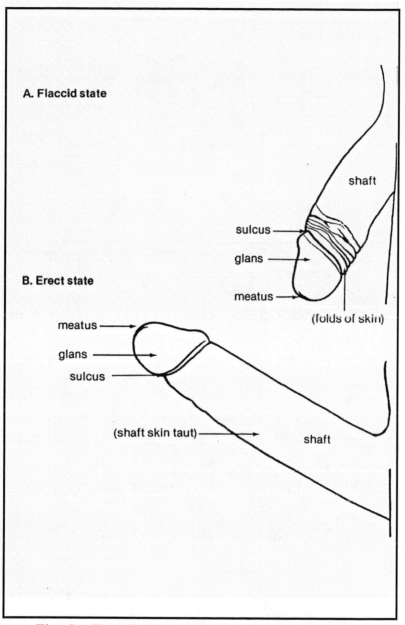

Fig. 8   Erectile Process in the Circumcised Penis

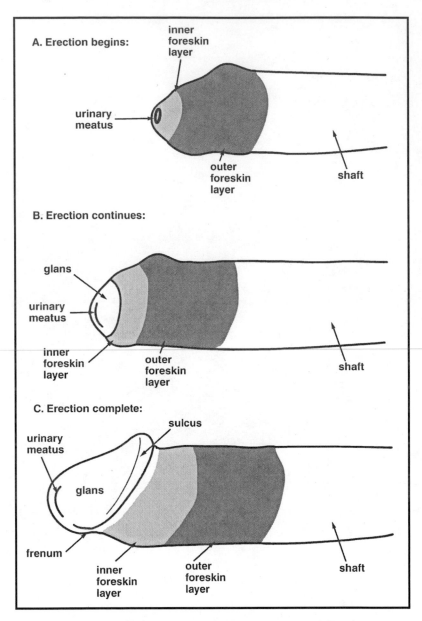

Fig. 9   Erectile Process in the Natural Penis

and its "sensitivity to light touch and pain are similar to that of the skin of the penis as a whole."[33] The foreskin inner surface is different. It is mucous membrane similar to the inner surface of the mouth, also rich in nerves and blood vessels. Between the inner and outer layers of the foreskin is a unique structure they call a "ridged band" that contains "specialized nerve endings."[34] The researchers conclude that the foreskin has several kinds of nerves and "should be considered a structural and functional unit made up of more or less specialized parts. . . . The glans and penile shaft gain excellent if surrogate sensitivity from the prepuce."[35]

The foreskin represents at least a third of the penile skin. It protects the glans from abrasion and contact with clothes.[36] The foreskin also increases sexual pleasure by sliding up and down on the shaft, stimulating the glans by alternately covering and exposing it. This can occur during masturbation or intercourse. Friction is minimized, and supplementary lubrication is not needed.[37] Without the foreskin, the glans skin, which is normally moist mucous membrane, becomes dry and thickens considerably in response to continued exposure. This change reduces its sensitivity.[38] In addition, the loss of a secretion called smegma of the inner foreskin layer removes natural lubrication. Oral-genital sexual activity is more common in the United States than in many other societies.[39] Could the lack of natural lubrication of the penis due to circumcision be a reason?

Only men circumcised as adults can experience the difference a foreskin makes. In the *Journal of Sex Research*, Money and Davison from the Johns Hopkins University School of Medicine reported on five such men. Changes included diminished penile sensitivity and less penile gratification. The investigators concluded,

> Erotosexually and cosmetically, the operation is, for the most part, contraindicated, and it should be evaluated in terms of possible pathological sequelae.[40]

Other men circumcised as adults regret the change.

I play guitar and my fingers get callused from playing. That's similar to what happened to my penis after circumcision.[41]

After the circumcision there was a major change. It was like night and day. I lost most sensation. I would give anything to get the feeling back. I would give my house. [This man's physician persuaded him to be circumcised by warning he could otherwise get penile cancer. When the man complained of the result, the physician replied, "That's normal" and would not help him.][42]

Slowly the area lost its sensitivity, and as it did, I realized I had lost something rather vital. Stimuli that had previously aroused ecstasy had relatively little effect. . . . Circumcision destroys a very joyful aspect of the human experience for males and females.[43]

The greatest disadvantage of circumcision is the awful loss of sensitivity when the foreskin is removed. . . . On a scale of 10, the intact penis experiences pleasure that is at least 11 or 12; the circumcised penis is lucky to get to 3.[44]

The sexual difference between a circumcised and uncircumcised penis is . . . like wearing a condom or wearing a glove. . . . Sight without color would be a good analogy. . . . Only being able to see in black and white, for example, rather than seeing in full color would be like experiencing an orgasm with a foreskin and without. There are feelings you'll just never have without a foreskin.[45]

After thirty years in the natural state I allowed myself to be persuaded by a physician to have the foreskin removed—not because of any problems at the time, but because, in the physician's view, there might be problems in the future. That was five years ago and I am sorry I had it done. . . . The sensitivity in the glans has been reduced by at least 50 percent. There it is, unprotected, constantly rubbing against the fabric of whatever I am wearing. In a sense, it has become callused. . . . I seem to have a relatively unresponsive stick where I once had a sexual organ.[46]

How can we explain the continuance of flawed reasoning in the medical claims and the discrepancies in beliefs of many physicians about circumcision pain and foreskin? One reason is that people want coherence and consistency in their beliefs and experience. If inconsistency occurs, called cognitive dissonance, we will tend to align our beliefs to fit our experience.[47] The experience of many physicians regarding circumcision is that they have performed it many times. Choosing to circumcise is a serious choice. After such a choice is made, people tend to appreciate the chosen alternative and depreciate the rejected alternative.[48] As a result, beliefs are adopted to conform with experience and support the decision to circumcise. Inconsistency can also be reconciled by altering our experience. That is, we may perceive and accept only information that fits our beliefs. The tendency to avoid new information increases when the discrepancy between beliefs and experience increases.[49] (Even after learning something new, people better remember information that supports established beliefs than conflicting information.[50]) Avoidance may lead to rigidity of thinking and dependence on dogma to counteract and subdue doubt. Another approach to reducing cognitive dissonance is to discredit those with an opposing view. Obviously, this response has nothing to do with the content and merits of opposing arguments.

The incongruity of circumcision beliefs goes unrecognized by those who hold them, as the double standard replaces consistency. For example, tonsillectomy used to be a routine procedure that was considered a cure for many childhood illnesses. Doctors stopped performing routine tonsillectomies when they learned that the surgery was of no benefit, had serious risks (including death), and removed tissue that served a health function.[51] It was determined that instead of surgery, treatment with antibiotics was often sufficient. But when the AAP concluded that there was no valid medical need for circumcision,[52] physicians ignored the statement and continued to circumcise. Part of the reason for this inconsistency was that physicians' behavior followed their beliefs. They continued to believe that circumcision had medical benefits or that, at least, circumcision did no harm.

Clearly, in and out of the medical community, several principles of logic and reason are violated, and some important factors are ignored when it comes to the issue of circumcision. False beliefs are substituted for basic facts and are adopted in the process of rationalization to defend the underlying attitude that circumcision is a good thing. These beliefs can be challenged with rational argument and changed. That is why medical claims supporting circumcision have changed over the years. However, the attitude in support of circumcision is not so easily affected because of its connection to strong emotions.

EMOTIONAL FACTORS

Using medical claims to defend circumcision may be an unconscious way for physicians to avoid the emotional discomfort of questioning their own circumcision. A survey of randomly selected primary care physicians showed that circumcision was more often supported by doctors who were older, male, and circumcised.[53] Other research has demonstrated that people will continue an endeavor once they have invested time and effort.[54] Perhaps, as Dr. Anand believes (see "Beliefs about Infant Pain" earlier in this chapter), some circumcising doctors are also seeking to avoid guilt feelings connected with circumcisions they have performed throughout the years.

Defending circumcision with medical claims also fits the tendency toward preventive medical interventions. This approach is often based on fear. A nurse for newborn infants reflected on her childbirth training, "I can't forget how much I was trained to expect that something *will* go wrong. . . . I was trained to be afraid."[55] If the physician is afraid that something will go wrong if he does not circumcise, then that fear further contributes to support of the practice.

There is additional evidence that emotional factors affect doctors' opinions about circumcision. Anne Briggs, childbirth educator, researcher, and author of a book on circumcision, wrote that "open hostility is not an uncommon reaction among physicians when faced with a challenge to circumcision thinking."[56] This kind of response confirms that some doctors who do circumcisions are emotionally invested in continuing to do them. A mother reported to the Circumcision Resource Center that she was "hounded" by obstetricians about circumcision after she declined circumcision for her newborn son.

Parents must also deal with emotional factors. According to a recent study, the decision to circumcise "is more an emotional than a rational decision."[57] It is often based on either of two fears: fear that their son will not be socially accepted, a social concern; or fear that he will get a disease or infection, a medical concern. If the medical concerns do not persuade parents, some doctors who strongly advocate circumcision will often cite social concerns (for more on this, see Chapter 3), a response that clearly involves issues beyond their field of expertise.

Appeals to fear often work better than other methods of persuasion.[58] This is particularly true when the source has high credibility. In general, fear is more likely to be used by advocates to influence others' decisions when the merits of their argument are weak. On a 1993 radio talk show, former Surgeon General C. Everett Koop defended circumcision by warning,

> If you have one little boy in your family who is already circumcised, you'd better circumcise the second little boy, because if you don't, neither one will know which one is normal.[59]

Although lack of knowledge about circumcision makes some parents vulnerable to this kind of appeal, others benefit from their own experience. Steven Dion, father of an older circumcised son and a younger intact son, explained his last circumcision decision in a television news interview. "We just felt, 'Why make the same mistake twice?'"[60] Dion changed his mind about circumcision after he learned more about it.

MALE ATTITUDES TOWARD CHOOSING CIRCUMCISION

In a study of parental circumcision attitudes, where the parents disagreed about the decision to circumcise, in the overwhelming majority of cases (89 percent), it was the father who wanted to circumcise.[61] Therefore, in studies of the views of both doctors (see "Emotional Factors") and parents, it is mainly men who are perpetuating circumcision. Why is this?

To find out why men choose to circumcise, I conducted a preliminary survey regarding male attitudes toward circumcision. My questionnaire was distributed to men attending a 1993 weekend men's conference called the Massachusetts Men's Gathering. The conference was attended by about ninety men, mostly between thirty and sixty years old. Fifty-six men returned the questionnaire (see Appendix B for sample questionnaire).

Based on responses to the questionnaire, the following inferences can be drawn for this group of men:

1. Circumcised men are much more likely than intact men to choose circumcision for their son.
2. Circumcised men are much less likely than intact men to know that the foreskin has a few purposes that benefit sexual sensation.
3. Circumcised men who do not know the purposes of the foreskin are more likely to choose circumcision for their son than those who know the purposes of the foreskin.
4. Circumcised men who don't know the purposes of the foreskin tend to minimize the size of the foreskin.
5. Circumcised men who tend to minimize the size of the adult foreskin are more likely to choose circumcision for their son.
6. How a man feels about his own circumcision has a strong impact on how he feels about circumcising his son. Those who feel better about their own circumcision are much more likely to circumcise their son.
7. Those circumcised men who feel better about their own circumcision tend to believe they are more well-informed about circumcision.
8. Some circumcised men who believe they are well-informed about circumcision are in fact not well-informed.
9. Seeing a circumcision can make it less likely that a circumcised man will choose to circumcise his son.

It appears that those who feel better about their own circumcision are more likely to underestimate what they are missing. Not choosing circumcision for their son would suggest disapproval of their own circumcision, a step they are not ready to take. Women obviously do not have to contend with the psychological effect of being circumcised when making a decision for their son.

This preliminary survey suggests that support for, or a neutral attitude toward, circumcision is based, at least in part, on a lack of knowledge about circumcision and acceptance of the general culture's circumcision beliefs. In that case, as more men learn the facts about circumcision, their dissatisfaction with circumcision will increase. This may lead to a decrease in the circumcision rate.

BEHAVIORAL FACTORS

While fathers may choose circumcision because of beliefs and attitudes, for the physician, there are contingencies that support circumcision, one of which is financial reward. Some physicians believe that as long as physicians are paid for doing the procedure, circumcision will be performed. Predictably, research confirms that expecting something positive (or negative) from an anticipated course of action affects motivation.[62] Surgeon Thomas Ritter, who wrote a book about circumcision, tried to discuss the practice with other physicians at his hospital. Responses included, "Most parents want the operation. I can make an extra $200. Why should I try to dissuade them?" An obstetrician argued, "If I don't do it, the pediatrician will, and he'll get the money."[63] Even Wiswell, who defends the practice of circumcision based on his research on urinary tract infection, noted in 1987 that he knew physicians who "look at a foreskin and almost see a $125 price tag on it. Heck, if you do 10 a week, that's over $1000 a week, and they don't take that much time."[64] Clearly, the financial incentive influences some doctors and is an important part of the issue.

Another factor that can affect physician behavior is that there may be negative consequences for a physician who does not comply with a request for circumcision. Such a response may antagonize the parents and require an extended discussion. In other situations, a refusal by the physician may create friction with hospital administration or peers.

COMMUNICATION FACTORS

Mental, emotional, and behavioral factors have an impact on communication regarding circumcision. The crucial effect of communication on the circumcision decision is illustrated in a study of 133 families who had recent male births. There was a tendency for those couples who had more discussion about circumcision to decide against it.[65]

Between Physicians and Parents

The traditional lower status of parents in their relationship to the doctor affects discussion of circumcision. As humanistic psychologist, Abraham Maslow, wrote, "A status of weakness or subordination or low self-esteem inhibits the need to know."[66] Consequently, the tendency for most parents is to defer to medical authority. The general high credibility of physicians also plays a role. A source of information that is considered highly credible can get away with poor evidence in persuasion.[67] In the words of one regretful mother, "The doctor was in favor of it. He didn't mention any problems with it. It seemed like it was the thing to do." For their part, some physicians rely on their authority to influence laypeople and may consciously or unconsciously discourage questioning.

Because of the emotional nature of the subject, communication between physicians and parents about circumcision often does not satisfy the requirements of "informed consent" which is applied to other surgical procedures. "Informed consent" means that a full and complete discussion with the doctor regarding potential benefits, risks, and complications of circumcision, as well as discussion of the alternative of no circumcision, must precede the parents' written authorization for the procedure. The usual lack of a complete discussion is borne out by the results of a study of medical school students. While learning the informed consent process, students were least successful in providing complete information in situations that involved emotional conflict.[68] In the case of circumcision, the physician may minimize the procedure's risks and complications and believe that there is nothing to gain personally from what might need to be a detailed explanation. Full disclosure of facts might even arouse animosity in parents and make the physician uncomfortable. For example, some mothers who had decided for circumcision were unhappy to hear their physician give them comprehensive information on circumcision risks and complications.[69]

Consequently, both doctors and parents often take the path of least resistance. A doctor might not raise the subject of circumcision; or he or she might offer advice that differs from his or her personal views, for example, opposing circumcision privately while being neutral with parents. A national study of 400 pediatricians and obstetricians indicated that two-thirds of doctors took a neutral position on circumcision when advising parents.[70] This approach can lead a physician to make conflicting statements. Richard Harris, a Chicago urologist, was consulted about circumcision by a Boston radio talk show. With reference to medical benefits, he offered the following separate remarks in the course of his brief interview with the host:

> There are indeed some benefits to circumcision.
>
> There are really no true medical indications.
>
> I don't counsel my patients that there is a really truly great medical indication.
>
> There are some benefits to it medically.
>
> I don't know that you could say that it medically definitely should be done.[71]

A neutral or contradictory response from a doctor does not encourage parents to question circumcision, the status quo, nor does it help them make a confident, informed decision. Even a clear statement that circumcision isn't necessary may not matter because parents may believe that physicians who do circumcisions must support the practice.[72] The fact that hospitals continue to offer the service also contributes to parents' belief that it is an advisable practice.

On their side, physicians believe that parents want circumcision strongly and cannot be influenced otherwise. This is a self-serving belief. Anne Briggs's research, and that of others, indicates that the physician's attitude strongly influences the circumcision decision.[73] If the physician strongly advised against it, the circumcision rate would drop dramatically. In one study, the circumcision rate was 20 percent when physicians opposed it and almost 100 percent when physicians supported it.[74]

Between Childbirth Educators and Parents

Most expectant parents attend childbirth education classes. What educators teach parents about circumcision is affected by educators' experience and attitudes concerning circumcision education. To learn about this connection, I asked a small group of childbirth educators to complete a questionnaire prior to the beginning of my workshop presentation to them on circumcision. The following results are based on 14 returned questionnaires:

1. Most respondents had seen a circumcision in person.
2. Asked if they would choose to circumcise a son, only one of the educators responded that she would have him circumcised for non-religious reasons (three were unsure).
3. Those who had circumcised sons regretted their decision, which they later concluded was not based on factual information.
4. Most respondents spent less than ten minutes on circumcision education in their classes.
5. Those who were more strongly opposed to circumcision spent more time teaching about it.
6. Most respondents agreed that their circumcision presentation should be "balanced."

Even among this group of childbirth educators, who are probably more likely to question or oppose circumcision than their peers (as demonstrated by their attendance at this workshop), the strategy of adopting a neutral position on circumcision is the preferred approach to educating parents. Based on their responses, there are several reasons for neutrality. Childbirth educators are wary of being accused of bias. They believe it is their responsibility to present balanced views of childbirth issues. In the case of circumcision, they are also sensitive to the feelings of expectant Jewish parents. Finally, if educators are not independent, but work for a hospital or other medical organization, their options for questioning standard practice are limited. As a result, some educators walk a fine line between their desire to inform their clients of the facts and their fear that the facts will upset their clients or their employers. The result of the balanced approach, in this case, is that expectant parents leave the class thinking that there are reasonable arguments on both sides of the circumcision issue. (See Appendix A for a sample circumcision information sheet.)

Does offering balanced arguments on both sides of the circumcision issue necessarily serve the best interests of the child and his parents? It may be easier to consider this question with the help of an analogy. Suppose we were planning to offer a class about the advisability of cigarette smoking. The dangers of cigarette smoking, unlike circumcision, are well-known. However, if the aim was to offer a class that gave balanced views of the smoking issue, the arguments against smoking would have to be diminished, and the arguments for smoking would have to be augmented. For example, rather than hear that cigarette smoking has been found to cause many diseases, we might hear something like cigarette smoking may lead to lung "problems" in rare cases. On the pro-smoking side, there would be inflated arguments about smoking being pleasurable and popular. The point is that to present a "balanced" review of the advisability of smoking would require omitting and distorting the facts that are known about it.

This is what happens with circumcision education. The circumcision information sheet (see Appendix A) at first seems to offer more arguments supporting circumcision than arguments against it. However, after reading the accompanying letter pointing out the errors and omissions in the fact sheet, one sees the arguments for circumcision evaporate, and the arguments against circumcision expand. Furthermore, both the fact sheet and circumcision education in general do not address psychological concerns, which are discussed in later chapters.

In addition to the question of how circumcision information is presented is the issue of taking a position on circumcision (to be discussed further in Chapter 8). Some of the childbirth educators who completed questionnaires confuse taking a position with taking away the parents' "right to choose." Clearly, whatever the childbirth educator says, the parents will make their own decision. These educators may be following the lead of the two main childbirth education organizations, the International Childbirth Education Association and the American Society for Psychoprophylaxis in Obstetrics (ASPO)/Lamaze. Neither of them takes a position on circumcision. Generally, their literature contains a balanced presentation that does not sufficiently warn expectant parents of the harm caused by circumcision (e.g., extreme pain, behavioral changes, risk of complications, and loss of protective, sensitive tissue, the result of which is diminished sexual pleasure) or confirm the lack of proven benefit. Although a balanced position on circumcision is perceived as being not biased, it alters the facts to serve a purpose other than providing the best information available on the subject. The other purpose of the balanced approach is not to offend. Facts are withheld or altered, intentionally or unintentionally, because of people's feelings. The end result is familiar: more damage is done by concealing the facts than by revealing them. In the case of circumcision, most infants are subjected to the procedure because their parents are not well-informed.

For the group of childbirth educators in the survey, observing a circumcision was associated with opposition to it. At the Circumcision Resource Center, we have also heard from adults who have witnessed circumcisions and consequently have chosen not to circumcise their sons. This is why some people feel that viewing a videotape of a circumcision should be included as part of circumcision education for expectant parents. The pictures would convey what no words could say.

LANGUAGE FACTORS

The words we use and the words we choose to avoid when talking about circumcision all serve to reinforce the practice. The word "circumcision" itself is a symbol for a specific surgical procedure, but based on surveys of adult knowledge, the meaning of the word and the impact of the procedure on the infant are often not clearly understood. We are reluctant to use certain other words to describe or identify what circumcision is. The word "circumcision," in effect, becomes a euphemism because it has less emotional impact on us than these other words. Words not typically associated with circumcision may stir uncomfortable feelings, yet a closer look supports the connection, regardless of the intent of the doctor or parent.

To mutilate is to damage or injure by removing a part or parts. Circumcision removes a normal, healthy, functioning part of the penis. It leaves a scar, a mark left after a wound has healed. A wound is an injury in which the skin is cut or damaged. Therefore, circumcision qualifies as a form of mutilation.

Trauma is an emotional shock often having a lasting effect. Research on infant responses to circumcision and, as we shall see in later chapters, trauma theory and clinical experience support the view that circumcision results in trauma.

To amputate means to cut off. Generally, other body parts are surgically amputated only if there is an incurable localized condition present that may threaten the rest of the body or result in a serious irreparable injury. In circumcision, the foreskin is cut off without such justification. Though the intention differs, circumcision is foreskin amputation.

Furthermore, the term "uncircumcised" suggests that to be circumcised is the norm, the standard. This assumption represents an American view. From a global perspective, to be "uncircumcised" is to be normal, natural, intact, the way males are born, and the way most of the world's males remain.

Even the word "pain" can limit our appreciation of what an infant feels. By definition, pain can range from "mild discomfort or dull distress to acute often unbearable agony."[75] Advocates of circumcision tend to equate circumcision pain with "mild discomfort" while the research indicates otherwise. In general, when circumcision is described as causing pain, people relate the word "pain" to what they consciously recall as a painful experience, for example, an injection or closing a door on one's finger. However, a normally conscious painful experience would be much less severe than the overwhelming pain of being circumcised (see Chapter 1). Circumcision pain, like any similar pain, is too extreme to be conscious.

Words used to refer to the infant may also support circumcision. Our society often tends to think of infants more as property than as people, and our language sometimes reflects this. Rather than calling little Samuel or Robert by name, we often say, "Where's the baby?" or refer to the newborn infant as "it." We replace the personal with the impersonal. The dehumanization of infants contributes to the deterioration of our protective instinct toward them. Contrarily, in a more general sense, research has shown that perceived similarity to victims increases our willingness to aid them.[76] Recognizing that infants are in many ways similar to us will affect our attitude toward them and toward circumcision.

DEFENSE MECHANISMS

Freud wrote, "The tendency to forget the disagreeable seems to me to be quite general."[77] The subject of circumcision is so "disagreeable" that many people will avoid it consciously and unconsciously. In psychoanalytic theory, defense mechanisms are unconscious ways of dealing with the "disagreeable," internal emotional pain and external experience that stimulates emotional pain. Two common defense mechanisms are repression and denial.

Repression relates to keeping memories, feelings, or impulses from conscious awareness (see Chapters 4 and 5). Denial involves a refusal to acknowledge certain aspects of experience.

To varying degrees, one can be open and aware of experience or closed and numb to experience. Our degree of awareness can be subject to unconscious control. For example, we may deny or avoid a potential threat or uncomfortable situation without being aware of it. By doing so, we avert anxiety and stress. We feel safer, but our perception is now distorted and restricted, and our emotional capacity and spontaneity are diminished.

Denial can be amazingly effective. Pediatrician Paul Fleiss did circumcisions for ten years and says, "I never heard the baby cry."[78] Dr. Gregory Skipper, a prospective father, recognized his denial after observing a circumcision.

> I watched a circumcision being performed and immediately, without any question, knew that there was no way that I could have my new-born son tortured in such a manner. It seemed like the first time that I had ever really watched the procedure, *even though I had done several dozen in medical school.* The baby was absolutely panicked and exhibited the most shrill and desperate behavior one could imagine! The pediatrician performing the procedure continued his mutilation as if nothing were happening. I almost vomited.[79]

The use of defense mechanisms by physicians and parents serves, in part, to protect their self-esteem. Recognizing that they are harming an infant might cause them not to feel good about themselves. Because protecting self-esteem sometimes takes priority over being accurate or correct, potentially threatening information may be reinterpreted or dismissed.[80] This can happen without awareness.

It is difficult to assemble convincing empirical evidence of denial since it is the evidence itself that is denied or interpreted to mean something else. A particularly noteworthy demonstration of the existence of denial is therefore an admission by one who has been in denial. An instance occurred in the course of my research on circumcision attitudes. A mother reported choosing circumcision for her son because "the doctor said it was best. We trusted this information." Years later after learning more about circumcision, this woman stated, "I feel like I've come out of denial and feel sad and guilty about my son's circumcision." She did not regret that she found new information about circumcision.

Denial, as previously stated, often involves adherence to certain beliefs. It may involve a tendency to minimize or trivialize the issue. This explains the behavior and responses of some doctors who minimize the pain to the infant or ignore the function of the foreskin. When I asked the editor of the *New England Journal of Medicine* about circumcision at a public forum, he replied that "it doesn't make any difference," meaning that it doesn't make any difference if one is circumcised or not. Parents who refer to the foreskin as "just a little skin" are using the same defense against anxiety.

Peg Guerra declined the option of observing her son's circumcision because the thought made her "a bit squeamish." She explained, "I'm frightened of it. I kept saying it can't be any worse than having my daughter's ears pierced when she was 3 month's old."[81] It seems that she was attempting to minimize both her own feelings and the experience of her son. Parents who choose circumcision do not want to believe they are causing great pain to their child.

Those who witness circumcisions may deny their experience. Indications of this denial can be detected empirically in the form of reduced physiological response.[82] In extreme cases a person may shut down physically by fainting. This has been observed at ritual circumcisions and hospital circumcisions.[83]

Studies, personal accounts, and our experience confirm that the ability of adults to deny experience is well developed. However, children cannot deny reality so easily because their defenses are weaker. I know of two adults who witnessed circumcisions when they were children; both were about eight years old at the time. I met Zipora Schulz following my presentation on circumcision at a Jewish conference. She related this story of her childhood experience at a ritual circumcision.

> I walked into the room by mistake. I saw it [the circumcision] happen. I remember the baby crying and crying for a long time. People seemed happy about it. It seemed horrible and insane to me.[84]

She insists that she will not circumcise if she has a son in the future. Jeffrey Felshman was also at a Jewish ritual circumcision.

> One detail remains in my mind almost 30 years later. Screaming. The screaming was like none I've heard from any baby before or since. My cousin's grandfather was a doctor . . . and he assured us kids that the baby didn't feel any pain. It also was the first time a doctor expressed an opinion to which I responded, silently, "Bullshit."[85]

That experience helped to give Felshman, who is Jewish, the courage to keep his own son intact.

An examination of pertinent medical and psychological literature, including surveys of parents, physicians, and childbirth educators, helps to explain the decision to circumcise.

WHY PARENTS AND PHYSICIANS CHOOSE TO CIRCUMCISE INFANTS

1. Parents are asked to make the circumcision decision but lack the proper knowledge. They tend to defer to the doctor's supposed knowledge.
2. Parents fear assumed undesirable future consequences for intact boys regarding social disapproval and disease.
3. Health claims supporting circumcision are believed, though they are based on flawed studies and faulty reasoning.
4. Physicians' and parents' false cultural beliefs that circumcision is not very painful and that the foreskin has no purpose are central to perpetuating the practice.

5. Because of discomfort and lack of knowledge themselves, many physicians and childbirth educators do not provide accurate and complete information to parents.
6. The use and exclusion of certain words helps to maintain public support for circumcision.
7. Both physicians and parents are subject to emotional repression and denial about circumcision.
8. Financial incentive is a motivating factor for some doctors to circumcise.

3

Social and Cultural Factors

Perpetuating Circumcision in America

No person knows his own culture who knows only his own
culture.

—Gordon Allport,
psychologist, researcher, and author

We are the only country in the world that circumcises most of its
male infants for nonreligious reasons.[1] Why is this the case? How
did this happen? A review of the historical background of our
circumcision practice contributes to an understanding of the
circumcision issue in America.

HISTORICAL CONTEXT

Circumcision was originally promoted in the United States in the
1870s.[2] To understand the reasons, it is helpful to examine the
social conditions of the time. Alexis de Tocqueville's *Democracy
in America*, published in 1840, is particularly useful for this
purpose. It is still considered to be one of the best accounts of
American society ever written. De Tocqueville's work is cited
frequently in *The Horrors of the Half-Known Life* by G. J. Barker-
Benfield and *Habits of the Heart* by Robert Bella and his colleagues, two contemporary major sociocultural studies of American beliefs and attitudes.[3] The American male of the 1800s was
described by de Tocqueville as insensitive, cold, and implacable.

He was said to be primarily driven by financial reward and had little concern for his destruction of the environment in pursuit of such rewards. Human relationships were seen as secondary to preserving male autonomy. Perhaps most important, child-rearing practices emphasized independence, self-control, self-denial, and breaking the child's will.

De Tocqueville also observed a tendency in Americans toward isolation. He used a new word, "individualism," to describe what he saw as a way of thinking and being that was potentially threatening and harmful to the developing society. The noted essay, "Self-Reliance," written by Ralph Waldo Emerson in 1841, exemplified the theme that troubled de Tocqueville.

In the previous century, the family had still worked together on the farm or in the shop. Now, in the nineteenth century, men worked outside the home, separate from women. Many men traveled west while the women stayed back east. With men out conquering the frontier, both men and women had less contact with each other. Perhaps the increased separation of the sexes led to increased masturbation. In any case, as part of this changing social environment, there were prohibitions against masturbation.

Masturbation phobia lasted from about 1830 to 1930, fueled by male ideas that grew out of Victorian attitudes, pervasive Puritan values, sexual guilt, self-doubt, and hostile public opinion. People became less able to disclose personal feelings to their family. Instead, they consulted advice columns in newspapers and manuals, and relied on counselors and physicians.[4] Best-selling books by male doctors, clergy, and industrialists warned about the supposed dangers of masturbation and exacerbated public fears.

It appears that some chose to exploit the situation for personal profit. Sylvester Graham, for instance, wrote in 1848 that disease was connected to sexuality. He explained his ideas in a book and advocated his own cure for abnormal sexual practices and excesses: Graham crackers and Graham flour.[5] In 1888 John Harvey Kellogg also wrote on the subject of sexuality and disease. He made a fortune from selling books persuading people that masturbation was a "disease." He blamed masturbation for thirty-one different ailments and identified "symptoms" of masturbation like shyness and insomnia. Kellogg "discovered" two cures: Kellogg's breakfast cereals and, for persistent masturbators, circumcision.[6]

It was not long before circumcision was advocated for infants to prevent rather than cure masturbation. The editor of the *Journal of the American Medical Association* took this position in 1928.[7] A circumcised child, it was believed, was less likely to handle his penis for cleaning or in response to irritation connected with the foreskin. It was also presumed that many physical and mental diseases that were believed to be caused by masturbation could be prevented by circumcision.[8] Since little was known about the origins of various diseases, it was difficult to refute claims implicating masturbation. Though the original masturbation theories were acknowledged to be without merit years later, circumcision had by then become an established practice in the upper classes, from which most physicians came. Little wonder that new medical claims were then put forth to justify it.[9] The foreskin itself was then blamed for various diseases. It is noteworthy that advocating circumcision to prevent masturbatory insanity, a historical claim, and to prevent urinary tract infection, a contemporary claim, both involve flawed logic and irrational fear, and establish no proven cause-and-effect relationship to justify the surgery. While the specific beliefs may change, the psychological process does not.

Other beliefs about the human body gained public acceptance around the turn of the century. The growth of advertising had much to do with this change. Between 1865 and 1900, spending for advertising increased tenfold. By 1919 the amount expended on advertising was five times that of 1900, over half a billion dollars a year.[10] Psychology was a new and indispensable tool that advertisers learned and used for manipulating how people thought about themselves. The purpose was to create demand for consumer goods. In order to market a highly profitable class of products for personal hygiene, people were first sold the idea that their bodies were dirty and needed frequent cleaning. Anxieties about contact with "dirty" immigrants fed the desire for cleanliness. (Product appeal was enhanced if it was "untouched by human hands" before it reached the consumer.) Thus, anything that could help keep one clean was valued, and another argument for circumcision was adopted. People were also sold the idea that the human body was a "machine." To be "running like a machine" was to be in good health.[11] Viewing the body in this way facilitated acceptance of a "design improvement" on the penis.

Changes in childbirth practices also contributed to the growing acceptance of circumcision. In the late nineteenth century, male obstetricians took control of childbirth from midwives. The methods used were simple and effective: propaganda and legislation. According to Barker-Benfield, men were motivated by "anxieties about themselves, their fear of the changing status of women, and their desire to conquer and control the innermost power of nature."[12] Women were persuaded that birth was dangerous and required a doctor in attendance.

Male doctors further increased their control over the birth process by changing the location of birth. In 1900 less than 5 percent of births were in hospitals. By the 1930s, 60–75 percent of all births in cities were taking place in hospitals.[13] As the number of hospital births in the United States increased, so too did the number of circumcisions. As early as 1920, the circumcision rate had climbed to about 50 percent (see Fig. 1, Introduction).

Later in the century, as American families became more isolated from each other and from relatives, popular knowledge about childcare decreased further. New parents had little experience with children and turned to "experts" who wrote books about childcare. As a result, individual writers could have a tremendous influence. However, just as in the previous century, the information and advice in these books was a function of the contemporary cultural environment.[14] For example, as pointed out in the previous chapter, Benjamin Spock advocated circumcision in 1946. To his credit, in 1976 he reversed his position, but by that time millions of parents had followed his earlier advice.

CIRCUMCISION IN OTHER COUNTRIES

The United States is not the only country to ever practice male infant circumcision on a large scale. Earlier in this century, circumcision was instituted in England, Canada, Australia, and New

Zealand, all English-speaking countries. Non-English-speaking countries apparently rejected arguments for circumcision as fallacious. The British circumcision rate peaked at something over 30 percent and then fell drastically in the 1950s. By 1972 the rate was less than 1 percent. The probable explanation is that British medical studies critical of circumcision caused the National Health Service to terminate payment for it.[15]

In the 1970s the circumcision rates in Canada, Australia, and New Zealand were about half the American rate. Circumcision remained covered by their National Health Services, and rates fell slowly after peaking. The difference was that British parents had to pay for circumcision while those in the other English-speaking countries did not.[16] The need to pay for the procedure apparently was a significant factor in reducing parental requests for circumcision in England. This connection is supported by others. In one study of 90 couples who chose circumcision and had insurance coverage, only 20 would have chosen it without insurance payment.[17] A report in a medical journal found that circumcision was 2.5 times more likely to be done if it was paid for by insurance.[18] Though some American insurance companies have discontinued coverage for circumcisions, most have kept their circumcision coverage intact. One HMO explains that "such coverage is preferred by the vast majority of our members. . . . In fact, there would likely be a significant consumer negative response if we refused to perform these."[19]

Economic factors supported American circumcision, yet cultural factors contributed also.

SEXUALITY, DENIAL, AND NORMALITY

The cultural causes of circumcision in America may be related to specific widely held values and anxieties. Traditionally, in a society shaped by Puritan ethics and views of sexuality, sexual pleasures have been considered immoral or dangerous; celibacy and virginity have been regarded as virtues. In general, our culture tends not to value pleasure. Often what is pleasurable is in conflict with what is accepted as right. Concerns about sexual morality can be a disguise for deep adult anxieties regarding sex. The sexual experience has the potential to be our peak physical, emotional, and spiritual pleasure. Failure to achieve this satisfying peak experience because of a variety of personal and social inhibiting factors may be associated with unresolved tension and repressed emotional pain.

For those who have accepted prevailing values and who continue to deny themselves sexual pleasure or experience conflict over sexual pleasure, it hurts to be reminded of their denied pleasure, and it is difficult to allow someone else to enjoy something that they cannot or do not allow themselves to enjoy. In particular, many adults tend to want to control the sexual feelings of the young. For example, some parents may prevent infants from touching their own genitals. In this way, societal attitudes and actions may serve to inhibit children's sexual activities. Parents and physicians may pass on the control of sexual pleasure to children in different ways. Circumcision is one of them. Because the foreskin is erogenous tissue with sexual functions (see Chapter 2), removing it negatively affects sexual pleasure. Though parents and physicians would undoubtedly disagree, the connection between circumcision and the control of sexual pleasure deserves serious consideration.

Societal sexual anxieties also contribute to parental misunderstanding about circumcision. Generally, people are uncomfortable talking seriously about sex. They avoid it or joke about it. This is particularly true concerning the penis. Asking specific questions is considered too embarrassing. As a result, certain information, ideas, and feelings are excluded from societal awareness.

Social conditions are often an extension of common family conditions. Families that are uncomfortable talking about sex reflect and reinforce the same limitation in the society. How do children know not to talk to their parents about sex? It is not said, but it is implicitly communicated. The same is true of circumcision. It is rare for children to talk to their parents about circumcision. If they do dare to mention the subject, the response probably would make it clear not to mention it again. Young children who are taught to repress feelings about circumcision become adults who continue to deny a part of their own experience.

Families tend not to talk about certain matters that are sexual or shocking because they carry too high an emotional charge and threaten stability. Similarly, while the society continues to subject male infants to circumcision, the society generally remains silent. Such behavior demonstrates that denial and repression apply to families and the society as well as to individuals.

This family and social denial is a form of collusion, in that we tacitly agree not to ask or tell about circumcision. It serves to encapsulate and conceal the anxiety and pain connected with the practice. Instead, we tell ourselves that circumcision is "normal," but sexual normality reflects group values. As Gordon Allport stated, "What is familiar tends to become a value."[20] Circumcision is now familiar, widespread, and continues to be the preferred choice of the culture. For example, in a study of 145 new mothers, most preferred circumcised men for various sexual activities.[21] (Not coincidentally, the subjects overwhelmingly chose circumcision for their sons.) This American preference is in strong contrast to the comments of a woman who immigrated to the United States from Sweden, where they do not circumcise. She wrote,

> When I first started dating here, I was surprised, confused, shocked and disappointed because almost all the men here are circumcised. I have always regarded circumcision as barbaric and ugly. There are many American ways I still do not understand, and perhaps I am still experiencing culture shock, but a whole penis can't be *that* bad, can it?[22]

There is another cultural factor that merits mention. Although Americans generally see themselves as independent and free from the demands of conformity, our behavior is often in conflict with this view. In the case of circumcision, it is conformity, perhaps as much as any other social factor, that contributes to the perpetuation of the practice. Let's examine this powerful human social phenomenon.

CONFORMITY

The importance of conformity in the circumcision decision is illustrated by a survey of parents of 124 newborn males born at a Denver hospital. The results showed that for parents making the circumcision decision, social concerns outweighed medical concerns. Parents' reasons for circumcising were based mainly on an interest that the baby look like his father, brothers, and friends. Only 23 percent of the genitally intact fathers had circumcised sons. In contrast, 90 percent of the circumcised fathers had circumcised sons. Fathers wanted their sons to "match," and there was a belief that the boy would want that, too. The authors concluded that the circumcision decision has a strong base in social and cultural issues.[23]

Social concerns were also a major consideration among parents making the circumcision decision in a study at a Baltimore hospital and published in *Pediatrics*. A group of parents was given special information on circumcision, based on the 1975 American Academy of Pediatrics Ad Hoc Task Force on Circumcision Report, which concluded that circumcision is not medically necessary. (There was no information on significant harm caused by circumcision.) A control group in the study was not given any special information on circumcision. The circumcision rates of the two groups were not statistically different. Parents found social reasons alone sufficient to choose circumcision. The researchers concluded, "Circumcision is a custom in our society; to change the attitude toward it is not an easy task."[24]

The medical profession sometimes takes advantage of this tendency to conform. For example, the American Academy of Pediatrics pamphlet for parents, *Circumcision: Pros and Cons*, states, "Many parents choose to have their sons circumcised because 'all the other men in the family were circumcised' or because they don't want their son to feel 'different.'" This type of statement is commonly used in literature provided to parents. Sometimes an inflated circumcision rate is included (e.g., 80 percent rather than 60 percent) to increase the inclination to circumcise based on the tendency to conform (see Appendix A).

Presumably, the medical profession should be offering medical advice on this surgical procedure, not sampling or distorting the opinions of laypeople.

The following personal account also demonstrates the medical profession's use of the inclination to conform to influence parents.

> When my wife was expecting a baby, I was undecided about circumcision, while she was against it. After my son was born, the doctor asked me if I wanted to have him circumcised. He reviewed arguments about hygiene and health, but I was still unconvinced. In a final effort to persuade me, he asked, "Don't you want your son to look like you?" That question was enough to help me decide. I told him, "I'm not circumcised."

Whether a child is circumcised or not, the benefit to the son of "matching" his father may be more imagined than real, as shown by this story from a mother named Lori Whitmore. When she was pregnant with her son, her husband wanted circumcision and she did not. During dinner with her in-laws, the subject came up, and her husband defended his position by declaring, "My father is circumcised. I'm circumcised. I want my boy to be circumcised like us." Her husband's father responded, "Wait a minute. I'm not circumcised." Despite his embarrassment, the husband held to his position.[25]

Parents rarely examine the logic of these issues. One who did was Jeffrey Felshman, a circumcised man who kept his son intact. Felshman's friend had argued that father and son should "match."

> I thought about it, and realized that while my friend was no dummy, his was a stupid argument. Of course the kid was going to look different. I should have him put under the knife so we could look more alike? The last time I saw my father's penis was when I was a child, but if memory serves, our members looked pretty damned different. His was bigger. I don't know if that's still the case (he'd probably say it is), but it didn't make much difference to me.[26]

Author Edward Wallerstein asks, "If a boy's father is tattooed or has an appendectomy scar, or wears eyeglasses, should the child be similarly provided?"[27] What about the son conforming to the different circumcision status of a potential stepfather or peers in another community if the family moves? Because circumcising to conform is easier to question than reasons not to circumcise (extreme pain, medically unnecessary, risk of complications, etc.), parents who choose to circumcise (conformity being the dominant reason) have less confidence in their decision than parents who choose not to circumcise.[28] However, the concern of parents that their son match peers merits further examination.

It would be helpful to know the feelings of intact men who do not match their peers. In 1992 *Journeymen*, a national men's quarterly magazine, did a body image survey of its readers. Out of 30 intact men who responded, only one reported being unhappy with his intact status. Since most of these men would have been in the minority in the locker room, their apparent satisfaction conflicts with parental expectations.

To explore the feelings of intact men who are unhappy, I interviewed five such men who contacted the Circumcision Resource Center. All five either had considered or were considering getting themselves circumcised. The benefit they perceived from circumcision typically was "to fit in more" or "to look more attractive." Three of the five were not aware of any disadvantages to being circumcised. If they remembered, the first awareness of their difference was at about the age of ten to twelve, except that one was aware at about age six. Two of the five remembered negative comments made by others about their intact penis. The same two men also recalled negative comments from sexual partners. Four of the men had never talked to anyone about these feelings before. One man had talked to his parents once about it, and he reported feeling frustrated and dissatisfied with that conversation. Three of the five had circumcised fathers. One of these three also had five intact brothers. Another with an intact father had one circumcised brother.

Three men reported being the only intact boy in their gym classes. Another reported that maybe one out of twenty or twenty-five was intact. One reported that about 10 percent were not circumcised. Extreme minority status was a sufficient condition to lead to negative feelings for one man. He did not report any negative comments from others and was aware of advantages to being intact.

Interestingly, circumcision status of the father did not seem to matter. Two men claimed that they had never seen their father nude. The other three had rarely seen their father nude and were too young to notice the difference. By the time they were old enough to be aware of the difference, they never again saw their father nude.

The three men who were not aware of disadvantages to circumcision were given factual information about the purposes of the foreskin, the history of American circumcision practice, and the negative feelings of some circumcised men. These men were contacted a few months later. They reported a significant decrease in discomfort about being intact, with some remaining ambivalence. The other two men who were previously aware of disadvantages to circumcision reported lingering "back and forth" feelings.

Another intact man who contacted the Center grew up hearing negative comments about his status.

> By the time I was about seventeen, I thought women wouldn't like a penis with foreskin on it. Then I thought maybe I'll be sexually inadequate. For years it did quite a job on me. . . . I got kind of ambivalent about it in the 1970s and 1980s. After I was married my wife enjoyed it, but I still had that uneasy feeling. I even had a problem urinating around other men. When I learned more about it in the middle 1980s that completely changed. Now I'm so grateful that I've got it.

Based on pertinent information, the following inferences can be made regarding the decision to circumcise for social or "matching" reasons:

1. The circumcision status of the father is not necessarily known or important to a male child.
2. A circumcised man who "matches" others may nevertheless have negative feelings about being circumcised (see Chapter 5).

3. It is not possible to predict prior to circumcision how a boy will feel about it later.
4. There is some indication that many intact men are happy to be that way, even though they are in the minority.
5. An intact man who is unhappy about it can choose to be circumcised, but this is rarely done. The estimated rate of adult circumcision in the United States is 3 in 1000.[29]
6. An intact man who is unhappy about his status may feel different after learning more about circumcision.
7. Extreme minority status was the main common external factor that contributed to negative feelings in the intact men I interviewed. This factor is much less of an issue for boys born today because of the lower circumcision rate (approximately 60 percent nationally, under 40 percent in some states[30]).

These two accounts from mothers of intact sons add another perspective to the discussion of choosing circumcision for social reasons.

My youngest son [seven years old] is completely content at being "different" from his father and [three] older brothers. When I explained circumcision to him, his face took on a frightened expression as he cupped his hands over his genitals and loudly declared, "That is never going to happen to me!!"[31]

When my eight-year-old son was five, he noticed a difference in the appearance of the other boys' penises. I told him that's because they had their foreskins cut off. He said, "That's horrible." He's very adamant about it.[32]

I asked the second mother if I could talk with her son, Michael. Because he lives in an area with a very high circumcision rate, he is the only boy in his class who is not circumcised.

RG: How did you first learn about circumcision?
Michael: My mom told me when I was little, and she didn't want that to happen to me.

RG: How do you feel about her not wanting to let it happen to you?

Michael: I'm glad 'cause it's scary. It's scary for a little baby.

RG: At school, do the other kids have foreskins, or are they circumcised?

Michael: They're circumcised.

RG: How does it make you feel when you see that they're circumcised?

Michael: Kind of sad, because they had it cut off.

RG: Do the other boys notice that you have a foreskin and they don't?

Michael: Uh huh. And they say my penis looks weird.

RG: What do you think when they say that?

Michael: I say, "No it doesn't. Yours looks weird." Then I tell them why there is still skin over mine and not over theirs.

RG: Then what do you say?

Michael: Some say they don't believe it. Some just walk away.[33]

It appears that if an intact boy is given proper information, it is possible to prevent a negative impact from extreme minority status in a group of circumcised boys.

A reasoned evaluation of the conformity factor by parents is unlikely. Consequently, conformity will likely remain a major component of the circumcision decision. Because it commonly affects behavior, social science researchers have extensively investigated the issue of conformity and have verified what we suspect: group pressure can lead people to abandon their own judgment and conform. In a well-known study, 76 percent of subjects conformed to the false consensus of a group, even though that consensus was contradicted by visual evidence.[34] In the case of circumcision, most parents do not know of a strong reason to keep a boy intact. Therefore, conformity is understandable. Furthermore, when a situation is ambiguous, people are especially influenced by the group, and the greater the ambiguity, the greater the influence of the group on the judgment of individual members.[35] The basic rule in social contact is to minimize differences and fit in. The risks of nonconformity may include dislike and ostracism. Conformists are more likely to receive praise and popularity. Our need for social approval drives our tendency to conform.

Conforming to group practice has been shown to be more likely when the group is large.[36] Because parents generally know that circumcision is a national practice, they do not feel qualified to question it. Having an ally helps people to resist conformity,[37] but for a variety of reasons most parents usually receive little or no support from friends, family, educators, and doctors for keeping their infant intact. Left on their own, parents find the implicit pressure to conform difficult to resist.

Social concerns for the son may be projections of the parents' own insecurities. It may actually be the parents who fear being different or making different choices for their son. One father expressed it well when he said,

> What was so difficult in leaving my son intact was not that my son would feel different in a locker room, but that I would feel different from him. I would then have to accept that I'm an amputee from the wars of a past generation.[38]

Physicians and nurses are also subject to the pressures of conformity. Many of them have witnessed or participated in circumcisions performed in hospitals. This may cause them to question the procedure, but as with all groups, there is a diffusion of responsibility.[39] The greater the number of people who see an emergency, the less likely it is that any person will become involved. It would take rare courage and conviction to intervene.

FEMALE GENITAL MUTILATION

The tendency to conform to socially accepted practice applies, of course, to all cultures. This cultural bias can distort perception and limit understanding. Sometimes we can learn more about our own culture through exposure to other cultures. Specifically, examining practices related to circumcision in other cultures provides a valuable perspective. Female genital mutilation (FGM) is another practice that involves holding a person down and cutting the genitals by force. At least 110 million women and girls are victims of FGM in Africa, the Persian Gulf, and the southern Arab Peninsula. Female infants are subjected to the practice in Ethiopia and Nigeria.[40] The mutilations are done without anesthesia and with crude cutting tools.[41] There are several types.

Female circumcision (sometimes used to refer to all types of FGM) is the least common type and involves the removal of the clitoral hood, which is analogous to the male foreskin. Clitoridectomy or excision is cutting off the clitoris. Infibulation, also called pharaonic circumcision, is removal of the clitoris and labia, and sewing up the genital area to prevent sexual intercourse. Author Hanny Lightfoot-Klein, who has studied female genital mutilation for sixteen years, explains,

> When it happens, it happens swiftly. She [a young girl] is seized and held down by several women who pinion her arms and legs to the ground. The operation is generally performed by midwives under the direction of women elders. . . . In a society where all women have been dealt with in this manner in early childhood, their condition is naturally regarded by them as nothing other than normal.[42]

In the cities of those countries where it is practiced, local medical doctors frequently support and perform FGM. The biological facts about female genitals are unknown.[43] It is revealing to learn the beliefs that are used to justify these practices and whether men or women support them. FGM is typically defended with rationales such as tradition, religion, aesthetics, and false beliefs about cleanliness and health.[44] For example, based on interviews with over 400 Sudanese men and women about the effects of FGM, both sexes supported it with reasons connected to tradition, honor, and cleanliness despite adverse effects on physical and psychological health. Adverse effects are attributed to other causes. Complications from FGM can lead to death.[45]

A survey of two Nigerian communities showed that although both sexes supported the practice, FGM was most important to fathers and grandfathers because of cultural tradition, because it reduces sexual response, and because it supposedly facilitates childbirth.[46] Those who gave the last point as a reason believed that additional cuts with a clitoridectomy enlarged the vaginal opening.

In a study of Sudanese college students, women favored FGM more than men did, using custom and religion for justification.[47] In a survey of 290 Somalian women who had some form of FGM, a majority defended the practice with religious reasons, and all said they would subject their daughters to it.[48]

A survey of men in the Sudan revealed that over 50 percent believed that FGM was a Muslim religious requirement, although according to Islamic theologians, this is erroneous.[49] FGM is not mentioned in the Koran.[50] In the same survey, women respondents defended the practice because it was thought to promote cleanliness, prevent immorality, and improve prospects of marriage. Clearly, female attitudes are affected by the fact that men make excision a prerequisite for marriage. Men want to assure faithfulness of women by controlling female sexual pleasure. Where infibulation is practiced, it is required by men because it assures virginity. After marriage the women are cut open for sexual intercourse.[51] The myths used to justify FGM obscure the real reason for the practice: it gives men control over women.[52] Women have come to accept these myths, as evidenced by their support for the practice.

An American woman who was born in Somalia was interviewed on the television program *Day One*. Though she had been infibulated, she insisted that it had no sexual impact. "It's the same thing. There is nothing different about my sexuality." It was also noted on the program that African women subjected to FGM rarely talk about it because of the strong taboo.[53]

Psychological problems resulting from FGM include sexual anxiety and fear, avoidance of sex, compulsive sex, and low self-esteem.[54] Anxiety is suggested by the experience of a Sudanese man who had sexual experience with mutilated and unmutilated women. He reported that the mutilated women were more interested in satisfying him, and the natural women were more communicative about their preferences.[55] The psychological effects of FGM are not usually disclosed by mutilated women because of denial and cultural conditioning. Such effects can include chronic depression, anxiety about the genitals, and fear of infertility.[56]

FGM in the United States

The practice of FGM has not been confined to Africa and the Middle East. Female circumcision, removing the clitoral hood, was "widely employed" in the United States between the late 1880s and 1937 to prevent masturbation.[57] It was performed on females of all ages up to menopause[58] and was occasionally used to stop masturbation in the 1940s and 1950s.[59] (Male circumcision has outlasted female circumcision because the decision is largely influenced by circumcised male doctors and fathers who support it. Recognizing male circumcision as a mistake reflects on circumcised males. See Chapter 2. There are also the effects of trauma, to be discussed in later chapters.)

Lay literature advocated female circumcision in the 1970s as a misguided treatment to improve sexual response.[60] As a result, an estimated three thousand female circumcisions were performed annually in U.S. hospitals in the 1970s and many more were carried out in physicians' offices.[61] As late as 1973, female circumcision was suggested in a medical journal as a treatment for frigidity.[62] According to the World Health Organization, in 1976 the United States was the only medically advanced country in the world that practiced female circumcision. The procedure was covered by Blue Shield until 1977.[63]

Clitoridectomy was practiced in the United States between 1870 and 1910 to stop masturbation and treat "hypersexuality" and cancer.[64] Female castration, the removal of ovaries, was performed from 1872 to 1910 and as late as 1946 to treat "mental disorders."[65] Barker-Benfield believes that the surgery was used to keep women in their place. Hysterectomies started in 1895. Women consented to these operations because they accepted the male belief that they had psychological problems caused by their sexual organs.[66]

Circumcision and FGM Compared

Contrasting the American practice of male infant circumcision and FGM can be useful. The following table provides a summary:

CIRCUMCISION AND FGM

Similarities
1. About 100 million procedures have been performed on current populations.
2. The procedure is unnecessary and extremely painful.
3. It can have adverse sexual and psychological effects (see Chapter 5).
4. It is generally done by force on children without anesthesia.
5. The practice is supported by local medical doctors.
6. Pertinent biological facts are not generally known where procedures are practiced.
7. The procedure is defended with reasons such as tradition, religion, aesthetics, cleanliness, and health.
8. The rationale for the procedure has been connected to controlling sexual pleasure.
9. It is believed to have no effect on normal sexual functioning.
10. The practice is accepted and supported by those who have been subjected to it.
11. The decision is controlled by men.
12. The choice may be motivated by underlying psychosexual reasons.
13. Critical public discussion is generally taboo where the procedure is practiced.
14. The procedure can result in serious complications that can lead to death.
15. The effects are hidden by repression and denial.

Differences
1. FGM is performed under worse operating conditions.
2. FGM has several forms and is typically much more severe.
3. FGM is often a prerequisite for marriage.
4. FGM results in more apparent adverse effects.
5. FGM is performed on people of a wider range of ages.

During a network television program on FGM, the reporter stated that the procedure is "nothing like male circumcision."[67] Yet, as we can see in the table, there are many more similarities than differences between the two practices. It is noteworthy that Americans generally accept male infant circumcision without question, yet the subject of FGM horrifies them. The fact that the two practices are defended with many of the same reasons in our culture and others raises additional doubts about the validity of these reasons and underscores the power of cultural influence on personal beliefs and attitudes.

> *Viewed quantitatively*, the extent of genital tissue destruction in the overwhelming majority of ritually mutilated women far exceeds the physical damage found in male circumcision. *On a qualitative level*, however, we are dealing with one and the same thing.
>
> Hanny Lightfoot-Klein,
> author of *Prisoners of Ritual: An Odyssey into Female Genital Mutilation in Africa*

SCIENCE, MEDICINE, AND CULTURAL VALUES

American sexual surgery on males and females has been based on supposed "rational" factors because Americans (men more than women) tend to value the intellect over the emotions. This preference is consistent with our general difficulty in being aware of and expressing feelings. One of the consequences of this condition is that when we don't feel, our thinking is affected. Excessive reliance on the intellect is a mistake because suppressed feelings limit our experience and can surface as false beliefs. Psychiatrist Wilhelm Reich wrote,

> Intellectual activity has often such a structure and direction that it impresses one as an extremely clever apparatus precisely for the avoidance of facts, as an activity which really detracts from reality.[68]

This appears to have been the case in thinking about circumcision. If they strongly support circumcision, physicians may simply dismiss new information that conflicts with their view.[69]

Consistent with cultural overreliance on intellect, we have been inclined to adopt science as the great arbiter between fact and fiction. This systematic approach to evaluating our experience is of value, especially since research has demonstrated that a surprising number of adults do not reason logically.[70] However, total reliance on science is unmerited. Though the scientific method is designed to help protect the scientific community and the public against flawed reasoning, the flawed reasoning of supposedly reputable studies has contributed to the confusion on the circumcision issue.

Our science is affected by our cultural values. As mentioned earlier, circumcision reflects a cultural value, and a principal method for preserving cultural values is to disguise them as truths that are based on scientific research. This "research" can then be used to support medical practices. This explains the claimed medical "benefits" of circumcision.

Circumcision is not the only questionable medical procedure currently performed in connection with childbirth. According to information published by the International Childbirth Education Association,

> A growing body of research makes it alarmingly clear that every aspect of traditional American hospital care during labor and delivery must now be questioned as to its possible effects on the future well-being of both the obstetric patient and her unborn child.[71]

Examples include birth with the mother on her back, use of drugs, forceps deliveries, routine episiotomy, and cesarean births. Researcher and anthropologist Robbie Davis-Floyd argues that routine obstetrical procedures are cultural rituals "designed to convey the core values of American society to birthing women."[72] The core values, according to Davis-Floyd, are a patriarchal system that uses scientific knowledge for purposes of control.

Cultural values also determine what we study and what we ignore. In the medical community, biological science is taken much more seriously than is social science.[73] Psychiatrist, infancy researcher, and author Daniel Stern reflects on his switch from pharmacology research to studying behavior:

> There is an assumption among medical people that if you can explain a piece of behavior on a biochemical basis, then you've understood it. And it took me a long time to realize that the behavioral level was not explicable in terms of the other, that it was a level unto itself and had just as much validity. Finally, I junked the whole thing and said I wanted to work at the behavioral level. Which, strangely enough, felt like a rebellion.[74]

Most of the research and debate connected with circumcision has pertained to medical claims, the "biological" component. However, the practice of circumcision cannot be understood unless the investigation includes the psychological and social aspects.

The fact that much research is funded by government and private foundations also limits the kinds of projects that receive support. These sources tend to avoid certain topics that are controversial, unconventional, or emotional. For example, researchers involved in a comprehensive national sex survey found that resistance to funding such projects was connected with "a palpable fear of what sex researchers might discover."[75] This may be a reason why the long-term effects of circumcision have not been studied.

In addition, there have been quality-control problems regarding what gets published in the medical literature. Indeed, the medical community itself has acknowledged that it has not maintained very high standards in its published work. Researchers and authors Charles and Daphne Maurer cite an editorial published in the *Journal of the American Medical Association*:

> In a study of 149 articles selected at random from ten widely read and highly regarded medical periodicals . . . less than 28% have sufficient statistical support for drawn conclusions.[76]

Maurer and Maurer explain why so much "nonsense" is published: (1) Experimental design and statistical analysis are not typically taught in medical school; and (2) medical schools discourage questioning of authorities.

Medical writers are not trained to perform and report on research. Colleagues do not know how to review reports properly and critically. Even if reviewers do find fault with someone else's work, it is "not desirable, let alone polite" to question authorities about their work.[77] As a result, the pressure to submit to authority causes young doctors to withdraw from critical analysis.

Medical education affects the way medical professionals handle the issue of circumcision in particular. According to pediatrician Paul Fleiss, "We didn't learn anything about foreskins or circumcision in medical school. I watched one. That was it."[78] Several other doctors have confirmed that they typically received less than one hour of instruction on circumcision in medical school. What they were taught (e.g., infants do not feel pain, preventing penile cancer justifies routine circumcision) has been refuted by further review and subsequent studies. Dr. Thomas J. Ritter cites several authoritative medical texts that contain misinformation and improperly advise circumcision.[79] I visited the bookstore for the Harvard Medical School. Textbooks were often incomplete or inaccurate on this subject. A clear picture or illustration of a natural, intact penis in an anatomy book was rare. Taylor, Lockwood, and Taylor, who reported on foreskin structure, also noted "the current tendency to eliminate the prepuce from anatomy textbooks."[80]

The lack of proper medical education adversely affects medical knowledge and practice. In a study at two Salt Lake City hospitals, surgeons listed phimosis (nonretractable foreskin after puberty) as the reason for 65 percent of circumcisions on young boys older than a month.[81] Since the foreskin of a boy is normally attached to the glans at birth and may not be retractable until as late as adolescence, true phimosis cannot be diagnosed in a young boy.[82] Nevertheless, some physicians are suspiciously quick to advise circumcision of young boys. One mother who brought her baby boy to a doctor reported, "When I told him that the baby had an older [intact] brother, he said, 'I have to see him, too. He probably will have to be circumcised within the next year.' That's without even seeing him!"

Wallerstein notes two surveys of doctors and reports, "Many, if not most, American physicians are ignorant of proper care of the foreskin."[83] Apparently, the editor of *Pediatrics* agreed when he published my letter under the title "Who Doesn't Know This?"[84] It explained proper foreskin care and the harm caused by doctors who force foreskin retraction. The letter was in response to frequent calls received at the Circumcision Resource Center from mothers of young boys who reported that their pediatrician had forcefully retracted their son's foreskin.

Because of the general deficiency in knowledge about circumcision and the foreskin, doctors' opinions about circumcision often have little or no clinical or scientific basis. Researcher Anne Briggs recounts,

> I have spoken with more than one doctor who defends the circumcision procedure with zeal and seems totally unconcerned by the fact that he does this without a shred of fact to support his position.[85]

The public is generally unaware of deficiencies in medical practice. One reason is that from the time they are in medical school, doctors learn that, in the words of one student, "We have to be good actors, put across the image of self-confidence, that you know it all."[86] Another factor is that the medical profession has control over much knowledge that people would find helpful. The medical establishment is not always open with this information, as noted by sociologist Laurel Richardson.

> By withholding information from the public—although perhaps unintentionally—medical and paramedical institutions prevent individuals from understanding their bodies, their feelings, and, hence, themselves.[87]

In the case of circumcision, withholding information is sometimes intentional. Dr. Christiane Northrup has discontinued her obstetrics practice. She reports,

I used to lecture in the childbirth classes in the hospital about how circumcision didn't need to be done. What would happen was the word would get back to the department that Dr. Northrup was making people feel bad. [Expectant parents who intended to circumcise were uncomfortable.] So they didn't invite me to speak. That also happened to a male obstetrician who used to do the same thing.[88]

In 1984 the American Academy of Pediatrics (AAP) published a pamphlet called *Newborns: Care of the Uncircumcised Penis*, which noted that the functions of the foreskin include protecting the glans and urinary opening from irritation and infection. By omitting this section from subsequent versions of the pamphlet, it appears that the AAP is concealing useful information about the foreskin that could influence the circumcision decision. I contacted the AAP to request an explanation for the deletion, but they could offer no reason.[89]

Brigham and Women's Hospital in Boston has the highest number of annual births of all hospitals in New England. In 1991 I sent a letter with documented references calling attention to errors and omissions in their circumcision information sheet that they distribute to expectant parents (see Appendix A). Dr. Steven Ringer, the author of the sheet, called the information provided "adequate" and added that taking a position on circumcision would limit the choice of the parents. This reason was similar to some responses from childbirth educators (see Chapter 2). He dismissed my letter by saying, "You read our information sheet differently than we read our information sheet." In 1995 the same inaccurate information sheet was still being distributed.

The medical community also withholds information from itself. Studies and opinions that are critical of circumcision are more difficult to get published than studies and opinions that support circumcision. For example, *Ca—A Cancer Journal for Clinicians* published an opinion piece called "The Relationship between Circumcision and Cancer of the Penis."[90] The article argues that prevention of cancer of the penis is a good reason to circumcise infants routinely. Though opposing points of view were submitted in response, no such view was published. My inquiry into this matter was ignored by the journal's staff and

American Cancer Society officers and advisory board members. The suppression of debate is incompatible with a healthy scientific environment, and it contradicts a statement by the journal's editor in a previous issue: "*Ca* does not wish to preclude discussion of controversial topics."[91]

Dr. John Taylor, who did research on the anatomy of the foreskin (see Chapter 2), chose to submit his work to a British medical journal. He had several reasons, but among them was the perception that the likelihood of acceptance and publication would be better with a British publication than with an American journal.[92] The lack of routine circumcision in England accounts for a different cultural attitude toward it.

It is appropriate to remind ourselves that any institution or profession has its problems and deficiencies. The psychological and social dynamics described here and associated with the medical community also occur in other professions. Like other professions and institutions, the medical community is a reflection of the larger society it serves. It adopts the standards that the larger community expects. It avoids the uncomfortable issues that the society avoids. This is a matter of survival. If it did not, it would risk losing credibility and acceptance. Consequently, the people who work in medicine shape their profession to conform to our culture. In a sense, they are us. They have our values and act, in most cases, as we would in the same situation. How many of us are willing to challenge prevailing beliefs and practices in our professions? Generally, we also tend to thoughtlessly obey authority, cling to old thinking habits, and reject new information that threatens our beliefs.

To this point, I have documented that about 3,500 infants a day are subjected to unnecessary, extreme pain and the risk of surgical complications. One long-term result of this procedure is diminished sexual sensitivity. Behavioral changes observed in infants are of unknown duration. It is time to look at the possible long-term psychological effects of circumcision.

4

Long-Term Psychological

Effects of Circumcision:

I. Early Trauma and Memory

My clients kept having memories of birth, something I had not
known was possible.

—David Chamberlain,
psychologist and president of the Association
for Pre- and Perinatal Psychology and Health

The atmosphere of denial and suppression surrounding the issue
of circumcision has had a stifling effect on research concerning
the long-term impact of the practice. A search of psychological
and medical literature yielded no studies on this issue, aside
from the study of infants aged four to six months in which it was
found that circumcised infants cried longer than intact infants
after vaccinations (see Chapter 1). Researchers from the University of Cambridge in England and Georgetown University Medical
School referred to this lack of studies as "particularly worrisome."
In their article published in *Developmental Psychobiology*, they
wrote,

> In view of all the evidence showing long-term behavioral, physio-
> logical, anatomical, and even neuropharmacological effects of
> "minor" events in early animal development, we would be unwise to

assume without empirical demonstration that the circumcision effects are short-lived.[1]

Based on available information, they concluded that circumcision "may have long-term physiological and behavioral consequences."[2]

Citing previous research on newborn memory, other investigators at the University of Washington School of Medicine reached a similar conclusion in a circumcision article published in *Infant Behavior and Development*: "It seems inappropriate, therefore, to make the assumption in the absence of direct evidence that there are *no* long-term consequences of the circumcision experience."[3]

REASONS FOR LACK OF INVESTIGATION

The suggestion for research on long-term effects of circumcision had been made and virtually nobody responded. Why? The answer may be a combination of cultural and emotional factors. There is the popular presumption that infants are not real people yet, not sufficiently developed to register the import of an event like this, and that whatever we do to them at this stage has no long-term significance. This belief is supported by the fact that people do not usually remember their infancy. What isn't remembered is assumed to be inconsequential.

This view neglects the powerful effect of the unconscious. Since Freud, it has been a generally accepted idea in psychology that the past influences present experience. Daily life and clinical work confirm this connection, and a long-term study noted a relationship between childhood environment and adult psychological health.[4] Nevertheless, while it is understood that some psychopathology originates in childhood, the long-term impact of experiences during infancy is not generally recognized and appreciated in mainstream psychological theory and practice. Efforts to publish important work in this area in American journals have met opposition.[5] Prevailing attitudes and assumptions have been major obstacles.

The overspecialization of professional practice also contributes to the neglect of circumcision as a topic of research. Circumcision is a medical procedure, and the medical community is generally not trained in or sensitive to the psychological ramifications of its work. Conversely, mental health professionals generally do not look at routine medical procedures in infancy as a possible cause of adult psychopathology.

Research on the long-term effects of circumcision involves potentially inhibiting emotional factors connected with one's own circumcision. Investigators typically study individuals and groups that exclude themselves. This is consistent with the traditional scientific idea of the "objective" observer and also provides a safe emotional distance from subjects. However, in the case of circumcision, most of the investigators are themselves circumcised. In addition, many work in professions and institutions that carry out circumcisions routinely. Investigating the negative long-term effects of circumcision could become personally, professionally, and culturally uncomfortable. Such a study could call the practice into question, a threatening possibility for researchers and grant providers that is safer to avoid than confront. That virtually nobody is willing to study the long-term psychological impact of circumcision is itself a long-term consequence of circumcision.

Cultural resistance to research on circumcision is compounded by the fact that a proportion of investigators are Jewish. They may be even less willing to question a practice that is identified with their ethnic and religious heritage. Non-Jewish investigators may be sensitive to offending Jews with research that could be perceived as critical of the practice. Regarding the medical profession's attitude toward circumcision, Dr. Steven Ringer at Brigham and Women's Hospital in Boston states that "the religious aspect of circumcision plays a significant role." According to Ringer, discouraging circumcision would put doctors "in a position of attacking religious belief."[6] This stance may be a case of using religion to obscure other motivations (see Chapter 2), but it illustrates that the religious factor complicates the issue.

Finally, and most important, there is very little public awareness yet of any problem here. It is tacitly assumed that circumcised men are either glad or do not care that they are circumcised, and that there is no connection between their present psychological state and the fact that they have been circumcised.

BIRTH AS TRAUMA IN PSYCHOANALYSIS

While there have been no studies of long-term effects of circumcision, there are such studies on birth. Therefore, we will look at the connection between birth and trauma, which has long-term effects. If it is plausible for a newborn infant to experience trauma at birth, then it is plausible that other extremely painful events of infancy, like circumcision, are also experienced as traumas. The concept of trauma, the psychic and emotional response to an uncontrollable, overwhelming event, will be discussed in a later section of this chapter.

The idea of birth as trauma is not a new one. In 1920 Freud wrote that "the act of birth is the source and prototype of the affect of anxiety."[7] More generally, he stated,

> The significance of infantile experiences should not be totally neglected. . . . On the contrary, they call for particular consideration. They are all the more momentous because they occur in times of incomplete development and are for that very reason liable to have traumatic effects.[8]

Otto Rank also wrote about birth trauma.* As a psychoanalyst and an associate of Freud, he also thought that birth was the first trauma, and he developed the idea further. Because Rank believed "the anxiety of birth forms the basis of every anxiety or fear,"[9] he connected birth trauma with many conditions including phobias, breathing difficulties, and epileptic attacks. Rank suggested repeating the birth trauma as a way to treat its effects. His ideas have remained of interest to various professionals and laypeople. Many psychoanalysts have questioned some of Rank's claims, but many also have believed that the experience of birth has lasting effects.[10]

---

*Contemporary clinicians conclude that birth is not inherently traumatic. Birth trauma is caused by many factors usually connected with medical interference. A few babies are born relaxed and smile shortly after birth.[11]

There is renewed interest in the work of Donald Winnicott, an English pediatrician and psychoanalyst. His experience included attending many childbirths, periodically observing infants, hearing maternal reports of infant development, and working psychoanalytically with children and adults. He concluded that a traumatic birth has serious consequences and is remembered. In 1949 he wrote,

> When birth trauma is significant every detail of impingement and reaction is, as it were, etched on the patient's memory in the way to which we become accustomed when patients relive traumatic experiences of later life.[12]

Winnicott found a connection between birth trauma and both behaviors and psychosomatic problems.

INFANT NEUROLOGICAL DEVELOPMENT AND MEMORY CAPABILITY

Resistance to the idea of birth trauma is generally related to disagreement about the degree of neurological development and memory capability of the newborn infant. Does a newborn infant have sufficient development to experience trauma, and could this experience have a lasting effect?

Early writing on neurological development contended that infant capabilities were very limited.[13] Even recently some writers have claimed that newborn infants are not capable of memory and that their experience has no lasting effect.[14] It is noteworthy, however, that these statements are not supported with research, documentation, or clinical experience. They have only the status of opinion. Such assertions are similar to those used to deny infant pain: "A baby's sense of pain is almost certainly duller than an adult's."[15] As noted in the first chapter, this belief conflicts with the latest studies as well as common observations of infants by their mothers.

The parts of the brain needed for long-term memory have been identified.[16] Anand and Hickey, in their often-cited review of the literature on infant pain, report that these structures "are well developed and functioning during the newborn period."[17] Based on five references to literature on infant research, they conclude,

> In the long term, painful experiences in neonates could possibly lead to psychological sequelae, since several workers have shown that newborns have a much greater capacity for memory than was previously thought.[18]

It is also important to remember that there are several types of memory, both conscious and unconscious.[19] For example, remembering the color of a friend's shirt at lunch uses a different type of memory than tying your shoes or recalling where you were when you heard of a shocking political assassination. As we will see in the next section, it is not just the intellect that can be involved with memory, but emotion and the body as well.

The debate over long-term memory in infants may be put in a different perspective by considering related literature on other species. Long-term memory has been demonstrated behaviorally in monkeys, rats, chicks, migratory songbirds, snails, fruit flies, and ants.[20] If these simpler animals have long-term memory, it would be biologically and rationally inconsistent to deny the capability of long-term memory in newborn infants.

It appears that from the developmental and neurological perspective, newborn infants are capable of experiencing trauma and retaining a memory of it. We have projected our own inability to consciously remember our infancy onto the infant. We do store memories of our infancy, but we generally do not have access to them. In a survey of psychologists, the majority agreed that forgetting was due to retrieval failure and not the loss of information from memory storage.[21]

CLINICAL EXPERIENCE WITH BODY-ORIENTED THERAPIES AND RESEARCH ON BIRTH IMPACT

Early memories have been accessed in adults in the process of treatment using various body-oriented psychotherapies. Wilhelm Reich was the first clinician to devise a biophysical approach to treating individuals who reported psychological problems. He first developed this theory and practice in the late 1920s. Reich understood, for example, that words can obscure the honesty of the body's expression and that how a person talked was more important than what a person said.

According to Reich, "psychic tension and relief cannot be without a somatic representation, for tension and relaxation are biophysical processes."[22] He called the body's tension and defenses against emotional expression "armor." Reich paid attention to and responded to the biological expression of armor.

> The total expression of the armored individual is that of "holding back." This expression has to be taken literally: *the organism expresses the fact that it is holding back.* The shoulders are pulled back, the thorax pulled up, the chin is held rigid, respiration is shallow, the lower back is arched, the pelvis is retracted and "dead," the legs are stretched out stiffly or lack expression; these are some of the main attitudes of total holding back.[23]

Reich found that the body holds repressed feelings and memories. Although Reich's later work stirred controversy, mainstream researchers have confirmed his early observations.[24] With the dissolution of the armor and expression of emotion, unconscious memories become retrievable.

These principles and practices have been used more recently by other clinicians, particularly in connection with gaining access to the birth experience.[25] The idea of birth as traumatic and having long-term effects has been investigated by Arthur Janov. An internationally known psychologist and author, Janov is director of the Primal Training Center in Los Angeles and has worked in the mental health field for forty years. In his work he focuses on deep emotional release as opposed to mental approaches to treatment.[26]

In what he calls primal therapy, patients relive early painful scenes including the birth experience. This reliving of the event Janov calls a Primal. It is facilitated by the therapist, who assists the client in expressing feelings and countering the many defenses that block feeling. Like Reich, Janov found that as the feelings are experienced fully and the emotional state is reproduced, the associated repressed memories can become accessible.

This connection between feeling experience and memory has been confirmed by many researchers.[27] The accounts of laypeople add further support. Becky Wakefield, a mother who contacted the Circumcision Resource Center, related that her six-year-old son was crawling through a tunnel made of snow when he said, "This feels like when I was born." In a like manner, sometimes a birth Primal can be facilitated by simulating the experience such as pushing against a pillow with one's head from a prone position. Simulating the birth experience to access the trauma was first proposed by psychoanalyst Nandor Fodor.[28]

For two years after Janov first saw clients reliving birth, he thought the experiences were "symbolic" and not genuine. He had no conceptual framework for understanding what he was witnessing. Over time he devised theories to match these clinical observations and client reports.

Janov concludes that trauma caused by obstetrical interventions and other causes can have a lasting impact. He believes that "the entire person is altered by repressed Pain,* and each level of consciousness is implicated."[29] The three levels are somatic, emotional, and intellectual. Repressing "Pain" is necessary because otherwise we would have either died at birth or we would be feeling the overwhelming "Pain" continuously. The "Pain" is stored in the body as tension while the repressive system protects us from it by keeping it unconscious. There is a very wide range in how this "Pain" impacts the individual. Many different pathological outcomes that affect behavior, physiology, and personality are possible.

According to Janov, obstetricians who have observed films and videotapes of birth Primals confirm that "the movements, facial expressions, breathing patterns, and sounds were all those of the newborn."[30] Clients who were born with a forceps show a corresponding mark on the head when they relive their birth.[31]

In his most recent book, Janov reports,

---

*Janov uses a capital *P* to signify denied, disconnected, intolerable pain, i.e., trauma.

I have seen many hundreds of patients reliving various kinds of birth trauma over the years. These patients, from some twenty countries, have gone through certain reliving episodes which cannot be faked. This has been demonstrated, for example, by the way the feet and toes are locked in certain positions, whether it be a Japanese or a Swede undergoing the reliving. We have made electronic measurements of the pulse, blood pressure, body temperature, and brain waves during the reliving session and found that all measurements rise enormously. In some cases, the amplitude of the brain waves doubles, the pulse rises to 200, and the blood pressure to 220, the temperature some two or three degrees in a matter of minutes—all this in a person lying fairly still, but in the grip of memory.[32]

Another innovative theorist and practitioner is psychiatrist Stanislav Grof. He has done consciousness research for over thirty years and has worked with both psychedelic and nondrug approaches to therapy. Grof, too, was skeptical of early clinical reports from clients connected with their births, but further experience led him to conclude, "In deep experiential psychotherapy, biographical material is not remembered or reconstructed; it can actually be fully relived."[33] Grof now accepts that many types of psychopathology are connected to the birth experience. Writing as one who has relived his own early experiences, Grof concludes, "We have been born only anatomically and have really not completed and integrated this process psychologically."[34]

Some of the theories and clinical evidence presented by Janov and Grof are similar to those of Leslie Feher, psychotherapist and president of the Association of Birth Psychology. Her clients relive the birth experience and connect the feelings to current experience in what she calls natal therapy. The following table is based on her summary of clinical experience:[35]

BIRTH EXPERIENCE	ADULT TENDENCIES
forceps delivery	dependency, headaches
delayed birth	impatience, feeling trapped
cesarean birth	undefined boundaries, learning difficulties
premature birth	resisting change, clinging
suffocation	asthma
major trauma	suicide, death anxiety

Feher makes it clear that these correlations are preliminary and are based on only a few clients in each group. Despite the limitations, she believes the consistency of the observed pattern justifies reporting. In a subsequent study of 71 adults, Feher administered a standard personality questionnaire and a birth questionnaire. The results showed significant correlations between type of birth and adult personality. Profiles were composed for six birth categories: natural, drugs, forceps, premature, cesarean, and breech.[36]

Thomas Verny, a Toronto psychiatrist, researcher, and author, has treated hundreds of patients affected by traumatic perinatal experiences. His clinical approach and experience with adults are similar to those of Leslie Feher. For example, he has noticed that people who were born by cesarean delivery have an intense need for physical contact; those who had umbilical cord difficulties at birth develop throat, swallowing or speech problems; and those born prematurely feel chronically rushed.[37]

There is further support for a connection between birth experience and adult behavior. Researchers investigated the relationship between birth trauma and method of suicide for 412 suicide cases. The results showed that those who chose a form of asphyxiation for suicide were more likely to have experienced breathing difficulties at birth; those who chose mechanical means were more likely to have had a mechanical problem at birth (e.g., breech delivery, use of forceps); and those who chose drugs were more likely to have been born from a mother who was given drugs during labor.[38]

The largest and most comprehensive study of the long-term impact of birth was reported by two researchers: Emanuel Friedman, professor of obstetrics and gynecology at Harvard Medical School and obstetrician-gynecologist in chief at Beth Israel Hospital in Boston; and Raymond Neff, assistant professor of biostatistics at the University of California at Berkeley. The study included 58,806 births from fourteen different hospitals. Children were followed for eight years with tests of mental, motor, and neurologic development, as well as examinations of speech, language, and hearing proficiency. The results showed that birth conditions can affect the child through at least the first eight years of life. For example, adverse effects were found for breech and cesarean birth, premature and post-term birth, umbilical cord complications, and the use of drugs and forceps during labor and delivery.[39]

MORE REPORTS OF PERINATAL MEMORIES

There are many cases in which hypnosis has been used to access perinatal memories. David Cheek, a retired obstetrician and hypnotherapist, has been particularly successful in this regard. He hypnotized ten adults whom he had delivered and asked them to describe their head and shoulder positions at birth. Cheek compared their reports with his notes, which he had made at the time of their births but had not seen in over twenty years. In all cases, the patients' reports of how they were delivered matched the written record.[40]

Psychologist David Chamberlain has heard hundreds of reports of birth memories in his clinical practice. He tested the accuracy of these memories recalled under hypnosis by experimenting with ten mother and child pairs. The children, mostly teenagers and ranging in age from nine to twenty-three, had no conscious memories of their own birth experience and had not discussed it with their mothers. The children and mothers were hypnotized independently and questioned about the birth. There were no leading questions, and the subjects spoke freely.

> Mother and child reports were coherent with each other, contained many facts that were consistent and connected, and were appropriately similar in setting, characters, and sequences. The independent narratives dovetailed at many points like one story told from two points of view. In some cases matching was uncanny.[41]

Rima Laibow is a psychiatrist in Westchester County, New York, who treats people through expressive, experiential approaches that facilitate retrieval of perinatal memories. She reports that when these memories were investigated, "the medical and other factors alluded to in the memories have always been corroborated by birth records, historical, and social factors surrounding the child's birth."[42] Laibow adds that these memories are spontaneous, unexpected, and not solicited.

More examples of early memory come from young children and have been noted in various psychological journals.[43] For example, a two-year-old verbally recalled a traumatic experience when she was three months old.[44] Other two-year-old children have asked about events related to their birth. They wondered why they were stuck in the heel (to obtain a routine blood sample) and why they were put in a plastic box (small bed in the nursery).[45] Laibow tells of her two-and-a-half-year-old son who questioned her about the patch over people's faces, the delivery room light, nasal suctioning, and other birth-related events.[46]

The following list summarizes the preceding information in this chapter regarding evidence of birth trauma and birth memory.

BIRTH TRAUMA AND MEMORY

Empirical research on newborn infants
• Neurological structures are well-developed and functioning.
• Memory capability has been demonstrated.

Birth memories of young children
• Children, usually two to four years old, have verbally recalled memories related to their birth.
• Documented reports of their statements sometimes include questioning of hospital procedures.

Empirical research on long-term effects of birth
• A comprehensive study has demonstrated long-term developmental effects related to birth experience.
• A study has shown a correlation between type of major birth trauma and method of suicide.
• Preliminary correlation has been shown between birth experience and adult tendencies and personality types.

Clinical experience in body-oriented therapies
- Some practitioners have observed clients reliving birth-related events.
- Measurements confirm that physiological changes accompany memory.
- Birth memories are corroborated by birth records.

Clinical experience in hypnotherapy
- Birth movements were remembered and matched the written record of the birth.
- Birth accounts of mother and older child pairs matched.

CIRCUMCISION MEMORIES

If it is possible for people to have perinatal memories, then it is reasonable to assume that it is possible for circumcised males to have circumcision memories, since circumcision is performed shortly after birth. Although there is no empirical research on circumcision trauma and memory, the other four categories of evidence in the previous list supporting birth trauma and birth memory can apply to circumcision. For example, Betsy Melber, a California mother of a seven-year-old boy, contacted the Circumcision Resource Center and related this account of a conversation with her son:

> My son remembered his circumcision when he was three. We were talking about when he was born. He remembered all kinds of details. He said, "I cried because they took me away from you" and "I cried when the doctor cut my pee pee with a scissors." He said it hurt, and he didn't like it.

Becky Wakefield's son also talked about his penis being cut when he remembered his birth at age six.

Author Anne Briggs reports that two mothers contacted her about circumcision memories reported by their children. One boy age four was asked if he remembered anything about his birth. He said, "No, Mommy, the only thing I remember is that my penis really hurts."[47] Another boy age four and a half hurt his penis when he tripped and fell. In the subsequent conversation with his mother, he remembered details of his circumcision. His account included the location of the straps that secured him, and that he was given something to suck after the procedure. Observations by the boy were confirmed.

David Chamberlain notes that some men can consciously remember their circumcision. Others remember under hypnosis. One of his clients gave this account in a hypnotic session:

> There's a sensation I've never experienced before. It's in my back, being drawn up, pulled in. I don't know where I am but I feel like my shoulder blades are not resting comfortably and my shoulders are pushing down. I can't bend them; I'm on something hard and cold! I feel my whole body arching now. I don't know what's going on. I hear babies crying and I'm crying too. I don't know why. Oh! They are pulling on my penis and I'm feeling some pain. (See Fig. 10.)

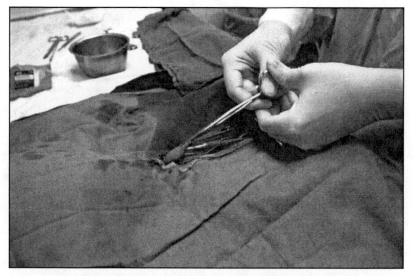

Reprinted by permission from The Saturday Evening Post

Fig. 10

It hurts there; I'm not sure why. There's a white robe; it's a doctor. They are holding my legs down, and my back is arched. They are cutting my penis and it hurts. It hurts! I feel my penis being pulled. I feel sharp points there. I'm hurting and my back is tight. Someone picks me up and holds me. I can't relax. I am stiff. My penis hurts; it burns. . . . I'm tired now. I cried hard. I'm all cried out. I'm trying to go to sleep.[48]

Author and childbirth educator Rosemary Romberg interviewed a father who had relived his own circumcision.

When I was in therapy I went through a sort of visualization, a re-experiencing of my own circumcision. I can't remember clearly what it was, but I know it was pretty awful. I felt at the time that I was just barely touching the surface of what it was that I experienced. Just think of being a man or a boy who is a little bit older and somebody holding you down and taking the end of your penis off. It's no different. Some people have a crazy idea that babies feel less and experience less than somebody who is older!! . . . It's a feeling of rage and anger that came out.[49]

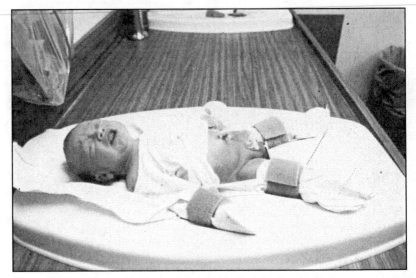

Reprinted by permission from The Saturday Evening Post

Fig. 11

Another man who had relived his circumcision had similar feelings.

> Anger is a pallid euphemism for what I felt. More accurate would be overwhelming fury, rage, and desire for vengeance, desire to torture, maim, and utterly destroy any human being who ever had anything to do with performing, ordering, or requesting circumcisions.[50]

Richard Schwartzman and Charles Konia are psychiatrists in eastern Pennsylvania who help people resolve past traumas. They practice a form of therapy developed by Wilhelm Reich. Schwartzman writes, "I have had patients who have relived the experience [circumcision] as evidenced by the severe pain felt at the site where the foreskin was cut." Schwartzman reports that he has had a total of twelve clients who have relived their circumcision.[51] Konia writes,

> I can tell you that from my clinical experience in treating patients who relived their circumcision as well as observing newborns being circumcised in the delivery room, *it is a nightmarish experience.* I shudder each time I witness patients going through the horror.[52]

Psychologist John Breeding recounts his personal therapy session during which he reexperienced his circumcision.

> The emotional experience . . . was horrible. I felt overwhelming fear, sweating and shaking for long periods. Intense rage also came up at times. I wanted to protect myself, but I couldn't. . . . I felt . . . terribly sad, engulfed in grief, despair and helplessness. I released emotionally for well over an hour and was finally spent, sad.[53]

The Circumcision Resource Center has had contact with several men who have relived their circumcision. In addition to feeling the pain, grief, and anger, they find themselves asking, "Why?" and "Why me?" These same questions are frequently asked by children who have experienced other traumas.[54] They try to make sense of their experience. It is particularly difficult for victims of trauma to accept that someone caused their experience.

CIRCUMCISION AS TRAUMA

If a newborn infant is capable of experiencing trauma, and if circumcision can be remembered, can circumcision cause trauma and have lasting effects? The *Diagnostic and Statistical Manual of Mental Disorders (DSM-IV)*, published by the American Psychiatric Association and the bible of mental health clinicians and researchers, could be helpful in answering this question. Its description of post-traumatic stress disorder (PTSD) includes, but is not limited to, the following items:

- It results from "exposure to an extreme traumatic stressor." This is an event that is beyond usual human experience.
- The response must include "intense fear, helplessness or horror."
- Examples of traumatic events include assault (sexual or physical), torture, and a threat to one's physical integrity.[55]

An assault is a physical attack. Torture is severe pain or anguish. It does not necessarily take account of the intention or purpose of the perpetrator but focuses on the act itself and the experience of the victim.

From the perspective of the infant, all the elements in this *DSM-IV* description of traumatic events apply to circumcision of a male infant: the procedure involves being forcibly restrained, having part of the penis cut off, and experiencing extreme pain. Based on the nature of the experience and the infant's response, circumcision traumatizes the infant and may result in some form of PTSD.

The question of an infant's capacity to experience trauma needs to be emphasized. John Wilson, an author with a national reputation for his research on PTSD, supports the view that PTSD can occur "at any point in the life cycle, from infancy and childhood to the waning years of life."[56] In addition, the *DSM-IV* states that the disorder "can occur at any age."[57]

Clinicians have documented that children are particularly vulnerable to trauma.[58] Psychic trauma seems to have a permanent effect on children, no matter how young they are when they are traumatized. Furthermore, psychopathology increases as the age of the child at the time of the trauma decreases.[59]

One important long-term effect of trauma is learned helplessness. Experiencing a traumatic event where no action can help may lead to a chronic inability to act. This has been demonstrated in rats.[60] Since rats are less developed than infants, and older children are more developed than infants, denying trauma in infants is inconsistent with recognizing the effects of trauma in rats and older children.

Because trauma is the response to overwhelmingly stressful events, it is reasonable to expect that virtually all organisms have a limit to the amount and type of stressful or harmful experience they can assimilate. Exposure to such experience beyond that limit would result in trauma. Based on research studies of many circumcised infants (see Chapter 1), circumcision exceeds that limit.

If circumcision causes trauma in the infant, it is certainly a physical trauma. Grof points out that based on his extensive clinical experience,

> memories of physical traumas appear to be of paramount importance. . . . and their significance exceeds by far that of the usual psychotraumas. The residual emotions and physical sensations from situations that threatened survival or the integrity of the organism appear to have a significant role in the development of various forms of psychopathology, as yet unrecognized by academic science.[61]

Grof cites anxieties, phobias, and sexual dysfunctions as examples of problems connected to physical traumatization.

The clinical experience of child psychiatrist and author Lenore Terr of northern California also supports the conclusion that physical traumas have a particularly damaging impact. The shock of such an experience is so strong that long-term symptoms often include a variety of characteristics that generally do not coexist. Traumas involving disfigurement are among those that "will most likely promote deep depressions and major character changes."[62]

CIRCUMCISION OF OLDER CHILDREN

Literature Reports

The possibility of circumcision causing traumatic effects in older children can be better explored because of easier access to the memory and the child's ability to talk. Two reports have studied the ritual as practiced without anesthesia on children in Turkey. In the first report, testing subjects between four and seven years old shortly before and after the ritual yielded this result: "Circumcision is perceived by the child as an aggressive attack upon his body, which damaged, mutilated, and, in some cases, totally destroyed him."[63] According to this study, circumcision resulted in increased aggressiveness and weakened the ego, causing withdrawal and reduced functioning and adaptation. Withdrawal is a defensive response individuals use to protect themselves against further attack.

In the second study, children were observed to be "terribly frightened" during the procedure, and "each child looked at his penis immediately after the circumcision as if to make sure that all was not cut off."[64] One eight-year-old boy fell "unconscious" during the cutting and subsequently developed a stuttering problem. A few weeks later, parents being interviewed reported that their children exhibited increased aggressive behavior and experienced nightmares. In the same report, adults were interviewed and recalled castration anxiety and other serious fears connected with their childhood circumcision, particularly if they had been deceived or forced by parents to undergo the procedure. Freud, who had a strongly critical view of circumcision, believed that it was a "substitute for castration."[65] Castration anxiety resulting from circumcision may be related to the finding that symptoms resulting from personal injury trauma often include fear of repetition of the trauma.[66]

The traumatic impact of surgery on children is well-established. For example, the psychiatric literature documents serious long-term effects resulting from childhood tonsillectomy.[67] Psychiatrist David Levy reviewed the case histories of 124 children who developed psychological problems after a surgical procedure. He observed that the younger the child, the greater the chance of adverse reaction to surgery. The most severe anxiety reactions were from two boys each of whom had surgery on his penis. One boy had a meatotomy (surgical enlargement of the urinary opening) at age four, and the other had a circumcision at age six. Both exhibited destructive behavior and suicidal impulses. The circumcised boy repeated, "They cut my penis," and "I wish I were dead."[68]

Personal Reports

Recent accounts of men circumcised as older children support the literature reports of long-term effects. Some of these accounts are from circumcised men who have contacted the Circumcision Resource Center seeking a safe place to express their feelings about circumcision. I led a support group for circumcised men, which included two men who were circumcised as older children. One man was circumcised at age ten without any advance warning or knowledge. He was in the hospital to receive treatment for another medical matter and woke up to find a bandage on his penis.

> I didn't have the skills, verbally or psychologically, to know and ex-
> press what was going on. It was too overwhelming at the time. I just
> didn't know how to handle it. I was too young. I didn't understand
> the effect until later in life. It made me less trusting. The terror and
> the sadness never got processed since the event never was acknowl-
> edged. Those two things had a consequent effect on any relation-
> ships. It made me less emotionally available as a person.

Another man in the group was circumcised at age four. He remembers the shock and pain. Because of anxiety about undressing around others, he avoids locker rooms. This man has recurring, upsetting thoughts about his circumcision and difficulty with relationships. Like most other men, he has never before spoken to anyone about his feelings concerning circumcision.

A Turkish immigrant to the United States described his child-hood circumcision as "worse than torture" in a 1992 telephone conversation and noted that subsequent distrust and aggressiveness were connected with the event.

Based on the available information, we can make the following statements about circumcision trauma and memory:

CIRCUMCISION TRAUMA AND MEMORY

- According to criteria established by the American Psychiatric Association in the *DSM-IV*, circumcision is a traumatic event.
- Because circumcision is a physical trauma experienced most often in infancy, it may have a particularly damaging impact.
- Circumcision and related feelings can be remembered or relived under special circumstances, usually in a therapeutic setting.
- Young children have remembered their circumcision experience and associated feelings and details.
- Circumcision of older children has resulted in increased aggressiveness, withdrawal, and reduced adaptation.

5

Long-Term Psychological Effects of Circumcision:

II. Adult Emotional Impact

A whole life can be shaped by an old trauma, remembered or not.
—Lenore Terr,
child psychiatrist and author

Research on infant neurological development, studies and established theories of trauma, and clinical experience suggest that infant circumcision may have long-term psychological effects. What are these effects? A critical part of exploring this question is to listen to what men who were circumcised as infants have to say about their circumcision. Then we will examine how these reports compare with the known effects of other traumas.

MEN'S ATTITUDES TOWARD THEIR OWN CIRCUMCISION

Little is known about the American male attitude toward circumcision. To learn about this attitude and what accounts for it, I conducted a preliminary survey of the male attitude toward circumcision in a group of men attending a conference called the Massachusetts Men's Gathering who did not have a particular interest in the subject. (This is the same survey I discussed in Chapter 2.)

Fifty-six out of ninety men at the conference returned the questionnaire (see Appendix B for sample questionnaire). Thirty-seven men (66 percent) reported that they were circumcised. Of this group, thirteen men (35 percent) who responded to the pertinent question stated that they wished they were not circumcised. This response rate may be higher than that of the general public because of a possible greater awareness of the issue in this group. Attendees to a men's conference are likely to be more sensitive to men's issues and to have had exposure to men's publications that might have discussed circumcision. Nevertheless, the results suggest that dissatisfaction with circumcision may be more prevalent than expected.

Based on questionnaire responses, all of the circumcised men who wished they were not circumcised had learned that the foreskin had a purpose. A significantly lower proportion of men (42–58 percent) who were either glad or didn't care that they were circumcised reported that the foreskin had a purpose. Men who were glad to be circumcised were also more likely to minimize the size of the adult foreskin. These results suggest that the more awareness a man had of the impact of circumcision (i.e., that it involves the loss of a significant amount of tissue that has a purpose), the more likely he would be dissatisfied with being circumcised. Conversely, those who knew less about the impact of circumcision were more likely to be glad (or not care) that they were circumcised. In the survey, most men were in this category.

PSYCHOLOGICAL IMPACT OF CIRCUMCISION ON MEN

Feelings of Dissatisfaction and Having Been Harmed

The dissatisfaction of some circumcised men can be described in detail. It has been expressed in an increasing number of letters from men all around the country to the Circumcision Resource Center and to several other organizations (see "Resources") that educate the public about circumcision. Moreover, in a recent issue of a major medical journal, twenty men signed a letter saying, "We are all adult men who believe that we have been harmed by circumcision."[1] We do not know how widespread the discontent is, but that these feelings exist at all is a noteworthy development and reason for concern.

Following are some statements about circumcision excerpted from letters written by dissatisfied circumcised men and received at the Circumcision Resource Center:

> I have felt a deep rage for a long time about this.

> My penis feels incomplete, deformed, maimed.

> Circumcision has given my life a much diminished and shameful flavor.

> The single most traumatic event of my life with the greatest psychological damage was my circumcision as an infant.

> Circumcision: it's taught me how to hate.

> Being circumcised has ruined my sex life.

> I feel violated and abused.

> I have felt unhappy about it all my life.

> I am very angry and resentful about this. I've had many physical, psychological, and emotional problems all my life.

> No one had the right to cut my foreskin off!

> I feel cheated at having been robbed of what is my natural birthright.

> I never mentioned it to my parents.

> I've always felt I'm missing normal male experience, and I'm embarrassed when in public dressing rooms.

> I feel like the best part of me was severed from my body, and I have ugly scars to remind me. I am so ANGRY!!

The responses of men dissatisfied with their circumcision tend to include at least one of the following feelings:

anger, resentment, revenge, rage, hate
sense of loss, deficiency, diminished body image
disbelief, lack of understanding, confusion
embarrassment, shame
sense of having been victimized, cheated, robbed, raped,
      violated, abused, mutilated, deformed
fear, distrust, withdrawal
grief, sadness, pain
envy, jealousy of intact men

Similar feelings were reported in a preliminary survey in which over 300 self-selected circumcised men responded to a request to document the harmful effects of their circumcision.[2] Over 80 percent of respondents cited emotional harm. Reports of negative reactions of men to circumcision are surprising to those who assume that circumcision is a benign procedure. How can the existence of such reports be reconciled with the fact that the majority of circumcised men do not express these feelings about their circumcision?

If circumcision has a long-term psychological impact, why don't we hear a lot more from circumcised men about how they truly feel? There are four possible reasons:

1.   Accepting circumcision beliefs and cultural assumptions prevents men from recognizing and feeling their dissatisfaction. A typical response is "When I was young I was told it was necessary for health reasons. I guess I just didn't question that. I assumed that was so."

2.   The emotions connected with circumcision that may surface are very painful. Repressing them protects men from this pain. A circumcised man recalled, "It was something I just didn't examine. I put it away in the back of my mind like a lot of guys do." If the feelings do become conscious,

they can still be suppressed. After learning about circumcision, another man said, "I don't want to be angry about this."

3. Those who have feelings about their circumcision are generally afraid to express them because their feelings may be dismissed or ridiculed. When asked why he had not revealed his circumcision feelings before, one man said, "I would be looked upon as strange or else people would toss it off lightly." Another said, "It's not something that anyone talks about. If it is talked about, it's in a snickering, comical way which I find disturbing. People laugh about it as if there is something funny going on."

4. Verbal expression of feelings requires conscious awareness. Because early traumas are generally unconscious, associated feelings are expressed nonverbally through behavioral, emotional, and physiological forms.[3] Attitudes about people, life, and the future may also be affected. An example of an attitude resulting from childhood trauma is "You can't count on anything or anyone to protect you."[4]

Lack of awareness and understanding of circumcision, emotional repression, fear of disclosure, and nonverbal expression help keep circumcision feelings a secret. John Breeding explains his new awareness and understanding after reliving his circumcision:

> I had a clear awareness that, already at one or two days old, I experienced a duality. In some way, there was a separation, at minimum a rudimentary split of mind and body, in which I desired, even felt obligated, to protect myself. That I could not, and would not be able to for many years, does not change the set-up. . . . Although I see similar processes everyday in my practice as a psychologist, it still amazes me that I could so completely repress such an intense experience. I am even more amazed as I look around at my fellow men, aware that most of them are circumcised and unaware of the powerful trauma repressed in their psyches.[5]

Body Image, Self-Esteem, and Shame

Though men may be unaware of the effects of circumcision, the fear that their penis is somehow deficient is reported to be widespread in our culture.[6] Commercial interests have responded to this concern. A 1995 issue of a popular national men's magazine contained ten advertisements for penile enlargement by various methods. (The American Urological Association concludes that they are not safe and effective.) One full-page ad proclaimed, "No man ever needs to feel inadequate again." Another asked, "Isn't it time to feel better about yourself?" Male preoccupation with the penis is also reflected in a survey of what men think women find attractive in men. The data showed that men greatly exaggerated the importance of penis size as a physical attribute that attracts women.[7]

Negative feelings about the penis are related to the idea of body image. Our body image includes value judgments about how we think our body looks to others and can have a great impact on how we live our lives.[8] In addition, the concepts of self and body image are interconnected and affect our personal psychology. A diminished body image can negatively influence a person's social and sexual life. Those who have a bodily loss fear the judgment of others and the weakening of personal relationships. For example, psychological, sexual, and social effects have been reported in women after a mastectomy. They felt less attractive, less desirable, and had lower sexual satisfaction after their surgery.[9] Poor body image can also affect motivation and reduce feelings of competence, status, and power. In addition, depression and suicidal attitude have been noted.[10] Though there are differences between the circumstances and age at the time of loss, the feeling that an important part of the body is missing is common to mastectomy and circumcision (for some men). The feeling of "not being a whole man" can be especially distressing. Perhaps the effects of poor body image help to explain why one unhappy circumcised man summarized his feelings by stating, "I often wonder how different my life would have been if I were not circumcised." Another man called circumcision "that one overwhelming experience that has colored my whole life since."

An aspect of oneself can be identified with a particular body part, as masculinity is typically identified with the penis. When that part is wounded, there often is a corresponding psychic wound to the self, a loss of self-esteem. About 60 percent of respondents to the previously mentioned survey of self-selected circumcised men, in which they were asked to document the harmful effects of their circumcision, reported that they did not feel natural, normal, and whole.[11] It seems logical to wonder how much of a connection there might be between low male self-esteem and circumcision.

Self-esteem is a vital component of psychological well-being, a fundamental human need that is necessary for normal and healthy development. Those with low self-esteem seek to avoid pain rather than to experience joy, tend to prefer the safety of familiar environments, and seek people with a self-esteem level similar to their own.[12] The connection between circumcision and low male self-esteem reported by some men suggests that circumcision could have a significant psychological impact on a man's life.

If we suffer from low self-esteem often we feel shame and project it by attacking the self-esteem of others. Because shame causes us to hide, it hurts us at least as much as any other emotion. Shame isolates us from others and ourselves. We reject ourselves before others can reject us. We feel flawed and unlovable. Being cut off from a part of ourselves becomes part of our self-identity.

A physical loss, like circumcision, can be a source of shame. Such feelings are often mentioned in letters from circumcised men. The following account, written by a man about his therapeutic session in which he relived his circumcision, offers another example of the connection between circumcision and shame.

> I suddenly realized that shame was a split common to all of humanity. . . . I had a strong feeling that shame is communicated at birth and has something important to do with sexual organs. . . . And then I felt a burning and itching pain around my penis and I realized that I was going through circumcision. . . . This was the deep source of

shame! . . . . I felt deeply ashamed of myself. . . . . I am so ashamed that
I am ashamed to be ashamed![13]

Because shame itself is kept a secret, it is another reason why we
do not hear from circumcised men about how they feel.

Neurological Effects

Circumcision may have neurological consequences as well. Trauma
results in dissociation, a cutting off or separation of the traumatic
experience and associated emotional pain from awareness.[14]
Dissociation is a psychological survival response somewhat analogous to numbing or deadening a part of one's body to stop an
excruciating physical pain. To preserve a semblance of attachment
to the mother, a child who has suffered trauma alters reality and
believes that the trauma never happened.[15] In altering reality, the
child is also altered. Based on neurological research, painful
experience and trauma in childhood can result in long-term
physiological changes in the central nervous system and neurochemical changes.[16] Two brain-imaging studies of adults with
histories of child sexual abuse reported reduced size of the hippocampus, a part of the brain associated with memory, and in a test
of verbal short-term memory, adults who had been abused had
lower scores.[17]

James Prescott, a developmental neuropsychologist and former
administrator for the National Institutes of Health, maintains that
circumcision affects brain development. The pain of circumcision,
he says, "limits and qualifies all subsequent experiences of pleasure," which are "experienced upon a background of genital pain
that is now deeply buried in the subconscious/unconscious
brain."[18] Related research indicates that the presence of a high
level of the stress hormone cortisol in the blood stream correlates
with deep memory imprinting in animals.[19] As was reported in
Chapter 1, after circumcision, the level of blood cortisol increases
by a factor of three or four times the level prior to circumcision.
Could such deep memory imprinting help to explain why empirical
research demonstrates that many men are aroused by sexual

images that contain violence and pain, and why pornographic magazines contain an increasing number of violent images?[20]

DISCOVERING CIRCUMCISION

The overwhelming majority of circumcised men were circumcised as newborn infants. The memory of this event is not in their conscious awareness. Consequently, the connection between present feelings and circumcision may not be clear. For example, a circumcised man wondering about its effects said,

> It seems to me that there's got to be a connection between circumcision and how I feel about my genitals and my sexuality. It just isn't reasonable to me that there wouldn't be a connection there. I think it's something that's so deeply buried that it's going to take more exploration on my part for me to get in touch with it. It's pretty disturbing that circumcision was the first sexual experience that I ever had.

Yet the men quoted earlier attribute many negative feelings to their circumcision. Is this attribution accurate, and how did it originate? I explored this question by interviewing men who contacted the Circumcision Resource Center and asking them when and how they first recognized their feelings. Based on their responses, the answer is in the impact of discovering one's circumcision as a child. If a child grows up in a community that has children of differing circumcision status, it is probable that the day will come when a circumcised boy will notice the difference. Under certain circumstances, this realization can have traumalike consequences such as recurrent unwelcome thoughts and images.

One man told of an indelible scene when he was four. He was with an intact boy who showed him his penis and explained circumcision to him. He was shocked and ashamed at what had been done to him and thought, "Why would somebody want to do that to me? They just chopped it off. It didn't make any sense to me." As an adult he thinks about it "every time I take a shower or urinate."

Joanne Dion told of an incident with her three-year-old circumcised son. While she was showing him his baby pictures, he noticed one with his penis intact and asked about it. After his mother explained what had happened, he expressed his displeasure by saying, "Doctors shouldn't have scissors."[21]

The man who stated near the beginning of this chapter that circumcision was "the single most traumatic event of my life" related this experience:

> My initial awareness came when I was about five years old and playing with the boy who lived down the street. I discovered that he had that skin and I didn't. I don't remember anything in terms of verbal exchange. It's now sixty years later, and the memory is still very vivid, the two of us sitting on his bathroom floor. It had a profound effect, an imprinting on my mind. Then, when I was about thirteen, I went swimming with a friend at one of the local lakes. When we were changing into bathing suits, I realized that he was uncircumcised. That, again, was a strong imprint. Probably those two early experiences were enough to be a very strong picture in my mind and cause a realization of my loss. I had no idea at the time of how traumatic it was. I only knew that there was something different, and I was thinking about it so much every day.

Another man remembered his childhood discovery:

> I've been angry about being circumcised since I was six years old. I was taking a hike in the woods with my older brother and his friend. We all had to use the tree. My brother said to his friend, "What's wrong with you?" His friend said, "It's not what's wrong with me. It's you guys." His mother was a nurse, and she knew better than to do it to him. We didn't know the terminology. We didn't understand it, but he told us that we were born the way he was, and then someone cut part of us off. I haven't talked to my brother about it over the years, but all my life I've been just dying for my chance to get my hands on that doctor that did it to me.

A typical case of discovering the difference is the following story:

The shock and surprise of my life came when I was in junior high school, and I was in the showers after gym. . . . I wondered what was wrong with those penises that looked different than mine. . . . I soon realized I had part of me removed. I felt incomplete and very frustrated when I realized that I could never be like I was when I was born—intact. That frustration is with me to this day. Throughout life I have regretted my circumcision. Daily I wish I were whole.

A man who first recognized his dissatisfaction with circumcision as an adult reported:

What changed my feeling about circumcision was recognizing that this was done to me without my consent at a time when I couldn't do anything to stop it. I don't see anything wrong with having the option. I just don't like the idea that someone made this decision for me. I'll never know how it feels to be uncircumcised.

An English boy's shock of discovering his circumcision is evident in this account written by his friend.

A Seven-Year-Old Boy Learns He Is Circumcised

For the last few years, since he moved in, I have become best friends with an eight-year-old boy, Gary, living next door to me. I am now seventeen but, despite the age gap, we both get along really well with each other, and I have just as much, if not more, respect for him than I do for friends my own age. I hope that we can continue this friendship as he grows up. About a year ago when Gary was seven, he and I began on a series of events that neither of us will ever forget.

We had arranged to go for a cycling trip in the forest, and I had stopped for a snack on one of the many forest picnic tables. He then caught me urinating and nervously asked why his penis was different from mine and all his friends' at school. We had both seen each other naked many times while changing for swimming or sports and also when he was bathing while I baby-sat for his parents. I had noticed fairly early on that he was circumcised, but I assumed he knew he was circumcised as he had never mentioned it before. However, he insisted on showing me his penis and what he meant. He wanted to know why his "skin was so much shorter than mine," and he was obviously unaware of the fact that a large amount of it had been cut off.

Not wanting to upset him, as I could tell he was worried about it, I told him that he had had a little operation on it when he was younger, expecting that to be the end of it. However, he was intrigued and wanted to know what had been done in more detail. I was hesitant to respond, not knowing why it had been done to him. Being the sensitive boy he was, he noticed this and begged me to explain further. I could see he could in no way be turned away from the fact now, so I began to explain what circumcision was and that it had been done.

I now had to explain that part of his penis had been cut off, not an easy task. I thought maybe he'd remember the operation, as I assumed it must have been done recently as they are not religious at all. [Generally, only Jewish male infants are circumcised in England.] He had no recollection of this, so I came to the conclusion that it must have been done at a very young age. The only kind way I could think of at the time was to say that a doctor did it because it was necessary.

He didn't believe me that a doctor would "do anything like that to a person," and wanted to know "the truth" (it seems even a seven-year-old can recognize how barbaric it is). He began getting into a worse state and so, believing circumcision to be an unnecessary, cruel, painful, and humiliating procedure for a boy to suffer and not wanting to mislead him, I told him the truth about what had been done to him. I was careful as I could not to upset him, but learning that his most prized part of his body had had the end cut off was bound to upset him. [For many men, the foreskin extends beyond the tip of the glans and is the "end" of the penis.] Gary began sobbing, and I could only comfort him, as the sobs turned into a heavy stream of tears, until he calmed down. This lasted for close to ten minutes. He was evidently very upset and I think also angry. I was now feeling guilty for causing this upset. We continued to talk, and while I wiped away his tears he begged me not to tell his parents that he had been crying, to which I agreed. We then returned home.

Later that evening, during dinner to which Gary had invited me to stay, he got up, shouted at his parents, "I hate you," burst into tears, and ran off up to his bedroom. Knowing almost certainly what this was about, I went after him, telling his parents that I would see what was wrong with him. He did not want to talk about it at first, but I felt it was important that he talk to someone. He was now more angry than upset that his parents would allow such a thing to be done to him.

It's now nearly a year since this all began, but Gary is now coping well. . . . It's been an emotional time for me seeing such a young and otherwise very cheerful boy distressed to such an extent, but Gary now understands virtually everything associated with the social and physical aspects of circumcision, although I've had to simplify some parts. He often says how he wishes he was not circumcised and asks me how it feels to be "normal." . . . It seems such a waste of a childhood having to worry . . . because of an unnecessary operation that he certainly now resents and that was performed on the most sensitive part of his body without his consent.

SYMPTOMS OF POST-TRAUMATIC STRESS DISORDER RELATED TO CIRCUMCISION

To further examine the psychological impact of circumcision on adults, building on the discussion in Chapter 4, I again refer to the model of post-traumatic stress disorder (PTSD) in the *Diagnostic and Statistical Manual of Mental Disorders (DSM-IV)*.[22] According to the *DSM-IV*, the symptoms of PTSD may be arranged in three groups:

1. Reexperiencing the trauma through recurrent and distressing thoughts, dreams, illusions, and actions or psychological distress and physiological reactions resulting from exposure to anything resembling some aspect of the event. Symptoms may be acute, chronic, or delayed.
2. Avoidance or emotional numbing, including avoidance of situations, stimuli, thoughts, and feelings related to the trauma, or a generalized withdrawal from others and reduced emotional response. Symptoms are generally chronic or delayed.
3. Increased sleeping difficulties, tendency to irritability and anger, hypervigilance, and exaggerated startle response. Symptoms are usually acute or chronic.

Acute symptoms are defined as lasting less than three months. If symptoms persist three months or longer, they are described as chronic. Symptoms that start at least six months after the traumatic event are called delayed. It may be years before delayed symptoms appear.

The symptoms of PTSD result from a variety of distressing events. Do some of them also result from circumcision? Let's consider the symptoms by group.

First Group of Symptoms

Reexperiencing the trauma of the circumcision event would be more likely to be an acute or short-term symptom for the infant rather than a common long-term effect because the event is not consciously remembered by the adult. However, as shown earlier, men who have significant childhood experiences or learn about circumcision later are susceptible to recurrent thoughts and distress about circumcision. This experience qualifies as a delayed response to the trauma.

Dreams have been connected with childhood trauma.[23] Three men who contacted the Circumcision Resource Center reported recurrent, distressing dreams that they felt were connected with their circumcision experience. The dream of one man contained a sudden change:

> I sense a warm sun, a clear clean lake, a few cooling breezes, trees, flowers, friendly creatures here and there. I feel myself gliding smoothly, erotically in a light canoe, or maybe wading or swimming lazily. Suddenly, the lake transforms into a solid glass, shattering at the same time, shattering around my body, through my body, driving into my heart, throat, head, the very center of my brain. It is a grinding, crunching, never ending horror, increasing into eternity.
>
> The nightmares recur for years, the theme always the same: lovely erotic liquid smoothness, flowing life, a new universe, suddenly transformed to the shattering, grinding, crunching horror. The specific dreams varied widely, but the feeling content was unmistakable. There was no clue to the explanation at the time or at any time during

my entire life, until I finally got into the circumcision memory itself. Then and only then did the entire horror fall into place.[24]

The connection between sadomasochistic behavior and childhood injuries or procedures has been noted in the psychiatric literature.[25] Do these disorders sometimes reflect a reexperiencing of the circumstances of circumcision? The common elements of sadomasochistic behavior and circumcision include pain and suffering, restraint or bondage, and sexual context. A circumcised man who believes there is a connection reported,

> I have had S-M (sadomasochistic) fantasies for as long as I can remember. I do not believe it is "normal" for 4-year-olds to have these kinds of fantasies unless they have been violated in some way. Although I looked for other explanations, circumcision seemed to be the only trauma that applied which could have produced this kind of response in me.[26]

Clearly, there are other factors related to sadomasochistic behaviors, since women also participate in them. For example, psychiatrist Thomas Verny found that a fetus's experiencing induced labor in the womb correlated with sexual perversions when the child matured.[27] Nevertheless, the great majority of people who participate in sadomasochistic practices are men, and any explanation of the behavior would need to include early experiences that are common particularly to boys.[28] Circumcision qualifies. (The fact that some intact men also practice these behaviors does not preclude the possibility that circumcision increases the chances that a male will exhibit these behaviors.)

Physiological responses clinically associated with PTSD reactions were evident in a few circumcised men who answered my question "Do you have any particular response to the sight of knives or scissors?" One man said, "I shiver with fear when I think about it—I cringe I guess." Another stated, "occasional fears of being cut badly, also with sharp glass and razor blades." A third circumcised man responded to my question with the following:

> I have an intense dislike for knives or scissors. At some point when I had my knives displayed in the kitchen, I realized that I couldn't stand the sight of those knives out in the open.

Other men responded with statements that indicate physiological responses: "My greatest fear to this day is having a knife pulled on me." For some men, the words "circumcision" or "circumcised" have an impact: "I hate that word. The sound 'cir . . .' makes me shudder." One man revealed: "Adrenaline shoots through me when I hear the word 'circumcised.' I freeze."[29] Another man said, "I couldn't be in the same room with talk about circumcision. I felt it up and down my spine."

An extreme physiological and emotional response was reported by a man who was given some articles and books on circumcision to look at.

> I read the materials and went into shock. . . . Finally coming to understand the full horror of what had been done to me, I essentially went crazy for about two weeks. I felt like a raw wound, my whole body and mind. I noticed I was walking around bowlegged, as if I'd spilled boiling water on my crotch. I spent my time pacing my apartment or curled up in bed; I could barely think or eat.[30]

Second Group of Symptoms

One of the reasons the symptoms of this group arise is as a defense aimed at preventing the first group of symptoms from developing. The avoidance symptoms associated with circumcision accomplish that purpose. The general lack of curiosity about circumcision is no accident. There is an aversion to learning potentially threatening new information. In addition, some men that call the Circumcision Resource Center intentionally avoid mentioning the "c-word." They ask if they have reached "the Resource Center." Envelopes have been received addressed to the "C. Resource Center." Generally, most circumcised men appear uncomfortable with the "c-word" and avoid it. One man related the following story:

I was driving in traffic on a multilane highway with cars backed up for miles. We were bumper to bumper and moving slowly. Then I noticed in my rearview mirror that there was a large gap with no cars in the lane immediately behind me. Over a period of half an hour, I observed that no car in my lane beyond the gap would approach my car from the rear. A few shifted to another lane. Then I remembered that I had a bumper sticker that said, "Stop Infant Circumcision." I wondered if the drivers kept their distance so that they or their passengers would not have to read my message.

Reduced capacity for emotional expression or numbing response is a more likely PTSD symptom as time increases after the traumatic event.[31] This finding supports the idea of second group symptoms being more prevalent in circumcised men, because a significant amount of time has passed since their circumcision. The degree of numbing is connected with the intensity of the trauma. The stronger the unexpressed feelings, the stronger the subsequent numbing would have to be. Based on physiological and behavioral studies (see Chapter 1), an infant's feelings connected with circumcision are extreme. An infant can be overwhelmed by them. Either he withdraws totally and goes into a state of shock, or he expresses what he can until he is exhausted and goes to sleep. Certainly there can be many reasons for reduced emotional expression in circumcised men. However, as we have seen in the last chapter in reading the words of the man who was circumcised at age ten ("It made me less emotionally available as a person.") and others as well, circumcision could be an important contributing factor.

Third Group of Symptoms

Irritability and anger are also connected with circumcision for some men. One of the predominant feelings a person has when a part of his penis is cut off by force is anger. Statements by circumcised men confirm that some of them continue to feel deep rage, hate, and resentment about having been circumcised. ("I have felt a deep rage for a long time about this.") Storing this anger requires living with strong opposing forces. When the containment is insufficient, there may be episodes of excessive and inappropriate anger, or even violence. Those who have been violated generally have a problem with anger and direct it either inward toward the self or outward toward others.[32] Clearly, many different experiences can be related to a feeling of being violated. For at least some men, circumcision is one such experience.

Other Symptoms

Associated features of PTSD, according to the *DSM-IV*, include "impaired affect modulation, self-destructive and impulsive behavior, dissociative symptoms, somatic complaints, feelings of ineffectiveness, shame, despair, or hopelessness; feeling permanently damaged; a loss of previously sustained beliefs, hostility, social withdrawal; feeling constantly threatened, impaired relationships with others, or a change from the individual's previous personality characteristics."[33]

At least a few of these symptoms have been reported or exhibited by circumcised men. Janov, noting that circumcision can cause "prototypic Pain" (core trauma with long-term effects), concludes that it can result in anxiety connected to the penis and contribute to behaviors such as compulsive masturbation and sex, or avoidance of sex.[34]

SEX-RELATED EFFECTS OF CIRCUMCISION

Impotence

The link between adult circumcision, the loss of sensitivity, and impotence has been noted in the medical literature.[35] Since infant circumcision also decreases sexual sensitivity (see Chapter 2), it is possible that circumcision is an unrecognized factor in the high rates of impotence in American men and, by association, has a negative effect on male psychological health as well. According to a randomized study of 1,290 men between forty and seventy years old, 52 percent reported some degree of impotence ranging from minimal to complete. This rate varied from about 40 percent at age forty to 67 percent at age seventy. Higher degrees of impotence were associated with increased levels of anger and depression. Lower self-esteem was also found in impotent men.[36] The psychological response to impotence would compound any preexisting psychological symptoms that have already been discussed.

Problems in Psychosexual Behavior

When I mentioned the topic of circumcision to a female friend, she said, "I'm not interested. I'm not a man." The connection between circumcision and its potential effect on women is unrecognized. Yet there are signs suggesting that investigation is warranted. *Medical Aspects of Human Sexuality* conducted a survey of over 400 physicians on the subject of male contributions to female sexual dysfunction.[37] The results indicated that female sexual response is often dependent on the male's psychological responsiveness. A significant number of respondents felt that male insensitivity and lack of verbal communication negatively affected female sexual response. Although other factors are surely involved, we do not know to what degree potential psychological effects of circumcision would also inhibit interaction.

Communication is generally recognized as an important component of sexual experience. By providing a pleasurable context, sexual relations facilitate revealing other aspects of oneself. This disclosure is potentially satisfying, strengthens intimacy, and is particularly valued by women. Based on the examination of 186 societies, pleasure and disclosure are fundamental to human relationships.[38]

Talk about sex in particular between partners contributes to sexual satisfaction. It also has a positive association with relationship satisfaction.[39] Because males are generally less expressive than females in this culture, the degree of intimacy in a relationship may be limited by the willingness of the man to self-disclose. As one man revealed, "No matter how close I feel to a woman, there's a part of me that is only mine, that I won't share. I never raise any woman's expectations about total intimacy."[40] Male self-concealment correlates with low self-esteem.[41] It is possible that self-concealment and unresolved issues about sexual matters could, in some cases, be related to circumcision and may negatively affect sexual experience and relationship quality.

It may be difficult for a man to speak honestly and personally if he is having sex for reasons that do not enhance intimacy. For example, he may engage in sex mainly to boost his low sexual self-esteem. In addition, a large majority of respondents in the study on male contributions to female sexual dysfunction believed that some men are overly preoccupied with the frequency of their partners' orgasms.[42] If circumcision contributes to low sexual self-esteem, then both conditions, in some cases, could be associated with circumcision on a deeper level.

There is much to learn about how circumcision itself affects women sexually. Knowledge and understanding of this question will have to wait until researchers investigate this area. The effects of circumcision on gay relationships is also an unexplored subject.

In summary, based on the PTSD symptoms as outlined in the *DSM-IV*, as well as clinical experience, related research, and statements from circumcised men who report a number of symptoms associated with PTSD, we have the following list:

POTENTIAL LONG-TERM PSYCHOLOGICAL EFFECTS OF CIRCUMCISION TRAUMA

1. Reduced emotional expression
2. Discomfort related to the topic of circumcision
3. Avoidance of intimacy
4. Distrust
5. Low self-esteem
6. Excessive or inappropriate anger
7. Recurrent thoughts and distress
8. Sexual anxieties, phobias, and dysfunctions
9. Limited capacity for pleasure
10. Physiological responses
11. Diminished body image
12. Shame

Other early traumatic experiences may contribute to these symptoms, and some circumcised men may not have such symptoms. With further investigation into this area, we can learn how circumcision affects the prevalence of these symptoms.

6

Circumcision and the

Mother-Child Relationship

> The tie is stronger than that between father and son and father
> and daughter. . . . The bond is also more complex than the
> one between mother and daughter. For a woman, a son offers
> the best chance to know the mysterious male existence.
> —Carole Klein, author of *Mothers and Sons*

Avoidance of intimacy is one of the most important potential long-term psychological effects of circumcision trauma. To explore more closely how it can develop, we will examine the first and fundamental intimate relationship: the one between mother and child. Though others may care for the child, the quality of the mother-child relationship cannot be duplicated, and its primary importance cannot be denied, particularly during the period just after birth. The relationship starts during pregnancy when the awareness, sensitivity, and responsiveness of the newborn infant develop, and the fetus and mother communicate physiologically. It is no accident that newborn infants recognize their mother's face in a few minutes and prefer her voice and smell, whereas recognition of the father and others comes later (see Chapter 1). Therefore, although the infant's relationship with the father and others is important, the quality of this principal relationship has profound long-term consequences.

The emotional bond connecting the infant and mother is called attachment. The importance of attachment has been well established

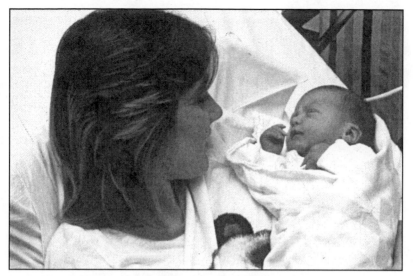

Reprinted by permission from The Saturday Evening Post

Fig. 12

in the literature for decades. A strong bond between mother and infant contributes to the child's mental and social development. The infant-mother relationship is a model for infant-peer relationships.[1] In addition, research demonstrates that securely attached infants are more curious and sociable with peers at two, three, and five years of age. The child's self-confidence and empathy are also connected with the quality of the relationship with the mother.[2] Attachment affects the body as well as behavior. Securely attached infants are more physiologically in tune with their mothers, and they have improved immune functioning and lower stress levels.[3]

    Many factors can disrupt the mother-child bond. For example, it can be disrupted by mother-child separation (including separations resulting from hospital policies). Numerous studies of monkeys have demonstrated that maternal-infant separation causes significantly more stress (as measured by the level of stress hormone cortisol in the blood) in the infant than in the mother, that even a thirty-minute separation is highly stressful for the infant, that high stress can be present despite a lack of crying, that infant contact with other monkeys during the separation does not relieve this stress, and that the effects of separation can last long after reunion with the mother.[4] Furthermore, it has been shown that human infants and children and monkey infants have similar behavioral and physiological responses to maternal separation.[5] Investigators have found that the response of young children to separation has two phases: protest followed by despair. Other responses include helplessness, hypervigilance, withdrawal, depressed activity level and heart rate, higher stress level, and suppressed immune response.[6] In addition to separation, child-hood maltreatment and trauma are also connected with poor attachment.[7]

Circumcision is traumatic primarily because of the overwhelm-ing pain. In addition, it typically involves a separation (to another room) from the mother, who is the main source of physical and emotional comfort and contact. For a young child experiencing trauma, a few minutes can feel endless. Separation from the mother contributes to the terror and emotional distress experienced by young children undergoing surgical procedures.[8] In addition, the lack of appropriate support during a childhood traumatic experi-ence can have long-term consequences on adjustment and func-tioning.[9]

Studies have already shown that circumcision can adversely affect mother-infant bonding.[10] As mentioned in Chapter 1, cir-cumcised infants can be more irritable. Since infant irritability at two days has been connected with insecure attachment at fourteen months,[11] the impact of circumcision on attachment may be more than temporary.

The long-term effects of impaired bonding have not received the attention they deserve. Some researchers have suggested that disrupted bonding in childhood can result in adult psychopa-thology.[12] There may be psychobiological and neurobiological consequences as well.[13] The research concerning the effects of disrupted attachment bonds can be summarized as follows:

Premature or inappropriate sudden disruption of attachment bonds, in addition to being subjectively painful, may lead to psychological disturbances, physiological disorganization, and ill health. Disturbances in attachment per se may result in skewed affective development, impaired parenting, and possible other forms of psychopathology, including child abuse.[14]

The long-term effects of disrupted attachment resulting from circumcision are difficult to assess, but could be very important. The following clinical reports, personal accounts, and references to empirical studies describe how circumcision can affect the mother-infant relationship. Suggestions about directions for future research are also included.

MATERNAL ANXIETY

The impact of circumcision on the child may start even before birth. Investigators have found a relationship between prenatal maternal anxiety connected with the birth experience and infant irritability.[15] One event described as "highly stressful" for the mother is circumcision, if she is in conflict about the decision and feels apprehension about subjecting her infant to the unnecessary, extreme pain.[16] Maternal anxiety about circumcision is particularly likely if the issue is not resolved between the mother and father. Family and cultural demands also have an impact. One mother who questioned circumcision said, "My mother felt so strongly about circumcision that she urged my friends to pressure me about it at my baby shower." Natalie Bivas, a Jewish parent, wrote, "I spent most of my pregnancy crying, vomiting, ruminating, and reading about circumcision."[17] Whatever the reason, if maternal anxiety and infant irritability are connected, a mother anxious about circumcision may be more likely to have an irritable child. Neither emotional state would be expected to facilitate bonding.

Circumcision can have an impact on the child in other ways. Research has shown that maternal anxiety during pregnancy affects the birth itself and the infant outcome.[18] The effects may manifest in a number of ways, including prolonged labor, delivery complications, and low birth weight. The following story illustrates the possible impact of maternal anxiety concerning circumcision on the delivery:

> A midwife was attending a very difficult home birth. The baby would not descend. They were at the point of moving from the home environment to a hospital, and they both wanted the home birth. In her wisdom, the midwife understood that this couple had not resolved their decision whether to circumcise their baby or not. The Jewish father wanted the boy circumcised. The mother, also Jewish, wanted to protect her baby. So the midwife whispered to the husband, "Tell her you changed your mind. We won't circumcise the baby." He did. The baby descended. The birth was spontaneous. He is an intact son.[19]

MOTHER-INFANT INTERACTION

Experiments with goats demonstrate that if the mother and infant are separated for a brief period after birth, the mother may neglect or reject her own offspring.[20] Similarly, early events affecting the human mother-child relationship can have long-term consequences on maternal behavior and child development. For example, diminished mother-child contact after birth (e.g., a glance and then thirty-minute feedings every four hours versus an hour of contact after birth, the same feeding schedule, and five extra contact hours during the day) has been associated with differences in maternal behavior toward the infant after one year and differences in maternal speech patterns and child speech and language comprehension after five years.[21] In addition, mother-infant separation has been disproportionately associated with child abuse.[22]

As stated in Chapter 1, changes in mother-infant interaction have been observed during the first twenty-four hours after circumcision. We do not know the possible long-term impact of these changes.

The effect of circumcision on mother-infant interaction is evident in this account by Mary Milvich about her experience around the birth of her first child:

> I shared a hospital room with a mother whose son was born within hours of my daughter. My roommate and I marveled at the identical personality traits exhibited by our newborn babies. Both were perfectly calm, never cried and gazed unwaveringly at our faces when we held them. We experienced that maternal closeness the mother feels when she realizes her baby knows her and accepts her as caretaker. . . . Delight in our new-found joys of motherhood was shattered the following morning. My roommate's baby had changed. He refused to nurse; he cried; he wouldn't be held. "He doesn't want me," my roommate pitifully told the nurse. "It's just the circumcision," the nurse told her comfortingly.[23]

Investigators have confirmed that circumcision may contribute to the failure of an infant to breast-feed.[24] The importance of breast-feeding to the emotional and physical health of the infant is often unappreciated. The advantages to breast-feeding over bottle-feeding include improved bonding, short- and long-term health benefits, and enhanced intellectual and neurological development (measured at age ten).[25] If circumcision interferes with breast-feeding, these advantages would be lost.

Some circumcised infants cry for extended periods and seem inconsolable. This response is possibly due to intrusive post-traumatic stress disorder (PTSD) symptoms connected with circumcision. Research and clinical experience have shown that infant crying is a valuable physiological process that helps to resolve earlier trauma.[26] However, the extended crying may exceed the tolerance level of the mother and cause her response tendency to change from an empathetic to an egotistic one.[27] In other words, she could become more interested in relieving her own distress (from hearing the crying) than that of her infant.

If a mother believes she is not able to relieve the cause of her infant's distress, she may feel a lack of competence and respond less or not at all. She may also think of the infant as having a "difficult" temperament and use that belief as a reason not to respond.[28]

Conversely, if an infant withdraws because of the trauma of circumcision, he will not communicate his needs, the mother will assume he is content, and his needs will not be met. Interaction between mother and child will be frustrating and less rewarding for the mother because she will receive only a limited response from her child. Clearly, the mother-infant relationship is a two-way social relationship that depends on the responsiveness of both. If either the mother or the infant is unresponsive, the relationship will suffer, and emotional disturbances may occur.[29]

The degree to which a mother recognizes and responds to her infant's behavior affects the quality of the mother-infant attachment bond. A strong bond requires the mother to be sensitive and responsive to infant vocal, facial, and body expressions.[30] The reduced responsiveness of the mother correlates with a high frequency of infant crying, insecure attachment, and delayed mental and social development of the infant.[31] Therefore, any effect that circumcision has on infant behavior and subsequent maternal responsiveness disrupts the mother-infant bond.

Of course, other factors affect the quality of the mother-child relationship. The mother's personality traits affect attachment,[32] and maternal responsiveness varies with societies as well as individuals. For example, in one study of mothers' responsiveness, American mothers ignored almost half of the crying incidents of their first child during the first three months.[33] When they responded, it was sometimes after nine minutes had passed. In hunter-gatherer cultures, the mothers typically responded within seconds to infant cries.[34] Crying, as noted earlier, is meaningful communication that signals the caretaker to help relieve some form of distress.

In extreme cases, the lack of proper responsiveness has been associated with parenting problems such as child abuse and developmental problems in the child.[35] For example, if the infant cries excessively, the parent may use violence to try to stop it. Limited responsiveness from the infant may also lead the parent to be abusive.[36] Circumcised infants tend to be less responsive and more irritable. We do not know to what degree circumcision contributes, along with other factors, to child abuse.

LOSS OF TRUST

Erik Erikson's theory of psychosocial development includes eight chronological stages. In the first stage, the core issue is basic trust in the caretaking environment.[37] This theory is supported by the clinical experience of psychiatrist Rima Laibow, who uses leading-edge techniques and reports,

> Events which impact upon the child's ability to trust mother may have long-term consequences in all areas of growth and development. . . . When a child is subjected to intolerable, overwhelming pain, he conceptualizes mother as both participatory and responsible regardless of mother's intent. . . . The consequences for impaired bonding are significant. . . . Circumcision is an enormous obstacle to the development of basic trust between mother and child.[38]

This statement, based on more than twenty years of clinical observations of children and adults who have relived perinatal experiences, calls on us to see the world through the eyes of the newborn infant. That world centers on the mother. As a result, even though the physician does the circumcising, and the father may have made the final decision to circumcise, the newborn infant connects the experience to the mother. Because the experience is repressed, the connection between the event and the mother is also repressed. The loss of trust and the disruption of bonding are connected.[39] Distrust is also associated with neurobiological changes.[40]

In a typical hospital circumcision, the mother is not a witness to the pain and helpless cries of her infant son. Consequently, she is not aware of how the procedure affects him or how it affects their relationship. In general, when a person is perceived to be responsible for inflicting pain on another, the relationship is adversely affected by the resulting distrust and emotional distance. Even when a person is not aware of the incident, the response of

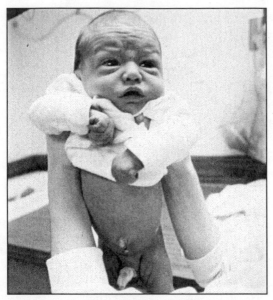

Reprinted by permission from The Saturday Evening Post

Fig. 13   Note the expression on this infant's face
as he is held after being circumcised.

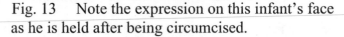

withdrawal and distrust by the recipient will affect the other person. Inevitably, the distrust of one person develops into mutual distrust and separation. It would seem that the deeper the pain, the deeper the distrust. The extreme pain of circumcision may engender deep distrust.

Infants themselves have exhibited behavior after circumcision that suggests distrust. The following personal account relates to the infant's ability to respond appropriately to the circumcision experience. Mary Conant, an obstetrical nurse, has observed circumcised infants who cover their genitals with their hands when their diapers are changed. Intact infants do not do this. One can plausibly infer from this that circumcised infants may fear further damage to their genitals and may not trust their caretaker.

Trust is a prerequisite for intimacy. Circumcision may disrupt the development of basic trust in infancy and impair the potential for intimacy in later life. One circumcised man who wrote to the

Circumcision Resource Center reported, "When I look deeper I find that my primary and overriding response to women is simply fear, and I see the same fear in nearly all the men in our culture." The possible connection between circumcision and difficulty with intimacy is consistent with theory and clinical experience associated with trauma. The withdrawal or avoidance of feelings related to intimacy is included in the second group of PTSD symptoms (see Chapter 5).

According to the psychological literature, the effects of the circumcision experience on the child's feelings toward the mother may be more than withdrawal and distrust. A thirteen-year-old boy in psychoanalysis was profoundly affected by his circumcision at two years, eight months and regarded his mother as a malicious attacker.[41] Similarly, in a study of twelve Turkish boys who were circumcised between the ages of four and seven, the children perceived their mothers as the mutilators and directed aggression at them.[42] More reports and studies would be helpful, but they are not yet available.

Some men report negative feelings toward their parents because of their circumcision. An analysis of information provided by 301 men who were dissatisfied with circumcision showed that 52.7 percent resented their parents because they felt that their parents had a choice and did not protect their son.[43] Though this report does not tell us how prevalent this feeling is among all men, it does confirm that such feeling exists, a noteworthy development.

MOTHERS WHO OBSERVED CIRCUMCISION

The typical hospital circumcision is done out of view of the mother in a separate room. However, a few are observed by parents, and many Jewish ritual circumcisions are done in the homes of the parents and observed by family and friends. Although some parents may report that this is a positive experience, this is not always the case. Women are more likely than men to report distress from hearing an infant crying.[44] Regarding circumcision, the father is more likely to deny his son's pain because it could remind him of his own circumcision feelings. Therefore, witnessing the circumcision and the infant's response can have a particularly shocking effect on the mother. Only recently have some parents been willing to describe their agonizingly painful experiences at their son's circumcision. Though further research is needed to tell us how common these responses are, the fact that they exist at all is reason for concern and reflection.

Some mothers have written about their experiences with circumcision during the previous year. "It was as close to hell as I ever want to get!" one wrote. Another related this memory:

> My tiny son and I sobbed our hearts out. . . . After everything I'd worked for, carrying and nurturing Joseph in the womb, having him at home against no small odds, keeping him by my side constantly since birth, nursing him whenever he needed closeness and nourishment—the circumcision was a horrible violation of all I felt we shared. I cried for days afterward.[45]

Melissa Morrison was having a difficult time seven months after she had watched the (nonritual) circumcision of her son:

> I'm finding myself obsessing more and more about it. It's absolutely horrible. I didn't know how horrific it was going to be. It was the most gruesome thing I have ever seen in my life. I told the doctor as soon as he was done, if I had a gun I would have killed him. I swear I would be in jail today if I did have a gun.[46]

Two other mothers have reported to the Circumcision Resource Center that watching their son's circumcision was "the worst day of my life." Another mother noted that she still felt pain recalling the experience about a year later. She wrote to her son:

> I have never heard such screams. . . . Will I ever know what scars this brings to your soul? . . . What is that new look I see in your eyes? I can see pain, a certain sadness, and a loss of trust.[47]

Other mothers clearly remember their son's circumcision after many years. Miriam Pollack reported fifteen years after the event, "The screams of my baby remain embedded in my bones and haunt my mind." She added later, "His cry sounded like he was being butchered. I lost my milk."[48]

Nancy Wainer Cohen recalled her feelings connected with the circumcision of her son, who is now twenty-two:

> I heard him cry during the time they were circumcising him. The thing that is most disturbing to me is that I can still hear his cry. . . . It was an assault on him, and on some level it was an assault on me. . . . I will go to my grave hearing that horrible wail, and feeling somewhat responsible, feeling that it was my lack of awareness, my lack of consciousness. I did the best I could, and it wasn't good enough.[49]

Elizabeth Pickard-Ginsburg vividly remembered her son's circumcision and its effect on her:

> Jesse was shrieking and I had tears streaming down my face. . . . He was screaming and there was no doubt in his scream that he wanted mother, or a mothering figure to come and protect him from this pain!! . . . Jesse screamed so loud that all of a sudden there was no sound! I've never heard anything like it!! He was screaming and it went up and then there was no sound and his mouth was just open and his face was full of pain!! I remember something happened inside me . . . the intensity of it was like blowing a fuse! It was too much. We knew something was over. I don't feel that it ever really healed. . . . I don't think I can recover from it. It's a scar. I've put a lot of energy into trying to recover. I did some crying and we did some therapy. There's still a lot of feeling that's blocked off. It was too intense. . . . We had this beautiful baby boy and seven beautiful days and this beautiful rhythm starting, and it was like something had been shattered!! . . . When he was first born there was a tie with my young one, my newborn. And when the circumcision happened, in order to allow it *I had cut off the bond.* I had to cut off my natural instincts, and in doing so *I cut off a lot of feelings towards Jesse.* I cut it off to repress the pain and to repress the natural instinct to stop the circumcision.[50] (italics added)

After several years, Pickard-Ginsburg says she can still feel "an element of detachment" toward her son. Her account is particularly revealing. That she "cut off" feelings toward her son by *observing* his circumcision suggests that her son may have responded similarly toward her by *experiencing* his circumcision. Furthermore, because she was willing to feel and communicate the intensity of her pain, we have a clue to why more mothers who observe their son's circumcision do not report such pain. Denial and repression may keep this extreme pain out of their awareness.

Observing their son's circumcision has left some parents with a deep feeling of regret. The following quotes are typical:

> I am so sorry I was so ignorant about circumcision. Had I witnessed a circumcision first, I never would have consented to having my son circumcised.[51]

> Always in the back of my mind I've thought, "I wish he hadn't been cut." I have apologized to him numerous times.[52]

> If I had ever known, I wouldn't have done this in a million years.[53]

> I felt as if I might pass out at the sight of my son lying there, unable to move or defend himself. His screams tore at my heart as his foreskin was heartlessly torn from his penis. Too late to turn back, I knew that this was a terrible mistake and that it was something that no one, especially newborn babies, should ever have to endure. A wave of shock coursed through me—my body feeling nauseatingly sick with guilt and shame. All I could think of was holding and consoling my child, but his pain felt inconsolable—his body rigid with fear and anger—his eyes filled with tears of betrayal.[54]

Some mothers who did not witness the circumcision have since regretted allowing it:

> The nurse came to take the baby for the circumcision. I have relived that moment over and over. If I could turn back the hands of time, that would be the one moment I would go back to and say, "I don't think it's a good idea. I need another day to think about it" and just hold on to him because I wasn't sure. I think if I had held on to him it might have turned out differently. I just shouldn't have let him go when I was so ambivalent. After they took him I went into the shower, and I cried.[55]

When they brought him back to me, I could see that he had been crying and had a glassy, wild look in his eyes. I think it was terror. I
didn't know what had been done to him, but I could tell whatever it
was, it hurt. I'll never forget that look. They probably shattered every
bit of trust he had. I'm very angry about it. I would never have done
that to my own son. No mother would take a knife to her child. When
I looked at his penis, I was again instantly sorry that I had allowed it
to be done.[56]

Even if a mother does not observe her son's circumcision, she
must look at his wounded penis every time she changes his diaper.
One mother reported, "I couldn't bring myself to look at him
when they brought him back. Every time I changed his diaper I
cried. It was so red and raw." Another mother recalled, "His penis
was red for so long. It just looked horrible to me." Do these maternal feelings toward his penis have an effect on the infant?

We experience guilt when we have harmed another person or
violated some rule. The Circumcision Resource Center has received letters from mothers who feel a deep sense of guilt for
having allowed their sons to be circumcised. In the words of one
mother, "I have a lot of stuff going on about not having stood up
for something that I knew intuitively was the wrong thing to do."

A mother of three sons related this story:

The first one, I didn't know, but I should have educated myself. The
second one, I should have insisted on no circumcision. The third one,
I insisted. It was as easy as that. Then my sister started having kids. I
talked to her about circumcision and brought her articles to read before each one. She had six boys. She circumcised five. Her last one,
she didn't. She finally came to realize that it's barbaric. It finally
sunk in. Now she feels guilty and complains to me that I didn't insist
that she not circumcise the other ones.

Donna Bigony, mother of a four-year-old boy, wrote,

There is a deep wound of guilt in my heart around my son's circumcision. Though not the only mistake I made in parenting, it is
certainly the gravest and the one I have the most trouble forgiving

myself for. . . . I've cried many times about my son's circumcision. Somehow I keep thinking I should have known better. How can I forgive myself for this one? And how can my son forgive me? How can I make it up to him? . . . I'm angry at myself. I'm angry at our society that condones and promotes this genital mutilation. . . . I just now realized that my son's circumcision wounded me as well as him. I carry his pain as well as my guilt.[57]

The *Diagnostic and Statistical Manual of Mental Disorders (DSM-IV)* includes the following personal experiences that may result in PTSD: "witnessing an event that involves . . . a threat to the physical integrity of another person; or learning about unexpected or . . . serious harm, . . . or injury experienced by a family member."[58] Witnessing the circumcision of one's son fits this description, and several of the previous statements of mothers suggest that they are experiencing intrusive PTSD symptoms. One mother actually described her son's circumcision as "a very traumatic experience" for her.[59]

The strong emotional responses of some mothers to circumcision raise the question of what possible effects their feelings have on their behavior toward their sons. Behavior changes could involve, for example, overprotectiveness associated with guilt or withdrawal connected with their own pain.

Whether they witness it or not, mothers who consent to circumcision are often left wondering what impact it may have on their son. As the child grows up, some mothers ask themselves, "Why is my son distant from me?" Based on the accounts of mothers' and infants' responses in this chapter, circumcision may be part of the answer to this question.

7

The Impact of Circumcision

on American Society

What's done to children, they will do to society.
—Karl Menninger,
psychiatrist, author, and
founder of the Menninger Clinic

Whatever affects us psychologically also affects us socially. In particular, if circumcision has long-term psychological effects related to post-traumatic stress disorder (PTSD) and disrupts the mother-child bond, then our society has been profoundly affected by this cultural practice. This follows because most American men are circumcised, and we have a patriarchal culture. In addition, the symptoms of PTSD, like rumors, can spread to others.[1] If certain behaviors, attitudes, fears, and beliefs are prevalent among circumcised men, then they also affect those who are not circumcised, both male and female.

The social contraction of PTSD symptoms is assisted by adult survivors of childhood trauma who may *want* to pass their symptoms on to others. This tendency has affected various writers and artists. For example, Stephen King acknowledges, "I like to scare people." Child psychiatrist Lenore Terr relates this desire to a childhood incident. When King was four he was traumatized when he witnessed a young friend being killed by a train. King's mother remembers the fear in her son's eyes after the event. King himself has no conscious memory of it.[2]

The spread of PTSD symptoms is also facilitated by the fact that people generally and readily conform to the standards of their social environment. Usually, in this country these standards are set by circumcised men. Just as individuals are not aware of how circumcision affects them, the society is not aware of how circumcision could affect us all. However, as this awareness increases, the potential social effects of circumcision will become more apparent.

It is important to understand that circumcision is not the only possible common early infant event that could result in PTSD and therefore have a social impact. For example, birth conditions (e.g., prematurity, cesarean or breech delivery, the use of forceps or drugs) can have a significant effect on adult personality (see Chapter 4).[3] Early disrupted bonding resulting from separation of the mother and child may also contribute to later psychological problems (see Chapter 6). *Because early trauma is common, PTSD symptoms are common and are not necessarily connected with circumcision. In addition, because so many factors help to shape a person's personality, some circumcised men may not have the traits and behaviors to be discussed.* We need to see each person as an individual and not stereotype a person's personality simply because he has had a certain experience.

Responsible researchers have learned to avoid claims of certainty and to qualify their statements in order to allow for unknown factors and possibilities. This is a sign of an open investigative mind. Similarly, rather than accepting or rejecting the ideas that follow, I invite you to hold open the possibility. The fact is that we do not know the validity of these ideas. An appropriate test would be to simply compare a circumcised group of men with a matched group of intact men for the various traits and behaviors. But we must ask the questions before they can be answered. And in order to encourage research, there must be plausibility in the questions. Accordingly, I have attempted to make the case for plausibility by applying related studies.

Before continuing, it may be helpful to clarify a few points of logic and meaning so that there will be no misunderstandings.

1. A statement that circumcision may or could contribute to behavior or social condition X means only that this relationship is a possibility. *It is a speculation, not a conclusion.* And though the possibility may be perceived to be small, it remains a possibility, particularly when there has been no pertinent study to suggest otherwise.
2. The speculative statement (or question) about the possible effect of circumcision *does not exclude the presence of other possible factors that may contribute to* X.
3. The fact that in the majority of individual cases circumcision does not lead to X *does not refute the speculative statement.* For example, if circumcision increases the incidence of X from 1 in 1,000 to 2 in 1,000, then the speculative statement is supported (and in this example, the change is significant) even though in the vast majority of individual cases, X does not occur as a result of circumcision.

If there are any doubts raised in connection with subsequent sections, please refer back to these points.

While I encourage researchers to explore the following potential relationships, I do not believe that the advisability of circumcision depends on any future research report. Enough is already known to justify discontinuing the practice. I believe the best application of the suggested research would be to teach us to appreciate the relationship between perinatal experience and adult social behavior. Then, perhaps, professionals and the public would be motivated to evaluate all perinatal interventions differently. For now, let's apply Menninger's statement at the beginning of the chapter to circumcision by examining how this practice may possibly relate to some current American cultural traits and social problems.

EFFECTS OF LOW MALE SELF-ESTEEM

As circumcised men learn that the foreskin is a vital part of their sexual anatomy, they may view themselves unfavorably compared to intact men. Males who compare themselves unfavorably with others of their group feel lower self-esteem. In addition, the male focus on sexual performance has a lot to do with male self-esteem.[4] As mentioned in Chapter 5, negative feelings about the penis are already prevalent among men. Moreover, if we accept what logic, research, and men circumcised as adults say, circumcision reduces sexual sensitivity and function (see Chapter 2). Consequently, whether men know the facts about circumcision or not, diminished male self-esteem is a possible result of circumcision.

Low self-esteem has personal and social consequences. Those with low self-esteem generally have a low opinion of others.[5] Low self-esteem is also associated with relationship dissatisfaction, poorer general health, high conformity, depression, drug use, and loneliness.[6] In an attempt to compensate for their low self-esteem, some males may adopt certain behaviors. According to a study of adolescents, males who fathered a child had lower self-esteem than those who did not.[7] In addition, half of the males involved with adolescent pregnancies are adult men. They are often six to twelve years older than their partners. Some of these men prefer girls as young as twelve years old to women their own age.[8] This pattern also suggests a lack of male self-esteem. Is unprotected sex a symptomatic behavior of circumcised males seeking to confirm their masculinity and elevate their self-esteem? Is circumcision one of the factors that helps to explain why the United States has one of the highest rates of unwanted teenage pregnancy among developed countries?

Generally, males try to restore their self-esteem by competing and telling themselves they are bigger or better than others. If they don't believe it on a personal level, they may become attached to a group that fulfills that requirement, whether it is a sports team, social club, or other association. As Gordon Allport states, "The easiest idea to sell anyone is that he is better than someone else."[9] Whether it relates to the penis or the personal computer, American men like to compare and compete. Mark Macgillivray, a management consultant and computer owner, says,

> Computers are the new lingua franca for would-be studs. . . . I remember crass boys in junior high school pulling down their pants

and having "big member" contests. Well, that's what it's like here [in a New York bar]. Guys will open a conversation with, "So, what kind of processor are you running?"[10]

In this game of competition and status, "the more megabytes; the more RAM; the bigger the hard drive; the more speed; the more a PC costs, the better"[11] and presumably, the higher the owner's self-esteem. Though men may gain the status they seek, it is never enough, because what they really want is the approval and acceptance they think status will give them. Women, acting more directly to satisfy these needs, seek connection with others, a much more effective way to foster self-esteem.

Male competition has a price: it is incompatible with altruism. With competition, the concern for the welfare of others that is normally expressed through acts like sharing, cooperating, and helping is replaced by an interest in being "better" than another and "winning." American children learn to be competitive very early and have difficulty shifting out of this mode. Highly competitive preschool children are less likely to share. In one study, seven- to nine-year-old children competed with their partners in cooperative games.[12]

Another detrimental product of the male focus on elevating self-esteem is that it tends to undermine female self-esteem. Women with high self-esteem may appear to be threatening to men. One way that men can diminish female self-esteem is by insisting on an unrealistic female physical standard. Generally, women then assume that they are inadequate when they do not meet this standard.

The more we look, the more we see that self-esteem has a significant influence on social behavior. While there are many causes of low self-esteem, circumcision could be one of them. If circumcision lowers male self-esteem (what's done to children), then there will be a motivation to restore one's self-esteem. This often involves attacking or diminishing the self-esteem of others (they will do to society). Research on the potential connections between circumcision and low self-esteem could be especially fruitful.

AVOIDANCE OF INTIMACY IN
MALE-FEMALE RELATIONSHIPS

The psychological effects of circumcision on men could have a further impact on relationships with women.* For example, low male self-esteem, distrust, and sexual anxiety can adversely affect communication and limit the degree of intimacy. In addition, sexual intimacy is a major component of pair bonding, and research has shown that male sexual activity increases when self-esteem is higher.[13] If circumcision lowers both male self-esteem and sexual sensitivity, it would tend to reduce male sexual activity and consequently weaken the pair bond.

Male-female relationships could also be affected in another manner. Some circumcised men feel a nagging sense that deep inside something is missing, but they may not know exactly what it is. If a man perceives the responsibility for this loss to be outside himself, anger is a likely response. If a man sees himself as responsible, then a lifelong search for what is missing may result. A man may seek to recover what is missing in himself through women. That is, a man may believe that if he finds the "right" woman, he will feel whole, or he will have whatever he thinks he is seeking: for example, passion, excitement, or sexual fulfillment. (Women with sexual experience before female genital mutilation noted decreased sexual satisfaction after it but did not make the connection. Instead, they searched unsuccessfully for men to satisfy them.[14])

Because no woman can make him feel complete, a man may withhold commitment. Continually seeking new women gives him hope. Of course, women also want passion and excitement with men, but if circumcision contributes to emotional numbing, then women's feelings are also affected. As a result, both men and women may feel something is missing from their relationships.

From a larger perspective, it would not be surprising if circumcision were found to have a negative effect on interpersonal relationships, since trauma commonly impairs a person's

---

*Some of this discussion could also apply to gay relationships.

relations with others. Harvard-affiliated psychiatrist, professor, and author Judith Herman writes that after a traumatic event "a sense of alienation, of disconnection, pervades every relationship."[15] This is not just a clinical observation. It is a social outcome. For example, we can look at the experience of combat veterans who suffer from PTSD symptoms that are similar to the symptoms experienced by people who have been traumatized in other ways. Vietnam veterans who have PTSD are less likely to marry and more likely to divorce than those without PTSD.[16] Adults with a history of child sexual abuse also have high rates of divorce.

More generally, there is evidence of increasingly widespread relationship problems between men and women. According to results of a national survey of 4500 women, 84 percent of them were emotionally dissatisfied with their relationships.[17] Over 90 percent of respondents who divorced reported that they were the ones to initiate the breakup. The main reason they gave was "loneliness and emotional isolation within the marriage."[18] They needed their husbands to be more communicative.

Studies on marital relationships support this finding. John Gottman, a psychologist at the University of Washington, has been researching marital relationships for twenty years. By conducting an oral history interview with a couple, he is able to predict with 94 percent accuracy whether the marriage will end in divorce.[19] In particular, he and his colleagues have noticed that the responses of the husband in the interview were the best predictors of marital success or failure. They have learned through additional careful observation and measurement of behavioral, emotional, and physiological responses of the husband and wife, what makes marriages work and what makes them fail. One important factor that affects marital success is balanced emotional responsiveness, both in low-level and high level emotional interactions. For example, they conclude that male withdrawal from conflict seriously weakens the marital relationship.

Research has shown that men have a lower physiological tolerance to emotional stress. This would account for the male tendency to avoid certain situations, such as marital conflict. One method men use to control their exposure to this emotional stress is to respond rationally rather than emotionally. Another tactic is to withdraw or stonewall during a conflict. Both behaviors can weaken the marital relationship by restricting communication and leaving conflicts unresolved.[20]

The following question remains unanswered: Why do men have a lower physiological tolerance to emotional stress than women? Is it a natural difference, or is the difference a product of environmental factors? If environmental factors are involved (e.g., cultural suppression of certain male emotions), we may never know the answer to this question. To test for natural differences, we would need to exclude the effects of environmental differences. How can we find test groups of men and women that were unaffected by exposure to cultural gender expectations and differences? This exposure starts early. Parents make distinctions based on the sex of newborns on the first day, and beginning sometime around age one year, male infants are touched less by their mothers than are female infants.[21]

One environmental factor that has an effect on physiological tolerance to emotional stress is trauma. Because emotional numbing is both a psychological and a biological response to trauma,[22] it would tend to reduce a person's tolerance. Emotional numbing can become the primary long-term characteristic of the traumatized individual.[23] As previously mentioned, the younger the child at the time of trauma, the greater the pathological effects.

Could circumcision be a contributing factor to unresolved marital conflicts and other relationship difficulties? Let's look at some national statistics to explore this possible connection. The age at first marriage is increasing, the divorce rate has doubled in the last forty years, and the single population is growing (see Figs. 14 and 15). The proportion of adults who have never married increased by 37 percent between 1970 and 1990. In 1994 the single and divorced population was 32.5 percent of the total population, up from 19.4 percent in 1970.[24] The American divorce rate is more than double that of western Europe, where circumcision is not generally practiced.[25] Though other factors are certainly involved, there appears to be a correlation between

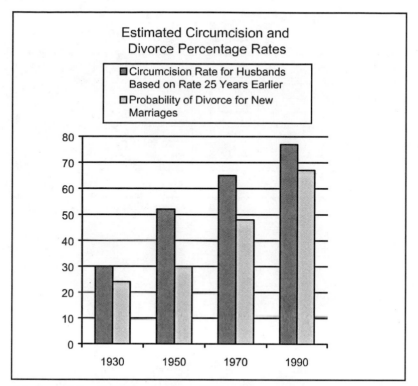

Data from Wallerstein 1980 and Gottman 1994

Fig. 14

Example: For 1970 marriages, the circumcision rate for husbands (25 years earlier, 1945) was 65% (see Fig. 1), and the probability of divorce for marriages begun in 1970 is 48%.

these increasing rates and prior circumcision rates (see Fig. 1, "Introduction").

However men have difficulty relating to women, women will feel their share of the consequences. In their desire to receive male approval, women may even feel responsible for some of the difficulties that are not necessarily their fault. We know that circumcision disrupts the bond between the mother and infant (what's done to children). It appears that circumcision could also

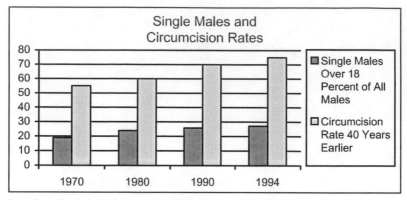

Data from *Statistical Abstract of the United States 1995* and Wallerstein 1980

Fig. 15

Example: In 1980, 24 percent of males over 18 were single. The circumcision rate 40 years earlier (1940) was 60 percent.

be a contributing factor to relationship difficulties between men and women (they will do to society). Of course, since there are many other factors that can affect individuals and relationships, difficulties in the relationships of circumcised men are not necessarily caused by circumcision, and particular relationships may not have such difficulties. With properly designed research studies, we could minimize the effects of other factors and examine the possible effects of circumcision status.

UNNECESSARY SURGERY

Though some surgery is necessary and lifesaving in some instances, at other times it is unnecessary and dangerous. In 1974 a Senate committee reported that 2.4 million unnecessary operations had been performed (not including circumcision), resulting in 11,900 deaths. In 1996 there are expected to be over 30 million surgical operations.[26] Comparing with rates in other countries emphasizes the problem. The rate of cardiac bypass operations in the United States is six times higher than in England. Hysterectomies in the United States are performed at a rate that is two to three times higher than in Europe. American cesarean births are performed at a rate that is 50 to 200 percent higher than the rates of most industrialized countries.[27] Why?

Behavior is linked to attitude. Cutting into somebody's body is serious business, yet the medical profession's attitude toward surgery sometimes seems to lack the appropriate sensitivity and caution. This view is supported by physician Robert Mendelsohn, who had practiced medicine for over twenty-five years when he wrote a critique of his profession titled *Confessions of a Medical Heretic*. In addition to having received many awards for excellence in medical practice and instruction, he was the national director of Project Head Start's Medical Consultation Service and chairman of the Medical Licensing Committee for the State of Illinois. In a chapter titled "Ritual Mutilations," he wrote,

> The first phase a new surgical procedure goes through is enthusiastic acceptance. . . . Once an operation is proved *possible*, its enthusiastic acceptance is guaranteed. Only after an operation has been around for some time and the real usefulness and *ab*usefulness have had plenty of chances to emerge from the fog of early enthusiasm does skepticism begin to seep in from around the edges.[28]

In addition to mentioning physicians' greed and ignorance, Mendelsohn offers this observation concerning why there is so much unnecessary surgery:

> Doctors believe in surgery. There's a certain fascination in "going under the knife" and doctors take every advantage of it to get people there. In America, what *can* be done *will* be done. Whether something *should* be done is beside the point.[29]

The tendency for some doctors to "believe in surgery" is demonstrated by a study that found that chances of circumcision increased if there were surgical interventions during the birth of the child.[30] This "fascination" with cutting is hardly a serious, prudent approach to healing using the least intrusive treatment. When the patient is an infant, there is an even greater insensitivity to the feelings of the patient. In general, based on physicians' behavior and attitude, it appears that the emotional effects and potential harm of surgery are not appreciated and that underlying psychological factors may help to explain this condition. For example, not only may there be insensitivity, but perhaps some physicians advise surgery on occasion because it will raise their self-esteem. Performing "successful" operations can improve how they feel about themselves. In any case, we need to consider all possible factors contributing to unnecessary surgery if we are to minimize it.

Adverse psychological effects of surgery have been investigated and reported in the psychological literature. Since circumcision involves cutting off a body part, it may be relevant to look at amputation to learn about psychological responses to surgery. Though the amount cut off in circumcision is much less than in other amputations, the qualitative and psychological significance are similar, and the comparison may be useful. Dr. Lawrence Friedmann, in his book *The Psychological Rehabilitation of the Amputee*, describes the emotional responses to amputation. They include anxiety, shock, grief, and anger. Depression, distrust, inhibitions, and feelings of inferiority are also common.[31] Amputees internalize society's view of them and may withdraw from society. The belief that someone else is responsible for the amputation may lead to strong resentment. There is also a feeling of "not being a whole person." Other researchers note a loss of body image and self-esteem, as well as fear of future economic, social, and sexual difficulties.[32] Some of these feelings may last a lifetime.

Studying amputees' emotional state is very difficult because they prefer to deny these painful feelings. Denying the significance and emotional effects of their disability serves to boost amputees' self-esteem. Overcompensation and excessive competitiveness and striving in vocational or avocational areas are related to this denial.[33]

Many of these feelings are either similar to those that have been reported by circumcised men or potentially applicable to circumcised men pending further study. Furthermore, medical attitudes toward unnecessary surgery are, in some cases, similar to those about circumcision. Examining other connections between the two may yield further understanding.

Unnecessary surgery may also be viewed in psychoanalytic terms. The expression of undesirable impulses through socially acceptable behaviors is considered to be a defense mechanism called sublimation. For example, as mentioned earlier, Stephen King's childhood trauma left him with the desire to scare people. If he habitually jumped out in front of pedestrians from concealed places, wearing a frightening costume, it would not be socially acceptable. However, by writing popular fearful stories, he sublimates his fear. Because the need for social acceptance has such a strong influence on how we behave, for most men, undesirable impulses connected with circumcision trauma would probably be sublimated rather than acted out in antisocial behavior. Of course, many factors help to account for unnecessary surgery. Yet, since most surgeons are circumcised males, could the high rates of surgeries by American physicians, in part, be a form of sublimation of feelings connected with their own circumcision? In other words, could their early trauma of being cut (what's done to children) be related to their attitude toward cutting others (they will do to society)?

CONTROL OF FEMALE SEXUALITY

The denial of female sexuality in America has been socially acceptable for many years. Over a hundred years ago, American men thought that women viewed sex only as a "distasteful duty" and "something to be endured." Among both the general public and physicians, it was not acceptable that women might want and enjoy sex. The early gynecologists, in particular, exhibited "profound anxiety" about female sexuality.[34] This denial of female sexuality served the purpose of helping to rationalize the removal of female sexual organs, described in Chapter 3. Decades later, an examination of nine gynecology textbooks published between 1963 and 1972 showed that female sexuality was still being denied. Two described most women as "frigid."[35]

In varying degrees, personal expression of female sexuality is still being suppressed by American society. Cultural values concerning sex can make women feel bad about themselves. For example, sexually expressive women can lose "respect" from men, and men may feel uncomfortable with women who initiate sexual intercourse.[36] Males project their discomfort onto women, who then feel the need to change their behavior to gain male acceptance. Clearly, the double standard still exists in the bedroom. If circumcision is one of the factors connected with male sexual insecurity, then it may also be connected with male anxiety about female sexuality. Studying this possibility could be an interesting research project.

The double standard also still exists in the operating room. Women, in particular, are subjected to excessive risk for unnecessary surgery in the United States.[37] Seven of the top eleven most frequently performed surgeries were performed exclusively on women. The most common surgery is the routine episiotomy performed on a mother during birth. A growing number of women view this obstetrical practice, which has no demonstrated benefit and only adverse effects,[38] as female genital mutilation. Hysterectomy is the second most common major surgery, and over 600,000 hysterectomies a year lead to 650–1100 deaths annually.[39] According to the National Center for Health Statistics, four obstetrical procedures comprised 18 percent of all surgical procedures performed in the United States. Some physicians are even advocating and performing "preventive" mastectomies on healthy breasts.[40] Others are reported to be surgically destroying female genitals without the prior knowledge or consent of the patient (see Appendix C).

Is there any connection between control of female sexuality through sexual surgery and male circumcision? A few facts suggest that there is a relationship. Virtually all cultures that widely practice female sexual surgery also practice a form of male sexual surgery, and men control both practices. Such is the case in the United States. In addition, as discussed in Chapter 2, circumcision diminishes sexual sensitivity and pleasure. It seems that those who have been denied the full expression of their sexuality (what's done to children) may unconsciously seek a way to deny others that pleasure (they will do to society), whether they use social custom, fear, ignorance, or sexual surgery. Finally, a study on the underlying reasons for FGM concluded that the motivation was psychosexual and included male fear of female sexuality.[41] This is a possible effect of circumcision.

Addressing male circumcision may be a prerequisite for dealing with female genital mutilation and unnecessary sexual surgery. Research into this connection is important because these practices adversely affect hundreds of millions of people worldwide.

ATTITUDES TOWARD PAIN AND STIMULATION

Surgical operations on the genitals cause extreme pain for both males and females. In the Bariba culture in West Africa, where female genital mutilation is prevalent, a social effect of the procedure is that females suppress their general response to pain.[42] Since beliefs and attitudes must accompany this lack of response, the women learn to associate indifference to pain with honor and consider it part of their cultural identity.

Suppression of pain response is also a trait among some African cultures that perform circumcision on boys approaching adolescence.

> They must submit without so much as flinching under the agony of the knife. If a boy cries out while his flesh is being cut, if he so much as blinks an eye or turns his head, he is shamed for life as unworthy of manhood, and his entire lineage is shamed as a nursery of weaklings.[43]

Perhaps the prohibition against normal response to pain is to protect everyone from feeling what is happening.

Our sensitivity to others' pain is related to our sensitivity to our own pain. When an infant is subjected to the extreme pain of circumcision with no one responding to his cries, he experiences our insensitivity to his pain (what's done to children). While other factors are also involved, could male infant circumcision contribute to the common American male attitude of indifference to one's own pain and, correspondingly, the pain of others (they will do to society)? This attitude can underlie certain common practices. The general and persistent tendency of physicians to withhold appropriate pain medications from children is related to the cultural attitude that tolerating pain is a sign of strong character.[44]

One who does not feel pain can be restricted in sensing other experiences as well. This is consistent with the long-term PTSD symptom of emotional numbing. Furthermore, one who is less responsive would need to seek a greater stimulus to achieve the same level of arousal. This is why some people who have emotional numbness seek dangerous activities to produce stronger sensations so that they can feel something.[45]

Since circumcision involves excessive stimulation (what's done to children) and subsequent potential numbing, it may also be one of the factors associated with the desire of men for increasingly greater stimulation (they will do to society), for example, loud music (men prefer music at higher volumes than women), video images (male undergraduates prefer hard-rock videos while females prefer soft-rock videos), and reckless or antisocial behavior.[46] Further investigation into these possibilities might yield valuable results.

PASSIVITY

The infant's response during circumcision is futile. As reported in earlier chapters, in studies that looked at infants' behavior after circumcision, some infants became less active.[47] Others have been observed to be in a state of shock after the procedure. Circumcision of older children has resulted in withdrawal and reduced functioning and adaptation.[48] The accounts of some circumcised men have also indicated an association between circumcision and withdrawal. This pattern of responses raises the question of the possible connection between circumcision and adult male passivity and a sense of powerlessness. Of course, the passivity of some is related to the excessive power of others.

Other studies also suggest a potential connection. Learned helplessness results from trauma.[49] It is characterized by a belief that one's responses have no effect on outcome, and it is associated with emotional numbing and low-self-esteem.[50] Learned helplessness also is connected with a pessimistic attitude, passivity, and depression.[51]

Because of its very nature, passivity is hard to evaluate as a social phenomenon. Perhaps the increase in television watching could be regarded as a symptom of increasing social passivity.[52] Of course, early experiences other than circumcision, as well as subsequent events, could contribute to passivity. In any case, the relationship of circumcision to social passivity remains a possibility that merits consideration for study.

REDUCED EMPATHY

Empathy is the universal human ability to experience the same emotions that someone else is experiencing. Newborn infants cry when they hear other newborn infants crying.[53] This is an empathetic response to the distress of another. With empathy we acknowledge, "I feel like you. I am like you." Despite the obvious differences, adults and infants are alike in fundamental ways. Both are human beings who need love and human contact. Both can experience a wide spectrum of emotions, including feeling hurt or angry when needs are not met. Both can suffer from extreme physical or emotional pain that may have long-term effects.

Empathy is the key to following the golden rule. When we feel empathy, we feel connected to others and treat them well. Without empathy we are separate and are more likely to mistreat others. It is no surprise that those who sexually abuse children seem to be incapable of understanding the harm they are causing their victims.[54] Apparently, those who circumcise also have little empathy for the infant.

An infant's survival depends on adult empathy. Crying, together with associated facial and body movement, are all the infant has to communicate distress to the caretaker. When no one responds to the infant's cries of distress, he gets the message that nobody cares about his feelings and that he is powerless and terrifyingly alone. Such is the experience of the circumcised infant. This lack of empathetic response is related to the limited ability of some adults to feel. If we do not have empathy for infants, they may not have empathy for us. Perhaps this is why circumcised men have such difficulty empathizing with circumcised infants. One male acquaintance, after reading the first chapter, remarked, "It hurts, and the baby screams. So what?" (It is usually the father that insists on circumcision. See Chapter 2.)

The degree of empathy adults feel varies considerably and is associated with other attributes. In one study, men who scored higher on a macho scale reported feeling more anger and less empathy for a crying infant than did less macho men.[55] Other research confirms that those low in empathy are more likely to exhibit aggression.[56] Low empathy is also related to general emotional numbing.[57]

A person's natural empathy is either nurtured or inhibited by environmental influences. Inflicting trauma on a child results in a reduced ability to empathize. For example, toddlers who were abused expressed no concern for crying peers and even attacked them.[58] However, sometimes those who have suffered painful experiences are more empathetic toward others. This response is possible when the pain is conscious. Either their pain was not severe enough to result in trauma, or they have made efforts to deal with their traumatic pain (more on this in the next chapter). Generally, circumcision pain is unconscious because it is overwhelmingly painful. As a result, there is usually no awareness of its effects on behavior. Circumcision may be one of those environmental influences that reduces empathy and consequently increases aggression.

ANTISOCIAL BEHAVIORS

Before examining some further possible social effects of circumcision, it is important to put the discussion in perspective. Most of the following American social problems also exist to varying degrees in countries that do not practice circumcision. Some also have existed here for many years before circumcision was first practiced. A few are as old as recorded history. *These problems are complex and are caused by many interdependent factors.* Because the prevalence of most of these problems in the United States is so high and, in many cases, still increasing, we need to look at any and all conditions that may contribute to them. Though we need definitive studies before reaching firm conclusions, we can use what is known to point researchers in potentially productive directions. In this context, let's examine how circumcision may relate to the critical American social problem of violence, keeping in mind Menninger's statement, "What's done to children, they will do to society."

Circumcision and Adult Male Violence

We are the most violent culture in the world. The American rate of homicides by men is about fourteen times that of Japan and eight times that of the countries that comprise the European Community (see Fig. 16). A violent crime is reported at the rate of one every sixteen seconds in the United States. According to a national survey, there were 10.8 million crimes of violence in the United States in 1994.[59] Public discussion of the reasons for the prevalence of violent crime tends to focus on social factors such as drugs, lack of a good moral upbringing, the availability of guns, television violence, the absence of fathers in the home, poor schools, lack of jobs, racism, and the decline of religion. To what extent would the effects of circumcision on men contribute to the high rates of American violence?

While there is no doubt that most of the social factors mentioned have an effect on behavior, little public attention is given to the impact of infancy on adult social behavior. However, long-term studies have demonstrated a connection. Temperament not only affected how infants perceived and responded to their environment, but it also predicted their future social development. For example, an angry temperament in infants correlated with later aggression at six to seven years of age, while increased fearfulness

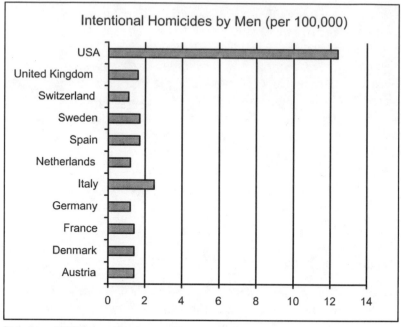

Data from *1994 Human Development Report*

Fig. 16

was associated with later reduced aggression.[60] In addition, defiant behavior at age three was associated with aggressive behavior at age six.[61] This report was consistent with earlier research that found that physical aggression directed at peers "was highly stable over the first 10 years of life."[62] Other studies had similar and complementary findings. Passivity at age three was found to be associated with dependent, conforming, and socially inhibited behavior at adolescence.[63] In an extended long-term study, boys who were more aggressive at eight years of age were found to be more aggressive at thirty years of age.[64]

Now let's examine what makes a child aggressive or violent in the first place. According to Dorothy Otnow Lewis, a psychiatrist who has done pioneering work for over twenty years on the causes of violent behavior, a child's prior experience is the primary factor.[65] For example, research shows that men who have been abused as children are more likely to be violent toward others later in life.[66] Male victims of child physical and sexual abuse are at a higher risk to be arrested for sex crimes as adults.[67] The behavioral reenactment of the trauma is a compulsion of some trauma victims.[68]

Problems during the birth experience have also been associated with adult violence. In a study that received national attention, investigators followed over 4,000 male infants to age eighteen. They found that those infants who had experienced both birth complications and early maternal rejection were most likely to have engaged in violence when they grew up. The authors suggested that "perinatal and early postnatal health care interventions could significantly reduce violence."[69] This conclusion is supported by the National Research Council study on violence.[70] Other studies have also found that perinatal factors were associated with violent behavior.[71]

Taken altogether, this work suggests that personality in general and violent tendencies in particular, may be determined in infancy and influenced by perinatal events.

Now let's see how circumcision relates to the discussion. An infant experiences this perinatal event as a violent and extremely painful act. Because it is a trauma, circumcision pain is repressed and stored in the unconscious. Research shows that pain can arouse aggression in animals and humans. People in pain are likely to be angry, though mental factors can modify their behavior.[72]

Furthermore, the overwhelming pain of circumcision leaves, among other feelings, anger that may be repressed or expressed. One mother of two circumcised teenage sons reported, "One son is angry and doesn't know it. One son is angry and does know it." As noted in earlier chapters, behavioral and temperamental changes in circumcised infants such as increased irritability have been observed, and circumcision of older children has resulted in increased aggressiveness. In addition, some circumcised men have expressed anger about being circumcised: "Over the past few years, I have discovered suppressed anger. If I could roll back time, I would kill to protect myself from this 'quick, painless, common procedure.'"[73] Over half of 313 respondents in the previously mentioned preliminary survey of self-selected circumcised men felt angry about circumcision.[74]

The repeated association of irritability and anger with circumcision warrants attention. Furthermore, the long-term effects of circumcision, like those of other traumas, are generally not in awareness but are evident in behaviors (see Chapter 5). Since violence is an expression of anger, and anger has been associated with circumcision, committing violent acts could be a behavior associated with circumcision. Moreover, low male self-esteem, a possible effect of circumcision, correlates with a high risk for homicide.[75]

Clearly, the majority of circumcised men are not violent. Because trauma is connected with a wide range of possible PTSD symptoms, a variety of associated behaviors is possible. Violence is only an extreme response. Furthermore, several factors inhibit violent behavior, including emotional repression and numbing. Fear that violence is not socially acceptable also limits its expression. The alternative is to express anger in less destructive, socially acceptable ways. Accordingly, if a man is circumcised, he is not necessarily violent. And an intact man is not necessarily nonviolent, since *there are many factors associated with violence.* However, if a man is violent, he may be more likely to be circumcised than someone in the nonviolent population. Therefore, in addition to child physical and sexual abuse, birth complications, early maternal rejection, and other factors, circumcision may contribute to violent behavior. This question could be easily studied (see Appendix E).

Not only are there many factors that may contribute to violence, but violent behavior can be exhibited in different ways, some of which may not be evident from crime statistics. This is illustrated by looking at Jews, a group with a high circumcision rate. Violent crime such as homicide is often a response to stress and is associated with poverty and income inequality.[76] The fact that most American Jews are not in a low-income category would contribute to reducing their rate of violent crime. However, other violent behaviors are not connected with income. A study by researchers associated with Hebrew Union College and the University of Southern California found that rates of Jewish domestic violence were comparable to rates in the non-Jewish community.[77] In addition, Jewish men reported similar rates of sexual aggression and courtship violence in a national survey of 6,159 college students enrolled in thirty-two institutions.[78]

Another approach to studying the potential connection between circumcision and antisocial behavior is by examining physiological changes of circumcised men. Emotional numbing is a symptom of PTSD and is associated with lower arousal. Experiencing early trauma such as circumcision could be a factor contributing to lower arousal in later life, leading to possible antisocial behavior. Researchers have found that significantly lower arousal of the central nervous system and the autonomic nervous system in adolescence is associated with criminal behavior in adulthood.[79] Sensation-seeking, a response to lower arousal, may also be connected with criminality.[80] Another factor in criminal behavior is rage, a response of emotionally numb individuals to high stress.[81] Again, research is needed to address these possibilities.

A look at circumcision and crime rates raises further questions about their relationship. The rate of reported violent crime has increased dramatically in the last thirty years (see Fig. 17).[82] Circumcision rates from the 1940s through the 1970s, when most of these violent criminals would have been born, were also on the increase. Is there a connection?

It is also notable that as the rate of violent crimes has increased, the average age of murder arrestees has dropped from 32.5 in 1965 to 27.0 in 1992.[83] The estimated circumcision rate was 56 percent in 1932 and 78 percent in 1965, the years when the average-aged arrestees of the years in question would have been born (see Fig. 1, "Introduction"). Is the increase in youthful involvement in murder connected in any way to the approximate 40 percent increase in the circumcision rate over this period?

In summary, the violent act of circumcision (what's done to children) may be an unrecognized perinatal factor that, in certain circumstances, increases the potential for adult violence (they will do to society). There are many contributing factors to the problem

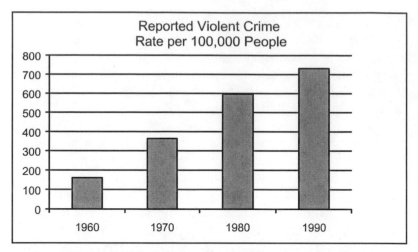

Data from *Sourcebook of Criminal Justice Statistics 1994*

Fig. 17

of violence. With research, the degree of connection between circumcision and violent behavior could be tested and perhaps other predisposing factors could be identified.

The most vulnerable potential victims of male adult violence are those who are weaker than and dependent on men. Therefore, let's examine forms of male violence that are directed at women and children.

Domestic Violence

In the United States, the most violent place is in the home. Domestic violence is the single greatest cause of injury to women. A national study reported that 12 percent of spouses had violently attacked each other in the last year.[84] In a survey of 4,707 male and female college students, about 35 percent had experienced physical aggression.[85] This violence is too often fatal. In 1993 29 percent of female murder victims were killed by their husbands or boyfriends.[86] In one cross-cultural study of the United States,

Ireland, and India, the United States had the highest rate of domestic violence.[87] Is there a relationship between the fact that every twenty-five seconds a male infant is circumcised and every fifteen seconds a man beats a woman?

Violence toward women is motivated by the male desire for control. First, a man uses socially acceptable methods of control, then threats of violence, and finally actual violence. Men who beat their wives view their behavior as justified punishment for their wives' failures to meet their demands.[88] They believe that a man is entitled to make the rules of his home and enforce them. This arrangement is based on the male's physical advantage over females and the economic dependence of women. It is also consistent with the historical belief that a man's home is his castle and that his wife is his property. These beliefs of abusive men are similar to those of some people who consent to or perform circumcisions because in both cases there is a sense of entitlement to force one's will on another who is physically and economically disadvantaged, and there is a perception that the victim is property rather than a person.

Low self-esteem, a possible effect of circumcision, can adversely affect behavior. Men low in self-esteem are more prone to jealousy in their relationships.[89] Jealousy is a precipitating factor in violence toward women.[90] Predictably, low male self-esteem correlates with a high risk for domestic violence.[91]

There may be other connections between the high rate of domestic violence and circumcision. It has been documented that exposure to violence in childhood is linked to later spousal abuse.[92] The child experiences circumcision as violent. Those who have been violated generally have a problem with anger and may direct it at others.[93] Some circumcised men who have reported anger toward their parents feel particularly angry toward their mother.[94] One man who wrote to the Circumcision Resource Center stated, "I know my mother never intended that I should be harmed, but it seems she never intended the opposite enough to question the idea." For others, their hostility toward women may be unrecognizable to themselves. One man who finally became aware of his "misogynistic way" reported,

For thirty years, my [intact] brother would ask me at least two or three times a year with real feeling and compassion, "Why do you hate women so much?" Always I would answer with the same sincere, hurt amazement, "Me. I don't hate women. I love women."[95] [This man changed after years of personal growth work.]

As discussed previously (see Chapter 6), if an infant being circumcised feels that the mother is responsible (what's done to children), the associated feelings of anger could more likely be expressed toward women (they will do to society). Most circumcised and intact men are not violent toward women, and other factors surely contribute to the propensity to be violent. Nevertheless, the possible connection between circumcision and domestic violence deserves study.

Rape

Rapists are also driven by anger and a desire for power. Many perpetrators view rape as a form of revenge. Because he tends to believe that all women are responsible for the acts of an individual woman, when a rapist is angry (usually inappropriately) at a woman he is involved with, he may direct that anger at a random woman by raping her. A convicted rapist acknowledged, "I wanted to take my anger and frustration [toward my girlfriend] out on a stranger, to be in control, to do what I wanted to do." Some rapists explain their actions by referring to their low self-esteem: "I would degrade women so I could feel there was a person of less worth than me." For others, distrust is a factor: "I hated women because they were deceitful." Perpetrators also are attracted to rape because it is stimulating. One described it as a "big kick" because of the "excitement" and "drama."[96]

Rape is an expression of a psychological dysfunction. Yet it is the most common of all violent crimes.[97] According to the U.S. Senate Committee on the Judiciary, as many as 2 million American women are raped each year.[98] Research indicates that most incidents go unreported. In a study of male college students, 15 percent reported having forced intercourse on a woman at least once.[99] Marriage seems to make little difference. One wife out of seven reported to an investigator that she had been forced to have sex with her husband.[100] In a survey of college students, 60 percent of the males responded that they would rape a woman in certain situations.[101] At current rates, 46 percent of women will be victimized by an attempted or completed rape sometime in their lives.[102] The incidence of reported rapes in the United States has increased sharply in the last thirty years and is about seven times that of countries in the European Community (see Figs. 18 and 19).[103] Why?

Could part of the answer relate to what happened to most American men when they were children? If Menninger's statement at the beginning of this chapter applies to circumcision and rape, we need to examine possible similarities between the two. By making this comparison I do not intended to distort the harm of rape, but only to increase our understanding of both rape and circumcision. Let's look at how they compare.

According to a booklet published by the Boston Area Rape Crisis Center,

Rape is an act of violence and control. . . . Rape is dehumanizing. . . . Rape is frightening. . . . The woman feels that her body is in danger. . . . Rape is an intrusion. The rapist invades the woman's body by force.[104]

From the infant's perspective, this description could apply to being restrained and having part of the penis cut off. Both rape and circumcision are acts of force directed at the sexual organs of the victim. The differences include the age of the victim and the nature of the act. In one case there is penetration; in the other there is mutilation. Interestingly, a noteworthy article critical of circumcision that appeared in the *Journal of the American Medical Association* was entitled "The Rape of the Phallus."[105] The fact that some circumcised men have used the word "rape" in referring to their own circumcision also raises the question of similarity.

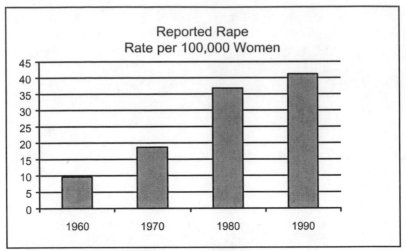

Data from *Sourcebook of Criminal Justice Statistics 1994*

Fig. 18

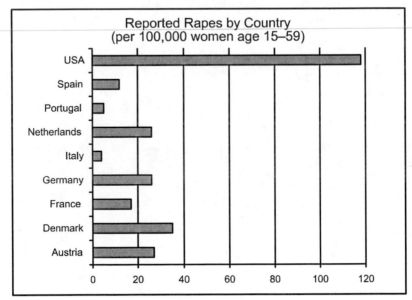

Data from *Sourcebook of Criminal Justice Statistics 1994*

Fig. 19

Similar acts suggest similar effects. The effects of rape are well-documented. Being raped, research indicates, takes a heavier psychological toll than most other traumatic events. Veronica Reed Rybeck of the Rape Crisis Intervention Program at Beth Israel Hospital in Boston reports that "the victim's beliefs about who she is and who she can trust are shattered."[106] Rape victims find it difficult to open up in intimate relationships. In general, they distrust men, avoid touch, and remain alone. Women react to rape differently depending on their own individual coping style. They may talk a lot about it and scream or keep their feelings secret and not talk about it for years. As with some circumcised men, there is a fear of not being believed, but maintaining silence is damaging.[107]

Linda Braswell, in her guide for rape survivors, writes,

> The single most terrifying reaction to being raped is the fear of being killed or mutilated. . . . [It often results in] a complete separation of mind and body. . . . Rape humiliates. The most precious and private parts of your body have been violated. . . . Rape itself may be a form of murder. It destroys one's will and spirit. It robs you of your self-respect. . . . Rape is the ultimate violation of the self, short of murder.[108]

How many of these descriptions could apply to the circumcised infant's experience?

Since rape is viewed as a traumatic event, it is not surprising that rape victims exhibit PTSD symptoms. The victim experiences intense fear, difficulty sleeping, hypervigilance, nightmares, shame, lower energy, irritability, anger, depression, and "heroic efforts" to repress the experience. Over time, intrusive symptoms diminish as numbing increases. Because of repression, victims don't recognize that behavior changes are caused by the rape.[109] Based on the psychological effects of circumcision discussed in Chapter 5, there is a similarity between the potential effects of circumcision and some of the symptoms experienced after rape. Similarities between the effects of circumcision and rape suggest that Menninger's statement in connection with rape is possible. The other effects of rape mentioned suggest similar potential effects for circumcision that could be determined from research.

Let's examine attitudes and beliefs to look for additional similarities. Rape tends to reinforce male power and dominance. "Macho" men are more likely to use force on a woman.[110] Some rapists believe that a woman has "no right to say no." In this respect, infants being circumcised are in a similar position. A belief in the inferiority of females is connected with rape. Male objectification of women is also a contributing factor.[111] Conversely, cultures that respect the status of women have few rapes.[112] The depreciation and objectifying of women and the dehumanizing of infants are analogous. In addition, rapists tend to believe in rape myths, such as that women really enjoy being raped.[113] This erroneous and self-serving belief concerning the victim's experience corresponds to the myth voiced by some circumcisers that infants do not feel pain during circumcision. Both rapists and circumcisers are oblivious to the physical, sexual, and psychological harm they are causing. In one study, only 2 out of 114 convicted rapists expressed any concern for the victim's feelings.[114] The statements of circumcisers suggest a similar indifference.

In summary, not only are there similarities between the act of rape and the act of circumcision, but there appear to be some similarities between the effects experienced by the victims of rape and the effects experienced by men who have been circumcised. Even some of the attitudes and myths are similar. Both rape and circumcision involve sexual organs and violence. Rape perpetrators' motivations and excessive, inappropriate anger reflect feelings of having been victimized themselves. It can be argued that in a broader sense, circumcision (what's done to children) could be considered to be a form of rape (they will do to society). The uniquely and excessively high rate of rape in the United States justifies research to examine the relationship between circumcision and rape.

Child Sexual Abuse

A particularly disturbing and common form of male violence directed at children is sexual abuse. In two studies of adult women, 38 percent reported having been sexually abused as children.[115] Another study reported a 45 percent rate.[116] These figures are surprisingly high, but they still underestimate actual rates because they are based only on reports of conscious memories that were admitted by women who agreed to be interviewed for the studies. Consequently, a conservative adjusted rate would be about 60 percent.[117]

To apply Menninger's statement, let's compare circumcision and child sexual abuse. It is first important to note that child sexual abuse is whatever the public defines it to be, depending on circumstances. For example, the child's response to the abuse makes a difference in how people feel about the violation. If the child objects strongly, the acts are considered more abusive. However, people rate acts as less abusive if they involve very young children.[118] Circumcision is not considered to be even remotely connected with child sexual abuse because it has social approval, the child is very young, the procedure is performed by respected professionals, it is not generally observed by the parents or public, and if it is observed, the child's sleeplike traumatic shock may replace protest. As a result, the public defines fondling a child's genitals as child sexual abuse yet cutting off a piece of the penis is not. Obviously, when the public determines what is abusive, cultural context is as important as the act itself. Considering the act of circumcision out of cultural context and recognizing its effects on the infant, it is an act of abuse. In fact, some circumcised men have used the word "abused" to describe their feelings.

A significant way that child sexual abuse differs from circumcision is that when the perpetrator is a person in the immediate family of the victim, the violation often recurs. The abuse is symptomatic of a seriously dysfunctional family, and such an environment would likely have other impacts on the child. On the other hand, circumcision is a single event that may be chosen by very caring, loving, and yet unaware and sometimes later regretful parents. A loving environment may have a neutralizing effect on part of the psychological impact of circumcision and help to account for the varying degree of long-term effects.

The effects of child sexual abuse may be compared to the effects of circumcision. If there are similarities, that would suggest that Menninger's statement could apply. Child sexual abuse has direct immediate and long-term effects on psychological functioning;[119] there is a high prevalence of PTSD.[120] As with circumcision, early symptoms may last throughout life, they may disappear, or they may resurface years after the trauma.[121] The initial effects of child sexual abuse include fear, anxiety, depression, anger, aggression, and sexually inappropriate behavior. Children may feel powerless to control their feelings and actions. In addition, child sexual abuse victims who are abused by a caretaker are devastated by the betrayal of trust.[122]

Long-term psychological effects include anxiety, fear, somatic complaints, guilt, problems with intimacy, nightmares, hyperactivity, aggression, and withdrawal.[123] Depression may be the most prevalent symptom in adult survivors.[124] Low self-esteem is also common.[125] In addition to sexual dysfunction, sexual behavior may be affected with tendencies toward promiscuity or inhibition.[126]

Adult survivors of child sexual abuse often view themselves and life differently than others. They may believe that they are damaged or fatally flawed. They may feel incapable of protecting themselves from harm, and fear impending disasters. Irritability and intrusive thoughts may also be present. They may believe that others are dangerous and not to be trusted. Conversely, they may not trust themselves and their ability to properly evaluate situations and make decisions. These tendencies can lead them to be passive or overdependent on the judgments of others.

In summary, child sexual abuse is such an overwhelming assault that psychological damage cannot be avoided. Consequently, to protect against the negative feelings, emotional numbing and denial are very common. As with circumcision, people may deny their abuse and their symptoms; they may be aware of just symptoms; they may be aware of both but find no connection; or they may know that their symptoms were caused by their abuse. These symptoms generally involve beliefs, attitudes, emotions, and behaviors. Adult symptoms may become part of personality traits.

Many of these same effects have been associated with circumcision, as has been discussed earlier in this book. Other effects of child sexual abuse may suggest directions for further research on circumcision. It is noteworthy that the most severe effects of child sexual abuse result from experiences that include, like circumcision, genital contact and force.[127]

Does circumcision of infants increase the incidence of child sexual abuse by adult males? This question has not been studied. However, men who sexually abuse children often exhibit low self-esteem and a sense of powerlessness, two symptoms that may be common among circumcised men.[128] In addition, child sexual abusers tend to have difficulty in getting their sexual needs met.[129] Perhaps sexual insecurities connected with circumcision could influence some men to turn to children because they feel threatened by adults. Finally, there is a strong connection between a history of child sexual abuse and male sexual abusiveness.[130] If circumcision is experienced by the child as sexually abusive (what's done to children), this relationship could apply (they will do to society). Obviously, most circumcised and intact men are not perpetrators of child abuse, and the causes of child abuse are varied. Based on the available information, research is warranted to determine whether circumcision is one of them.

Suicide

Childhood trauma often results in anger later in life. Sometimes this anger is directed at oneself rather than others.[131] Other self-directed responses have been noted. Judith Herman writes, "Long after the event, many traumatized people feel that a part of themselves has died. The most profoundly afflicted wish they were dead."[132] In extreme cases, such feelings can lead to suicide.

The suicide rate among young people has increased dramatically in the last few decades, particularly for males. Between 1950 and 1990 the suicide rate for males fifteen to twenty-four years of age increased by a factor of 3.4 (see Fig. 20). In addition, the 1990 rate was 5.6 times the corresponding female rate.[133] Male suicide is connected with social isolation, restrained emotional expression, and shame.[134] For some men, these factors may also be associated with circumcision. As reported in Chapter 4, a boy circumcised at age six had suicidal impulses and repeated, "I wish I were dead." How can we rule out circumcision as one of the factors connected with male suicide unless we investigate that possibility?

Sudden infant death syndrome (SIDS) is the sudden, unexplainable death of an infant under one year of age. It is the leading cause of death for infants of this age and accounts for about 6,000 deaths annually. No one knows why about 60 percent of SIDS cases are male.[135] Other countries have reported both higher and lower rates than the United States, but cross-cultural comparisons can be misleading because of unreliable data.[136] The possibility that circumcision is a factor contributing to SIDS needs to be studied. If circumcision is comparable to rape, and rape "destroys one's will and spirit," how do we know that SIDS is not, at least in some cases, infant suicide?

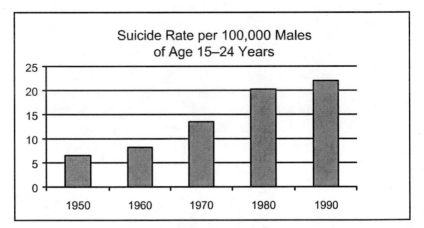

Data from *Sourcebook of Criminal Justice Statistics 1993*

Fig. 20

Theft

Even though it does not usually involve physical violence, theft is a violation of social relationships and a serious problem in the United States. Based on a national survey, there were 12.2 million thefts in 1992, and the rate has been increasing (see Fig. 21). Thefts are reported at the rate of one every four seconds.[137]

Many of us know what it feels like to have something stolen. Reactions may include shock, helplessness, rage, and a sense of being violated. If the stolen item was considered valuable, we may grieve the loss, or we may defend against the grief by denying the item's importance.

From the infant's view, circumcision may be considered to be "stealing" the foreskin from the owner (what's done to children). While some circumcised men have expressed grief about the loss of their foreskin, most deny the importance of what was taken from them. Obviously, like other social problems, many factors are involved in theft, but this question has not been investigated: Is there any connection between our high rate of circumcision and the high rate of theft (they will do to society)? Perhaps there also is a connection between circumcision and the relatively recent use of the expression "ripped off."

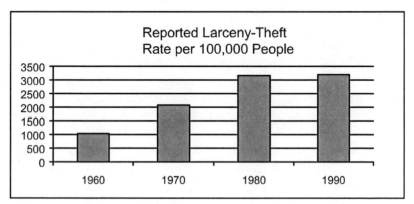

Data from *Sourcebook of Criminal Justice Statistics 1994*

Fig. 21

INTERRELATIONSHIPS OF SOCIAL PROBLEMS

All things are connected.
—Chief Seattle

Some antisocial behaviors are connected with the divorce rate. The lack of a father at home is associated with behavior problems among elementary school boys.[138] With the loss of an income earner from the home, children are now more likely to grow up in a low-income environment, which is related to higher rates of child abuse and violent crime.[139] Suicide and homicide rates are also strongly associated with the rising divorce rate in the United States.[140] Divorce is believed to be one of the most stressful events in an adult's life. Perhaps that high level of stress is what connects the incidence of divorce with rates of violence.

Evidently, anything that weakens male-female relationships can have multiple social consequences. As discussed earlier in this chapter, research shows that married men who are less emotionally expressive are more likely to have unresolved conflicts and to subsequently be divorced. If the potential long-term effects of circumcision trauma, such as emotional numbing and distrust, contribute to unresolved marital conflicts and divorce, then circumcision could play an indirect role in some antisocial behaviors.

WARFARE

Like individuals, societies can direct their anger inward or outward. Warfare is a form of externally directed social violence. It generally has social approval. All the factors that may increase the incidence of personal violence can contribute to a society's propensity to engage in war, for example, distrust, low self-esteem, sensation seeking, lack of empathy, depreciation of others, a history of violence, desire for control, emotional numbing, and physical (military) superiority. How many of these factors apply to our national psyche?

Though all I am doing is suggesting possibilities and calling for research, some readers may still feel that I am saying that circumcision is the cause of all the world's problems (or something similar). I am not. Those who have carefully followed my discussion know that this is an overstatement of my ideas. Others may take this polarized view because of the difficulty in discriminating between shades of meaning on a very complex and emotional topic. Rather than dealing with their discomfort stimulated by these ideas, some may exaggerate my position so that they can then reject it by calling it too extreme. Of course, if someone accurately understands my position and disagrees with it, that is another matter. Then I would expect to hear reasonable arguments (although there is no research to support such arguments at this time) on why it is virtually impossible for circumcision to have any social impact.

Another possible response to these ideas is to dismiss them because they are "just speculation" and not "proven." This response depreciates the value of asking serious questions whose answers could have wide applications. It may be driven by an underlying fear of knowing, resulting in avoidance. The implication is that if we dismiss the ideas, then we do not do the research. For those who must have a conclusion now, it is this: the potential social impact of circumcision has been ignored and avoided for too long. We need to investigate the questions raised here. I trust that there *are* some researchers who will find some of these questions intriguing and important enough to explore.

8

The Lessons of Circumcision

> If we are to have real peace, we must begin with the children.
> —Gandhi

For many readers, this book is an introduction to much new information. This chapter serves to both summarize and explore the meaning of some of the ideas previously presented. Further investigation of these issues could contribute to our understanding of the powerful impact of circumcision as well as other perinatal experiences. It could teach us much about ourselves and possibly provide answers to individual and societal problems. There is no single way to address all questions. Multiple approaches are needed (see Appendix E).

At the same time, we know a lot more about circumcision and associated matters than is generally thought. What researchers have learned about infants, for example, is often not reflected in how we treat them. This is a tragedy for the infants and for all of us.

INFANTS ARE REAL PEOPLE

The typical attitude toward infants was perhaps illustrated by an incident a father related to me concerning his two-and-a-half-year-old son. He asked his son to put the milk in the refrigerator. After his son did this, the father for the first time thought, "He's a real person. My son is a real person!" Evidently, it was both his son's understanding of language and his ability to perform a customary physical act that led the father to this realization, but what about the first two and a half years of his son's life? Apparently, he had not previously been considered to be a "real person." People might say he was "just a baby." It is convenient not to consider the infant a person who has feelings. Then parents have license to do what they want with the infant.

Are we prejudiced when it comes to infants? Perceived differences are used to justify prejudice. We assume that when things look different, they are different. In comparing a newborn infant to an adult, we find many apparent differences: age, size, skin color, vocal and body language, intelligence, responsiveness, eating habits, body proportions, physical coordination and strength, interests, and personality, to name a few. Consequently, we tend to view infants as being very different from ourselves, and our attitudes and behavior can demonstrate our prejudice. This preexisting prejudice toward infants continues to play a major role in the practice of circumcision.

Despite the differences, infants are real people. When we deny an infant's humanity, we deny our own humanity. Our prejudiced view of infants says more about us than it does about them. The perceived differences are used to justify adult ethnocentrism, a view that adults are superior to nonadults. Our prejudice serves to conceal our own feelings of inferiority and low self-esteem.[1] Thus, we are part of a self-perpetuating cycle. We experience prejudice as infants when we are subjected to it by adults. When we become adults, we view infants (and other apparently dissimilar groups) with prejudice. We pass on to others what we ourselves experienced.

We also falsely attribute our own feelings or traits to infants, an act called projection. For example, the belief that infants don't remember is a projection of our failure to remember our own infancy. (We do remember, but the memories are generally unconscious.) If we think infants don't feel, it is a projection of our own lack of feeling. When we are not open to infant signals, we assume that infants do not communicate. Therefore, before evaluating the abilities of infants, we might conduct some self-examination.

Our understanding of the human infant has undergone a revolutionary change in the last twenty years because of innovative research. We are learning how to design experiments that give infants an opportunity to teach us who they are. As a result, we are discovering that infants are much more capable than we thought possible. Even though infants are relatively helpless, without verbal language, and totally dependent on adults for their well-being, they are much like us, and they feel deeply. The latest research on infant development confirms that human infants are very aware, sensitive, perceptive, and responsive to their environment. All senses are working, and infants seek sensory stimulation. Purposeful movement has been observed within minutes of birth. Facial expressions are similar to those of adults. Smiling has been observed at birth. Cries are meaningful and can express specific feelings and needs.

The behavior of infants is rational, and they are enthusiastic learners. Infants have specific preferences, and they can even evaluate their experience. Their memory and learning abilities have been demonstrated from various behavioral experiments and physiological responses. Their ability to learn a given behavior and respond to obtain a reward suggests mental activity and anticipation. The more we discover about infants, the more we discover about ourselves. There is great potential that as we learn and implement what we learn, we can give the next generation a much better start in life.

The research further suggests that rather than just consulting the "experts" on infant care, we should be paying more attention to the infant. Pediatrician T. Berry Brazelton agrees: "The question parents ask me the most frequently is 'How do I know I'm doing the right thing?' I tell them, 'Watch the baby. He'll tell you.'"[2] We can trust infant responses as authentic and meaningful. Based on numerous studies, the infant's response to pain is similar to or greater than that of the adult. In particular, an infant's behavioral response to circumcision is a powerful personal communication of overwhelming pain. Adult intentions and beliefs regarding circumcision and infants do not diminish infant circumcision pain. If the infant's communication were being received, it would make clear that circumcision is not something we should be doing. Changes in behavioral responses following circumcision indicate that the experience is remembered.

Recognizing the infant as a person has important implications, not the least of which is recognizing infant autonomy. Infants have preferences, wants, and needs. Adults can choose to dismiss many of these because of the overwhelming physical power and control they have over the infant. Such adult behavior teaches the infant that one must have physical power to get what one wants or needs. But if adults instead recognize the infant as a person, there is a relationship to consider. Ignoring the infant's needs solely because one has greater physical power and control weakens the relationship, because the infant's feelings do matter. All this applies to circumcision, which is done by force without regard for the infant's feelings. He gets the strong message that the world uses force to hurt him and that physical power matters more than feeling and relationship.

The idea of infant autonomy conflicts with most parents' beliefs, but isn't it the parents' inherent responsibility to care for the infant, which includes satisfying the infant's needs and protecting the infant from pain? Generally, most parents were not given this kind of care when they were children. Parents face the challenge of examining what they believe about child rearing and how they choose to treat their children instead of simply enforcing their will with their power. If we want our children to treat others with respect and consideration, whatever their physical or social standing, then we need to treat our children that way starting from birth.

Much of what is done in hospitals to newborn infants violates maternal instincts. Many mothers have called our office and related their stories of abandoning their impulse to stop what was being done to their baby. When we fail to trust and act on our impulses, we forfeit our personal power and become victims of our own fear. Parents need to be aware of the impact of their choices and make them prudently. In some cases, protecting the best interests of their child may require that the parents make an extra effort to verify questionable information, and the result may be a decision that goes against "standard practice."

CIRCUMCISION TRAUMA AND EFFECTS ON ADULTS

This book has documented the work of eight clinicians who have independently and directly observed the long-term effects of circumcision and other perinatal trauma through clients who have remembered or relived such events. Those clinicians are Arthur Janov, Stanislav Grof, Leslie Feher, Thomas Verny, Richard Schwartzman, David Chamberlain, Rima Laibow, and Charles Konia. There are probably hundreds of other practitioners who use comparable methods and have had similar experience. Psychologist David Chamberlain reports that thousands of people around the world have remembered their birth.[3] Some reports of perinatal memories have been corroborated. Yet many medical and psychological professionals are affected by a cultural bias and restricted by a theoretical framework that does not accommodate such experience. More research is needed, but it is also time for more professionals to take note of the work that has already been done and to reevaluate outdated theories and assumptions.

What we know of the infant's neurological development, trauma theory, clinical experience, and research results all support the conclusion that circumcision is a trauma. Like other traumas, the experience of circumcision is repressed but may be remembered or relived under special circumstances. Some men report long-term psychological effects of circumcision. These effects are typically connected with childhood scenes when the lack of a foreskin was recognized in comparison with intact children.

Circumcised men are missing both a part of their bodies and a part of their experience. While the conscious mind may not be aware of this, the body "knows" and "remembers" by storing tension connected with repressed emotions. The fact that most circumcised men are not aware of associated effects does not necessarily mean that the effects are not present or are insignificant. The feelings of dissatisfaction expressed by some circumcised men could remain repressed among many more circumcised men. Some harmful effects may not be connected to circumcision because they appear many years after the precipitating event. In addition, other men may be reluctant to disclose their dissatisfaction because of a sense that these feelings will not be believed or taken seriously.

Long-term psychological effects associated with circumcision can be difficult to establish because the consequences of early trauma are only very rarely and under special circumstances recognizable to the person who experienced the trauma. However, lack of awareness does not necessarily mean that there has been no impact on thinking, feeling, attitude, behavior, and functioning, which are often closely connected. In this way, an early trauma can alter a whole life, whether or not the trauma is consciously remembered. As discussed previously, it is now well established, for example, that adults who were abused as young children suffer adverse behavioral responses connected with their early trauma.

In addition, psychopathology is not always detectable by trained clinicians. The effects of circumcision trauma can be chronic and so deeply embedded that it is very difficult to distinguish them from personality traits or effects resulting from other causes. As with other traumas, the psychopathological outcome may vary, but the reported and behavioral symptoms of circumcision trauma appear to be consistent with the symptom pattern of post-traumatic stress disorder (PTSD). Adult symptoms could be considered delayed psychological effects of circumcision. The most common chronic symptom is probably emotional restriction, an inability to express feelings of varied intensity. Furthermore, because circumcision is common, its effects are common and are interpreted as normal. This view is analogous to the outdated belief that the limited behavioral responses of newborn infants were normal when in fact their capabilities were diminished by the effects of drugs and routine medical interventions.

Other likely symptoms associated with circumcision are avoidance of circumcision-related stimuli (usually the topic itself), problems with intimacy, and reduced self-esteem. These are common symptoms in trauma victims who appear to have normal functioning. In addition, the lack of control and betrayal of trust that circumcised men experienced as infants may, at least in some cases, be connected with a degree of distrust and a desire for control. If the effect of circumcision is similar to that of other physical traumas, then the individual's character can be changed by the experience. Obviously, the adverse sexual impact of circumcision can only expand and compound the psychological effects. The combined sexual and psychological effects on men probably have an indirect effect on women and others in relationships.

As a society, we do not acknowledge the severe pain that circumcision causes infants, although it is amply documented. The discovery that some men feel harmed by circumcision, whatever the prevalence of this feeling, is a warning that we should heed. It seems that as we come to realize the long-term effects of circumcision on adults, we will reconsider our attitudes and actions regarding the practice. This is unlike, for example, our attitude toward the rape of adolescents. We don't wait to ask how rape will affect their adulthood or old age. We recognize the gravity of the act itself. The same standard should apply to assessing such acts involving infants.

CIRCUMCISION AND DISRUPTED BONDING

Secure attachment is necessary for proper development. The disruption of attachment bonds may lead to stress, various forms of psychopathology, as well as neurochemical, physiological, and behavioral changes.

Determining the long-term disruptive effect of circumcision on bonding is complicated by the fact that disrupted bonding is so common in American infant care and child rearing. For example, although it is widely accepted that optimum care for an infant requires almost constant contact with the mother,[4] this level of caretaking is not typical in America. Not only are the mother and infant often separated in the hospital after birth, but half of all infants have mothers who work outside the home.[5] By contrast, in a hunter-gatherer society, the infant is in contact with the mother 70–80 percent of the time during the first year and the rest of the time with someone else.[6] Extensive nonmaternal care of infants in the first year is associated with insecure infant-mother attachment.[7] (See the beginning of Chapter 6 for a discussion of the primary importance of the mother-child relationship.)

Conclusions that secure attachment requires both that the mother have close contact with the child and that she be responsive to infant communication may seem obvious to some, but these conclusions challenge the beliefs and lifestyle of others. Cultural change will be required in order to support optimum infant care. Public education on the importance of secure attachment is needed because if the bonding does not happen, the infant will suffer, whether that suffering is actively expressed or not.

Research has demonstrated that the quality of attachment is influenced by both the infant and the mother and that the social dynamics of the mother-child relationship are similar to those of other two-person relationships. How one person feels and responds affects how the other feels and responds. The adverse and direct effects that circumcision can have on mother-infant interaction, including the infant's failure to breast-feed, have been confirmed by studies. In some cases, improper parental response may be connected with changes in infant behavior following circumcision, and these changes can contribute to weak attachment. Clinical experience, child development theory, and infant behavior suggest that circumcision can impair bonding by having a negative effect on the infant's ability to trust.

In addition, a mother's lack of secure attachment with her new child may contribute to maternal depression. Whatever the reason for poor attachment, adverse consequences are likely to follow. When attachment is weak, a parent is more inclined to neglect or harm the infant.

Because most parents do not observe their son's circumcision in the hospital and are not aware of what he has experienced, the prolonged crying, irritability, or withdrawal that may result are not usually viewed as being associated with the practice. However, some mothers do make the connection. If newborn infants remain with their mother after birth, attachment is more secure, and the mother may be more sensitive to changes in her infant after circumcision. Furthermore, a number of mothers have observed their son's circumcision. Some of them have recurrent and distressing thoughts and recollections of the event; in particular they don't forget the screams of their son. Their statements suggest that they may have intrusive post-traumatic stress disorder symptoms. The negative impact of circumcision on attachment is perhaps as evident from these mothers' distressed responses of regret and guilt, as it is from the infants' behavioral changes.

As more mothers speak out about their experience with circumcision, the disrupting effect of circumcision on mother-child bonding will become more apparent. Because of the far-reaching developmental implications, the potential effect of circumcision on the quality of the mother-child relationship and subsequent relationships may be one of the most important adverse impacts of the practice.

AMERICAN MOTIVATION TO CIRCUMCISE

Parents who agree to the circumcision procedure for their newborn son are typically not aware of important information and, as a result, cannot give true informed consent. Those men who most strongly insist on circumcision for their sons are least aware of the effect their own circumcision has had on them physically, sexually, and emotionally. American parents don't know what they don't know about circumcision. Furthermore, it is not just information that is lacking, but also experience. Parents consenting to a circumcision generally do not see the procedure being done. Those that do see it are often horrified.

Considering the seriousness of the circumcision decision, the lack of awareness is alarming. It raises the question, "Why didn't you know?" Virtually everyone has heard about circumcision, but few bother to examine what it really is. The lack of curiosity is no accident. Avoidance of the issue by circumcised men is a likely PTSD symptom that can be transmitted to others. It signals an iceberg of underlying emotional factors that are generally connected with fears, anxieties, pain, sexuality, and threats to self-esteem. Together they contribute to a compulsion to repeat the trauma. Therefore, circumcision is not typically done just for assumed health reasons. Instead, many interdependent psychological factors account for the continued American practice of circumcision.

Existential psychologist Rollo May wrote, "It is dangerous to know, but it is more dangerous to not know."[8] The danger in knowing about circumcision is that one is then vulnerable to feeling the associated emotional pain of what has been done. The greater danger is that without this knowledge we will continue to circumcise and cause more pain. Knowledge gives us the ability to make better choices.

Many parents confuse their intention concerning circumcision with the effects of circumcision. They believe that as long as no harm is intended, no harm can occur. This does not necessarily follow. Parents do not know what they are choosing, and physicians do not feel what they are doing. The separation of the decision maker from the decision implementer helps to perpetuate the pain.

In studies involving physicians and parents, men are more likely than women to choose circumcision for the newborn. Based on the results of a preliminary survey, the following factors make it more likely that a man will choose circumcision for his son: he is circumcised himself; he is glad he is circumcised; he believes he is well-informed about circumcision when he, in fact, is not; he has never seen a circumcision; he does not know the purpose of the foreskin; and he minimizes the size of the foreskin.

A so-called neutral or balanced presentation of circumcision to parents is preferred by physicians and childbirth educators, but it does not provide accurate and complete information to those who need to make the decision. It appears that few involved in the circumcision decision are aware that circumcision can have a long-term effect on sexual experience and functioning. In addition, the use and exclusion of certain words in the educational literature and in public discourse help to maintain general support for circumcision. Based on this study, the mention of possible long-term psychological effects should now be included in information provided to parents.

Communication between the physician and parents is often insufficient for informed consent, largely because of emotional discomfort with the subject. The discussion may instead include incorrect tacit assumptions by doctor and parent about what the other really wants or means. These assumptions tend to lean toward the decision to circumcise. The parents' lack of expertise leads them to defer to the doctor's supposed knowledge, thus contributing to communication deficiencies and a decision to circumcise. Although doctors do not require that parents choose circumcision, and parents believe they are freely making their choice, doctors do exercise control over the parents' decision by controlling information.

Some doctors may use emotional arguments to persuade parents. Both physicians and parents are subject to emotional repression and denial about circumcision. These defense mechanisms unconsciously distort their ideas and perceptions about the practice. The doctor's motivation may be connected to the fact that he is circumcised and has performed many circumcisions. Financial incentive is a motivating factor for some doctors to circumcise. For most doctors, however, conscious and unconscious emotional factors seem to be primary. The father's preference for circumcision may be connected with his own circumcision or the fact that his other sons are circumcised.

One way to justify inflicting pain and suffering on others is to believe that otherwise more pain and suffering will follow. Using this strategy to defend circumcision requires minimizing or denying the harm caused by circumcision and producing overstated medical claims about protection from future harm. In fact, the "treatment" is worse than the potential "disease." Justifying the practice of circumcision with warnings of worse outcomes (unlikely or rare conditions such as infection, cancer, etc.) if it is not done is a certain indication of fallacious reasoning. The medical arguments used to support circumcision are based on untenable logic, flawed science, and incomplete information. The social myths are equally irrational and incongruous. How can foreskin be insignificant and yet noticed by others in the locker room?

In other circumstances, adults are generally sensitive to the pain and suffering of children because of children's vulnerability and innocence. For this reason, the welfare of children is sometimes used for political purposes. Virtually no one wants to hurt a child, but by allowing circumcision we are the ones who are doing the hurting. It is a hard pill to swallow. We do not want to acknowledge our mistake and all that it implies. Thus, avoidance of guilt explains the tenacity with which people defend the practice of circumcision and the ongoing denial requires the continued ignorance of facts and the acceptance of false beliefs.

SCIENCE AND MEDICINE

According to the medical profession's own analysis of its literature, flawed studies are not the exception. This is explained by the observations that medical investigators generally are not adequately trained to do scientific research, and that the pressure to submit to authority constrains their critical thinking. Regarding circumcision, instruction and textbooks are incomplete or inaccurate. Improper medical education has resulted in a significant proportion of doctors who do not know some basic facts connected with circumcision. Like the whole culture, the medical community has avoided and distorted the facts about circumcision.

Rather than trust ourselves and our experience, we often rely on science—instrumentation, data, studies. The quest for obtaining more "objective" data regarding people becomes increasingly impersonal. For example, in research on attachment, mothers are sometimes referred to as "attachment objects." Similarly, a physician may prefer to assess a patient's condition by observing instrumentation connected to the patient rather than by observing and communicating with the patient. In this way, researchers often assume that only observations that are measurable are important, and consequently they ignore what they can't measure. The infant's cry was not accepted by the medical community as meaningful communication until it could be measured!

As a society, we need to question our blind acceptance of science and our belief in "objective" reality. There is no such thing as objective observation, because observations are made by people who have inherent theories and expectations about how things should be. Studies defending circumcision make this abundantly clear by ignoring vital information (such as the functions of the foreskin) that conflicts with their observations, results, and conclusions. Some research is reliable, and other research is not. The record shows that we cannot depend on scientific and medical professionals to accurately and completely evaluate a cultural practice such as circumcision.

The study of behavior can help us to understand ourselves, but in the medical community there is greater interest in neurochemical and biological components of behavior rather than in social science approaches. Hormone levels are relatively easy to measure, but behavior is too complex to be reduced to such relatively convenient measurements. In addition, because medical educators take biological science more seriously than social science, physicians starting clinical practice have little training in or appreciation of the importance of social science to their work. They do not view their profession as having socially constructed limitations and distortions, and their behavior as being a product of psychological processes. As Erik Erikson said, "the best minds have often been least aware of themselves."[9] Unrecognized psychological factors enter into physicians' beliefs, attitudes, and behaviors regarding circumcision.

The practice of circumcision is partly the result of distorted medical priorities regarding emotion. Emotion has an even lower value in the medical world than in the general society. Doctors tend to measure pain rather than feel pain. One medical journal article evaluated circumcision based strictly on a cost-utility analysis,[10] as if we have no better way to make the decision. The wholesale dismissal of feeling is related to a limited ability to feel. It is a mistake. Feeling is a form of knowing. Reason and emotion complement each other. William James, an early pioneer in the field of psychology, went so far as to say, "Feeling is everything." If doctors would feel what they are doing as well as know what they are doing, they would make better decisions and be less likely to cause unnecessary pain.

The medical community has had limitations in other respects. For example, controversies require full and open debate. The misunderstanding of doctors about the foreskin is evidence that full and open debate has not occurred on the circumcision issue. It appears that information and observations that do not fit prevailing ideas are dismissed. A notable example of this occurred in the field of genetics. Decades ago Barbara McClintock reported that she had observed genes "jumping" positions within cells. Her work was rejected by colleagues for thirty years because the idea of "jumping genes" was impossible according to the prevailing paradigm. Finally, her work was accepted, and she was awarded the Nobel Prize in 1984.[11]

The lack of feeling and the lack of open discussion among physicians may be connected. Increasing one can facilitate the other. Support for open discussion in the medical community would encourage students and physicians who are inclined to challenge unexamined beliefs, practices, and procedures to speak out. Likewise, consumers need to ask more questions of doctors, and doctors need to respect those questions. Open discussion will benefit everyone and bring us closer to optimum solutions.

Even with full debate, the overwhelming pain and harm of circumcision cannot be "proven" to those who do not or cannot feel. No amount of data or studies will suffice. However, if we could see, hear, and feel what was happening during circumcision, we would not need any studies to tell us what to do (see quote of Dr. Gregory Skipper, Chapter 2). We would know instinctively not to do it. We would know that circumcision is a serious surgical procedure, not the trivial one it is purported to be. Because it is unnecessary surgery, the burden of proof in the circumcision debate rests with those who advocate it. They must show that it is both safe and effective. Neither has been demonstrated.

ETHICS AND MEDICINE

Like all professions, medicine has its own ethical code and principles of conduct. One rule of conduct is "First, do no harm." Removing a normal, healthy body part and causing unnecessary pain is doing harm. Some doctors who circumcise acknowledge the associated pain and then dismiss it by saying, "It only lasts for a minute," implying that it is acceptable to subject an infant to unnecessary pain as long as it is temporary. (In one study, the time required for the procedure ranged from six to forty minutes.[12])

However, there is strong evidence that the pain has lasting effects. Even if it did not, this careless attitude about inflicting pain violates the ethical principles of the medical profession. It also violates general moral principles to subject anyone, particularly a defenseless infant, to any unnecessary pain for any period of time. As recently reported in the *New England Journal of Medicine,* "Failure to provide adequate control of pain amounts to substandard and unethical medical practice."[13] Furthermore, circumcision without anesthesia is inconsistent with ethical guidelines that prohibit performing surgical procedures on laboratory animals without anesthesia.[14] Based on these standards and given that there is no effective and safe anesthetic that will eliminate circumcision pain, all circumcisions would be prohibited.

According to the Hippocratic oath, another important principle of medical practice is that the patient's welfare shall be the doctor's first consideration.[15] In the case of circumcision, doctors generally tend to ignore this rule, while parents falsely believe they are following it. When I visited Dr. Steven Ringer at Brigham and Women's Hospital in Boston, he defended circumcision by saying that "within the community at large, at the present time, there is not a tremendous amount of support for saying to parents you shouldn't do this." For Dr. Ringer, regarding the issue of circumcision, community attitude seems to supersede the patient's welfare. Isn't it the medical profession's responsibility to lead rather than follow regarding community health care standards?

Lawrence Kohlberg's writing on moral development can be applied to thinking about social attitudes surrounding circumcision. According to Kohlberg's stages of moral development, someone who acts based on what is expected by others is exhibiting a conventional level of morality.[16] This is the level of moral reasoning that is most common in our society. A person acting at this level primarily values social approval and adheres to the moral rules and conventions of society. Physicians receive social approval by taking a safe, neutral position on circumcision and doing the surgery if requested. Circumcising an infant is an example of conventional, socially acceptable behavior that is in conflict with universal moral principles.

A person who acts according to universal moral principles would exhibit what Kohlberg calls a postconventional morality, the highest level of moral reasoning. Few people choose to follow self-chosen universal ethical principles rather than the conventional principles accepted by their society. To do so puts one at risk of being ridiculed, ostracized, or worse. Most people would rather condemn the whistle-blower instead of examining their own behavior. Nevertheless, a growing number of doctors and nurses refuse to participate in circumcisions because the procedure conflicts with their ethical principles, and hospitals such as Parkland Hospital in Dallas and Highland Hospital in Oakland no longer do circumcisions. After performing circumcisions for ten years, one day pediatrician Paul Fleiss finally heard the "agonizing cry" of an infant he was circumcising. He realized what he was doing and stopped performing circumcisions. "You just should not be cruel to babies."[17]

A physician who agrees to circumcise is complying with a request to inflict pain on another human being. Professor Stanley Milgram conducted a series of experiments at Yale University to find out how far people would go in obeying a command to inflict pain on another person.[18] Most subjects obeyed the command to continue shocking a confederate, who really received no shocks, up to the danger level. In a subsequent experiment, Milgram found that a subject could be induced through group pressure to inflict greater harm on an innocent person than the subject did when he or she acted alone.[19] Since physicians recognize that peers generally agree to circumcise, that awareness probably contributes to physicians' willingness to comply with the request.

Similar to the arrangement in Milgram's experiments, when physicians perform their first circumcision, they are directed by a superior. Given the past and current cultural and professional environment, only an exceptional doctor would refuse to comply with the senior doctor's instructions. There is no cruel intent, only denial and self-deception. Once a physician does a circumcision, he or she has crossed an emotional line from which it is exceedingly difficult to retreat. A range of potential PTSD symptoms may take hold, since such symptoms can be experienced by participants as well as victims of trauma. In a study of Vietnam veterans, all those who participated in atrocities had PTSD symptoms years later.[20] Those who participate in circumcision trauma may deny inflicting harm as a way of protecting themselves against an outbreak of delayed PTSD symptoms.

Because the infant's experience of circumcision has been compared to torture in the medical literature,[21] let's consider what the medical profession has to say about physicians' involvement in torture. According to a publication of the British Medical Association,

> The standard established by the World Medical Association—the Declaration of Tokyo—gives little scope for ambiguity on whether or not doctors should become involved in torture [of prisoners]. It makes clear that "the doctor shall not countenance, condone or participate in the practice of torture or other forms of cruel, inhuman or degrading procedures.[22]

Why do doctors get involved in torture? The reasons include devaluing a victim group, training, fear of the consequences of refusing to cooperate, "bureaucratization" of the medical role, and an inadequate understanding of medical ethics.[23] All of these reasons apply to circumcision.

When a Uruguayan psychiatrist was questioned about his participation in torture, he responded:

> I was confined to my function. I ignored other aspects and there were some aspects I didn't want to know about. . . . It wasn't my purpose. I am a doctor.[24]

As with doctors who circumcise, this doctor's choices were reduced by the fear of knowing.

To defend against moral culpability and guilt, physicians have convinced themselves that they are not responsible for circumcision. They claim that they simply defer to parental requests and act as if they have no choice in the matter. George Denniston, a physician specializing in preventive medicine who has served with many medical and professional organizations, asks, "Since when does a trained surgeon take the advice of uninformed laypeople as to whether or not he should operate?"[25] Circumcision is the exception. However, the same doctors would refuse to perform other types of unnecessary surgery on infants. For example, if a parent requested that the infant's toes or ears be cut off for no apparent reason, the physician would decline. An exception to fundamental principles and practice signifies danger.

Most physicians do not consider circumcision to be an ethical issue. With enough social support and tacit agreement, people can be incredibly blind to their own ethical violations. Rudolph Hess, a German officer who participated in the mass killing of Jews during the Holocaust, did not think what he did was an ethical issue. At the Nuremberg trials he said, "I really never gave much thought to whether it was wrong. It just seemed a necessity. We just never heard anything else."

There is no medical journal article that examines the ethics of male infant circumcision. (Earlier citations have been from other sources or articles on pain.) However, "female circumcision" is the subject of two such opinion articles. In one article the writer comments, "No ethical defense can be made for preserving a cultural practice that damages women's health and interferes with their sexuality."[26] Because of the complication risks, in addition to potential psychological and sexual impact, a similar statement would apply to male infant circumcision.

In the other article, the writer, a female philosophy professor, argues that the physician has a duty only to provide "medically appropriate and necessary services," not all possible requested medical services.[27] According to her, the physician is not a "moral eunuch" and may refuse to provide services for ethical reasons. This would also apply to a woman requesting circumcision for herself. On the matter of a woman requesting circumcision for her daughter, the writer believes that the physician should refuse for ethical reasons, regardless of related cultural values and traditions. The writer concludes by expressing the same views on male circumcision. "To argue differently is to be guilty of discrimination on the basis of sex. . . . Both involve what in other contexts would be called nonconsensual mutilation of a minor for nonmedical reasons."[28]

CULTURAL AND SOCIAL PERSPECTIVES

Why did circumcision gain widest acceptance in the United States? There was a unique combination of social and cultural factors that made people in this country particularly inclined to accept circumcision. Among them were influential writers and medical professionals who promoted it, a health insurance system that continued to pay for it, pervasive sexual anxieties, and the power of conformity.

The existence of the practice of circumcision appears to be symptomatic of a deep American insecurity. Our willingness to go to the extreme of participating in cutting off part of our son's genitals may be due in part to alienation that is widespread in our society. Alienation breeds conformity. Researchers have shown that lonely subjects have less confidence in their opinions and are less willing to disclose them.[29] This condition makes them vulnerable to conformity. By relieving the sense of isolation, conformity gives us the illusion of the connectedness we seek. Actually, conformity can displace connectedness.

Conformity persists when there is self-doubt. With their doubts, conformists view personal responsibility as a burden and gladly trade it for being told what to do. They tend to trust authorities and "experts" rather than themselves. The problem with experts is not that they can be wrong, but that most people believe they are right. Conformists are subject not only to authoritarian error but also to authoritarian manipulation. The American conformists' dilemma is that autonomy is also valued, but because they doubt themselves and fear rejection, autonomy is hard to achieve. This fear of disapproval and rejection is the social reason for the enduring tenacity of circumcision.

Generally, most of us believe that a person who is natural, genuine, and different will not be accepted. We have forgotten and numbed ourselves to the deep emotional pain that accompanies the choice to hide our true selves. Let's remind ourselves that being true to ourselves is critical to how we feel, and that people who are true to themselves often earn not just acceptance, but the respect and admiration of others.

Circumcision exemplifies our tendency to raise our children to be like us, socially acceptable rather than who they really are. It is our society that needs to change, not our children. We can make important contributions to social change when we make important child-rearing decisions. Rather than thoughtlessly imitating the countless decisions of others who did not reflect on their decisions, we can instead give additional consideration to the child's wants and needs and to our own instincts. Recalling the feelings and experiences of our own childhood can also help us to make better decisions for our children.

We are social beings. Socialization involves adopting the standards of the group. It matters what others think and do. But doing something only because others do it is not sufficient justification to perform any act, particularly one that involves inflicting pain. Behavior needs to involve self-evaluation and awareness of responsibility at some level. If we simply pay attention to ourselves, we will be better able to resist conforming to the practice of circumcision, and to other practices that do not meet our needs or improve the quality of our lives. We may discover that the best of what we know has been inside us all along and was not learned from others. Furthermore, becoming more connected to our inner selves will facilitate becoming more connected to others. We are then able to communicate more deeply, for example, which can strengthen our connections with others, increase our confidence, and reduce the appeal of conformity.

Cultural arrogance makes it harder to reconsider our actions and admit our mistakes. Americans are raised with the idea that we are "the greatest country on Earth," the most advanced, and the most compassionate. Compared to other countries, we need to believe we are right and that we know best. Reconsidering circumcision as a tragic mistake conflicts with these easy assumptions. As a result, we honor the suffering and pain we have endured but deny the suffering and pain we have inflicted. Being honest with ourselves as a culture will relieve us of this pressure to maintain a compensatory, inflated image of ourselves.

Our arrogance is apparent in another respect. Circumcision involves altering the human body. Those who would circumcise implicitly suggest that they know better than nature, God, or whatever power created us and our world. Their actions imply that what is natural is either defective and needs correction, or that it can be improved by human intervention. Invariably, this attitude gets us into serious trouble.

Our materialistic view of the body gives rise to medical materialism and reflects our cultural materialism. Foreskin, we tell ourselves, is "just a little piece of skin." But we are more than our material body, and the impact of circumcision is not just material. It is also psychological and social. When the bond between child and mother is disrupted, the bond between child and humanity is disrupted. Consequently, it is not only the child who is wounded during circumcision. We are all wounded: the parents, the physicians, the community, and the society.

Circumcision is an act of diminishing. By removing a normal, useful part, circumcision diminishes the penis. When we diminish the penis of an infant, we diminish ourselves. The associated repression and denial diminish our awareness.

The continued denial of feelings and information in any area makes us vulnerable to the same kind of blindness in other areas. Clearly, awareness is crucial for maintaining and improving the quality of life. Our experience with circumcision teaches us that rather than just paying attention to the unusual, we would do better to pay more attention to the commonplace. What other beliefs and practices would benefit from close examination? What is the possible social impact of a 25 percent cesarean rate?

Circumcision has a ripple effect that permeates America. It is a source of shame. The way we attempt to alleviate the shame of circumcision is to see to it that others are also circumcised. The denial is contagious. Because our individual and national self-esteem are threatened, the silence continues. There are strong indications that we pay a price for this silence in personal and social terms.

Inquiry and disclosure are healthy. In the last twenty years we have learned much about child sexual abuse that was previously hidden. Who would deny that we are better off to know about child sexual abuse than not to know? The increase in media attention to child sexual abuse may be associated with decreased prevalence.[30]

By avoiding open acknowledgment of circumcision, we hold on to our pain, guilt, anger, shame, distrust, fear, and isolation. Our internal conflicts are related to our external conflicts. There is a list of societal ills that needs to be scrutinized for potential connections to circumcision: homicide, rape, and unnecessary surgery, for example. The United States, with its uniquely high rate of circumcision, leads the industrialized world in these categories. Obviously, circumcision is not the sole cause of these problems, but it could be a significant and unrecognized contributing factor. Even if the effects of circumcision were a factor in just a small percentage of these incidents, it would be well worth studying the possibilities.

We recognize violence as a social problem but respond generally with only more security and protection for ourselves and punishment for offenders. If we are going to reduce adult violence, we must reduce violence directed at children. We would do well to direct resources toward prevention, starting with more attention to the perinatal period. Simply educating young adults about proper perinatal care and reducing interventions before, during, and after birth could be an effective measure for reducing the incidence of adult violent behavior and a variety of associated problems.

Generally, circumcision is a practice that is originated by men, chosen by men (see Chapter 2), performed by men, and defended by men. (Since circumcision is allowed by women, they share in the responsibility for continuing it.) Men also control the medical institutions that manage childbirth. Because circumcision occurs shortly after birth, it is also a childbirth issue. The care of a newborn infant and mother requires the most sensitive, empathetic, and responsive human beings. The maternal instincts and experiences of women uniquely qualify them for this important responsibility.

For the welfare of newborn infants and society, control of the childbirth experience and its associated concerns needs to be returned to women.

HOPE FOR HEALING

> Your pain is the breaking of the shell that encloses your
> understanding.   —Kahlil Gibran

Healing the Emotional Harm of Circumcision

Once we have acknowledged the facts about circumcision, strong feelings may start to surface. Some people may choose not to express their feelings about circumcision at all. Others may feel content to talk quietly about them. Still others may feel as if they could explode. All options should be respected.

If one experiences a divorce or the death of a loved one, for example, people generally understand and can respond appropriately. Two factors that make healing from circumcision more difficult than recovering from many other painful experiences in life are that it is both a physical and emotional trauma, and that there is little social acceptance of feelings related to circumcision.

For those who choose to explore their feelings, I offer a few general guidelines. Since most feelings connected with circumcision have been kept hidden, social support is necessary to overcome this isolation. Whatever our involvement with circumcision, it can be helpful to share feelings in a safe environment with a trusted partner or with the help of a mental health professional. It will probably be necessary to select potential partners or clinicians carefully to ensure that they are emotionally supportive of feelings connected with circumcision. Because some of the feelings of circumcised men are related to sexuality, support from a sexual partner is especially important.

Feelings associated with circumcision can be so strong that they may frighten you with their intensity. However, expressing them will not hurt you. The worst has already happened. Trust your body. It knows how much you can feel and will not let you go any further than that point. For those who tend to rationalize the control of their feelings, trusting the body and not the head is a frightening step. Use your partner's support to confirm that you are safe.

Why go through it? The feelings are there whether we choose to express them or not. If we do not deal with them directly, they will continue to affect us indirectly. As with the expression of more common feelings, there is a sense of release and relief from emotional expression. We discover that it is holding on to the feelings that has hurt us and not their expression. Their expression actually feels "good," no matter how "bad" the feeling is. Releasing them will help us to open blocked energy, increase our ability to trust, enhance intimacy, and regain a sense of personal power.

Sharing secrets can be a transformative experience. It is as if the world is lifted off our shoulders. Simply being heard or receiving the feedback of others can dispel years of fearful illusions and create a new bond of trust. Rather than feeling it necessary to prove one's manhood and worth, being heard can facilitate being accepted for who one is, and, even more importantly, it can improve self-acceptance. Acknowledging and grieving the loss caused by circumcision can help to recover at least some of the emotional part of ourselves that has been cut off. (For information about recovering the physical/sexual part, see "Resources.") The safe release of feelings can also purge us of emotions that may have driven us to hurt ourselves and others. Recognizing that deep conflicts and anxieties have existed for a reason and are a proper response to the early trauma can also contribute to healing. Surviving early trauma is a triumph for the human spirit.

Talking honestly and personally about circumcision has the potential to improve relationships. Whether an exchange about circumcision between sons and parents would be of value depends on the individuals involved. Movement toward resolution requires that each one be open to feelings about circumcision. Sometimes one party is not ready for such sharing. For example, heartfelt apologies by parents may not be appreciated by a son who does not recognize that he has been harmed. A son seeking acknowledgment of his feelings about circumcision from parents who are not ready to hear them presents a more volatile situation. In a few cases, there may be a risk of disrupting the relationship. Sometimes openness can be facilitated by providing literature on circumcision to an uninformed parent before disclosing one's feelings. If openness is there, making healing the goal will increase the chances of a mutually satisfying outcome. While talking about circumcision can be emotionally stressful, expressing these feelings can also result in a breakthrough that renews the relationship. For example, in some cases, witnessing the pain and regret of their parents can help soften the anger and increase the trust of circumcised men, at the same time as it relieves parental guilt.

With so many men affected, there is much potential for sharing circumcision feelings among men. This can be a significant step toward male bonding and intimacy. Women, too, have an important role to play. Generally, the importance of the support of women cannot be overestimated. Female understanding and compassion are vital to men as they feel increasingly sensitive and vulnerable to feelings about circumcision. The rewards for this support can be considerable for both men and women.

Working through our personal pain in connection with circumcision makes it easier to appreciate the larger context of the practice. Because we were born into a culture that has practiced circumcision routinely, we have been subjected to extremely powerful psychological and social pressures to continue the practice. It is the hurt child in us that wants people to be perfect as parents, doctors, or whatever. When we want others to be perfect, we give them only two options: either pretend to be perfect or risk rejection. Most choose to pretend and hide their weaknesses, their mistakes, and their humanity.

Repression and numbing ourselves to our pain are part of the human condition. They are the rule, not the exception. They even serve a vital purpose: they allow us to survive. Yet once we survive the original painful events, these defenses then limit our quality of life and our capacity for growth. When we become parents, they inhibit our ability to meet our children's needs.

Eventually, if we are to learn from and move beyond the tragic mistake of circumcision, we will need to have compassion and understanding for ourselves, physicians, parents, and others. This can be a difficult step to even imagine for those whose anger may be just starting to surface, but circumcised men are not the only ones in pain. There is more than enough direct and indirect pain associated with circumcision for all of us.

An essential component of healing is forgiveness, both for ourselves and others. Concerning circumcision, we as a society are a long way from that day. Rushing forgiveness is counterproductive, as it will deny other feelings their full expression. It will come in due time. Meanwhile, the main point to consider is that our pain can serve to bring us together rather than to keep us apart.

Healing involves taking responsibility. Whereas physicians and some circumcised men place responsibility for circumcision with parents, some parents and circumcised men point the finger at physicians. Certainly, medical personnel and institutions have thus far failed to address the problem of circumcision. However, I believe that to hold the medical community (or any other group) solely responsible for the practice of circumcision would be a serious mistake. A person, group, or institution only has as much power as other people give it. Circumcision is a social problem in which the whole society is complicit. We have more power individually and collectively than we usually are willing to acknowledge. Our reluctance to accept our power is connected to our reluctance to accept responsibility. However, our belief in our powerlessness does not absolve us of our responsibility. Consequently, I believe that all of us as a society share in the responsibility for circumcision. Rather than just complain that the medical profession does not meet our expectations, we would do better to expand our awareness, and then to accept responsibility for what we know and experience.

Preventing Future Harm

> Never doubt that a small group of committed citizens can change the world. Indeed, it is the only thing that ever has.
> —Margaret Mead

Circumcision knowledge and awareness come with an ethical challenge. When the welfare of a newborn infant is at issue, neutrality is unacceptable. One must take a stand. It is easier to take the side in support of circumcision because nothing is required except silence and passivity. Silence gives implicit permission for more circumcisions. Passivity is complicity. Although circumcisions number in the thousands daily, it is the magnitude of the silence and passivity surrounding the practice that is truly astounding. To be opposed to circumcision requires action. With the acceptance of power and responsibility comes the need for action.

It is not just for the infants that we need to act; it is also for ourselves. Circumcised men in particular may have a special need to give meaning to their feelings by taking some sort of social action. Taking action to prevent others from being victimized aids recovery. This benefit has already been demonstrated with those who were raped and then worked to prevent others from being raped.[31] In addition, becoming involved in the issue of circumcision offers a person an opportunity for purposeful creative expression that can open up new levels of experience. Speaking one's truth is a powerful act. There is a sense of freedom in following inner guidance rather than only what is popular. Just as the fear to express oneself spreads to others, the courage to express oneself also spreads to others. That is why expressions critical of circumcision will continue to grow at a surprising rate.

The instincts that we have ignored are what have the power to unite us. Acting on one's best instincts with the knowledge that these actions can deeply affect others' lives provides surprising energy and satisfaction. In this way, we become connected to something beyond ourselves. As we change, a part of the culture changes, and there is an effect on the whole. What kind of a society would we be without circumcision? I have suggested some possibilities. Let's find out.

Circumcision may be the most important, simply preventable American psychological and social problem. It is important because it causes excruciating pain to over a million new people each year. It is simply preventable because all that needs to happen is for parents to keep their newborn sons' healthy bodies intact. It's simple, but it's not easy to accomplish. For some, questioning circumcision might disturb their core beliefs and lead to the recognition that they should question everything. As long as they do not trust themselves, that is a step they may not be willing or able to take. Therefore, we must be realistic about the obstacles and know that some people will not listen, and many will need time or will need to hear about circumcision repeatedly before the message begins to penetrate their defenses. One man reported after he read an article questioning circumcision, "I said to myself, 'Don't think about it.' It's easier to laugh it off and push it away." Six weeks later he returned to the article and allowed himself to feel more about it. Then he called someone to talk about it and got involved.

Psychological research suggests what approaches would work best in attempting to influence people's attitudes. For example, for a maximum change of attitude in others, it is best to have a message that deviates only moderately from the listener's viewpoint.[32] This guideline can be adjusted to suit particular speakers and listeners. Those with higher credibility can make more extreme statements designed to influence attitudes.[33] The more committed a listener is to a position, the smaller the discrepancy must be between that position and the message for maximum change of attitude to be achieved.[34] Consequently, depending on your credibility and your listener, a moderate message will usually have the best chance of affecting another person's attitude.

On the other hand, the message about circumcision is so simple and so universally acceptable that many people (including my elderly father) do not need to be persuaded. They get it immediately: don't hurt babies. The task, then, is to disclose the simple facts, appeal to their protective instincts, and trust that many people will eventually come to this conclusion themselves. We know that we are in a position of strength. Patience and persistence will be rewarded. How long will it take? That is up to all of us. For those to be circumcised, time is of the essence.

Some people may have difficulty being motivated about the circumcision issue. They value only what they perceive affects them personally and directly. If they are circumcised or have circumcised sons, the typical attitude is, "It's done, and there is nothing I can do about it." After learning more about circumcision, one mother told me, "It's too late now. My son is circumcised."

204 CIRCUMCISION: THE HIDDEN TRAUMA

By withdrawing to our own little worlds and leaving the rest of society to take care of itself, we make a costly mistake. To think that newborn infants can be subjected to circumcision without its having any impact on others ignores the interconnectedness of all life. When a baby boy's sexuality is not safe, no one's sexuality is safe. If the previous generation had taken action, we would not be a circumcised society today. What we do today for the next generation can help restore our integrity, affirm our connectedness to others, and prevent needless pain.

When we are open to our feelings, we are powerful and gain strength as we connect with others. Betty Katz Sperlich was asked where she and other nurses at her hospital in Santa Fe got their strength to put their jobs at risk, take an ethical stand, and oppose the practice of circumcision by refusing to assist. Sperlich replied without hesitation, "We get our strength from the babies." Infants are not as helpless and powerless as some people think.

Another who is speaking out is Melissa Morrison, who chose circumcision for her son because "it was something that was just done." She watched the procedure and now deeply regrets her decision.

> People need to know what they are doing to their babies. I didn't know. And ignorance is not an excuse. I'm embarrassed about what I did, but I am not about to hide it. I'm talking to my girlfriends; I'm talking to mothers. If somebody says to me they are having a little boy, I will beg them not to do it. If it helps just to save one little baby's penis, then it's worth it.

Perhaps the biggest lesson from circumcision is that the practice provides shocking evidence that we can cause extreme but unrecognized pain to those we love. It reminds us that we often do not pay attention to the many ways we can hurt not just our children, but also each other. Only when we stop hurting each other will we create the world of love, trust, and peace that we seek. Let us begin—with the children.

Appendix A

Sample Hospital
Circumcision Information

This information on circumcision was distributed to expectant parents by the Brigham and Women's Hospital in Boston, the hospital with the highest number of annual births in New England. My letter responding to this information follows.

FOR YOUR INFORMATION

Considerations for Non-Ritual Circumcisions

Upon entering the hospital prospective parents are asked, if their newborn infant is male, whether they would like their son circumcised. Although circumcision is one of the most common operative procedures performed in American hospitals, most parents have little factual information about this surgery.

Newborn circumcisions became common in the United States after World War II. Today the procedure is a somewhat controversial one. This procedure is practiced in few European, Asian or South American countries.

In 1975, the American Academy of Pediatrics Task Force on Circumcision concluded: "There is no absolute medical indication for routine circumcision in the newborn." In 1978, the American College of Obstetricians and Gynecologists endorsed the position of the Academy. In order that parents can make a more informed decision, we have summarized the current information on circumcision.

The decision to circumcise or not to circumcise a son is a personal one, but it should not be made without some thought. Parents are encouraged to discuss this decision with their obstetrician or pediatric health-care provider.

WHAT IS CIRCUMCISION?
Circumcision is the surgical removal of all or part of the foreskin of the male penis. The procedure is usually done by the mother's obstetrician after the first day of the child's life. Newborn circumcisions are most frequently done for traditional, cultural or religious reasons.

ARGUMENTS FOR CIRCUMCISION:
Cleanliness—Perhaps the major benefit of circumcision is that it makes cleanliness easier. A normal secretion, a cream-colored, waxy material called smegma, is formed under the intact foreskin. Smegma allowed to accumulate between the tip of the penis (the glans) and the foreskin can irritate and may lead to an infection. A well-performed circumcision may prevent this build-up of smegma. In the uncircumcised male, gentle retraction of the loose foreskin during bathing also prevents the buildup of smegma. Circumcision does not eliminate the need for proper hygiene; it simply makes it easier.

Decreased incidence of infection—In 1985 a clinical study demonstrated a decreased incidence of urinary tract infections in circumcised male infants. In this well controlled study of 2,502 male newborn infants there was a 20 fold greater incidence of urinary tract infections in the uncircumcised versus the circumcised male (4.12% vs. 0.21%).

Custom—At the present time, circumcision of the male infant is an American custom, with eighty percent of male newborns in this country being circumcised. It may be important for some children not to look different from their peers, or from their father. For this reason, some parents may wish to have their child circumcised.

Prevention of paraphimosis—On very rare occasions mothers retract the still-tight foreskin of the penis too vigorously in an attempt to cleanse away smegma. The foreskin, if left retracted, can sometimes act as a tourniquet, shutting off the blood supply to the end of the penis. This condition, known as paraphimosis, may need to be surgically corrected. Circumcision prevents paraphimosis from developing.

Prevention of cancer of the penis—Cancer of the penis, an extremely rare condition, is less common among circumcised men. At the present time, it is usually found only in elderly men with poor hygiene. There is evidence that proper hygiene provides as much, or nearly as much, protection as circumcision. The risk of developing cancer of the penis is less than that of suffering a major complication of circumcision.

Prevention of cervical cancer in females—Circumcision was once felt to reduce the incidence of cervical cancer in the male's sexual partner. Recent studies done in the U.S. and Britain have shown no significant relationship between the circumcision status of the male and the incidence of cervical cancer in females.

ARGUMENTS AGAINST CIRCUMCISION:

Pain—Frequently parents asked if circumcision is a painful experience for their baby. Experiment and common experience certainly suggest that it is. However, the procedure is quick—usually lasting less than five minutes. The infant is strapped to a circumcision board. No anesthesia or analgesia is administered. The use of local anesthetic distorts the operative site, making an unsatisfactory circumcision too likely. The risk to the baby of general anesthesia is not justified. To prevent aspiration, infants are not fed for two hours prior to circumcision.

Surgical risk—Circumcision is a surgical procedure and like any surgical procedure there are risks inherent in it. The complications of circumcision include hemorrhage, infection, surgical trauma, and ulceration or narrowing of the opening of the urethra (meatal ulceration/meatal stenosis). The great majority of circumcisions are performed without any complications.

Expense—There is a cost attached to any circumcision performed. This includes a charge made by the hospital for the use of its circumcision room and, if a private obstetrician is involved, a physician's fee. Because a number of health insurance plans do not provide coverage for the costs of a routine circumcision, which they consider not to be medically necessary, the procedure will involve an out-of-pocket expense for some patients' families.

October 24, 1991

Dr. Steven Ringer
Medical Director, NICU
Brigham and Women's Hospital
75 Francis St.
Boston, MA 02115

Dear Dr. Ringer:

I have recently received a copy of the hospital information sheet on circumcision provided by Judith Gundersen of the Childbirth Education Office. The information differs from other medical information which I have found. I offer this other information to you for your consideration and would be interested in your response.

ARGUMENTS FOR CIRCUMCISION
Cleanliness—The American Academy of Pediatrics pamphlet titled *Newborns: Care of the Uncircumcised Penis* states, "The foreskin is easy to care for. The infant should be bathed or sponged frequently, and all parts should be washed including the genitals. The uncircumcised penis is easy to keep clean. No special care is required! No attempt should be made to forcibly retract the foreskin. No manipulation is necessary." In contrast the hospital information sheet describes cleanliness as a "major benefit" and advises "gentle retraction of the loose foreskin." The AAP pamphlet states, "They [infant smegma, shed skin cells] escape [from under the foreskin] by working their way to the tip of the foreskin." If smegma can "escape" then how can it accumulate? What is the incidence of infection related to the accumulation of smegma in the infant?

Decreased incidence of infection—The 1985 study referred to appears to be one made by Thomas Wiswell. In a subsequent larger study Wiswell observed urinary tract infection of 0.11% in circumcised male infants and 1.12% in uncircumcised male infants (1). Martin Altschul, MD, in a study of 25,000 infants found a urinary tract infection rate of 0.12% among intact male infants (2). If a study is to be referenced why select one of relatively smaller size with higher incidence of infection? Many doctors have questioned Wiswell's findings. Several questioning letters appeared in *Pediatrics* as follow up to his reports (3).

Custom—According to the National Center for Health Statistics the national circumcision rate (1988) is 58%, not 80%. The rate of circumcisions of male infants at Brigham and Women's Hospital is 55%. There is no evidence to suggest that looking like peers or father is important to children. In any case, it certainly cannot be predicted at birth for which child this will be an issue. Whatever the child's circumcision status, over 40% of his peers will differ.

Prevention of paraphimosis—As stated earlier, the foreskin should not be retracted or manipulated. It is not clear how this constitutes an argument for circumcision.

Prevention of cancer of the penis—According to the American Academy of Pediatrics 1989 report on circumcision, "In developed countries where neonatal circumcision is not routinely performed, the incidence of penile cancer is reported to range from 0.3 to 1.1 per 100,000 men per year." It is not clear how this constitutes an argument for circumcision.

Prevention of cervical cancer in females—If there is no significant relationship between cervical cancer in females and circumcision, then it is not clear how this constitutes an argument for circumcision.

ARGUMENTS AGAINST CIRCUMCISION
Pain—There is no mention of post-surgical pain or psychological trauma. A study published in the *New England Journal of Medicine*, November 19, 1987, called "Pain and Its Effects on the Human

Neonate and Fetus" by K.J.S. Anand and others, includes a comprehensive review of over 200 references related to infant pain. Several studies are cited that found alterations in behavioral responses of circumcised infants.

> It was therefore proposed that such painful procedures [as circumcision] may have prolonged effects on the neurologic and psycho-social development of neonates. . . . The persistence of specific behavioral changes after circumcision in neonates implies the presence of memory. In the short term, these behavioral changes may disrupt the adaptation of newborn infants to their postnatal environment, the development of parent-infant bonding, and feeding schedules. In the long term, painful experiences in neonates could possibly lead to psychological sequelae, since several workers have shown that newborns may have a much greater capacity for memory than was previously thought.

Surgical risk—The AAP report states, "The exact incidence of postoperative complications is unknown, but large series indicate that the rate is low, approximately 0.2% to 0.6%." This exceeds rates of urinary tract infection in some studies. Other sources report complication rates as high as 38% (4,5).

No mention is made of the most obvious argument against circumcision: the loss of the foreskin. This omission implies that the foreskin has no useful purpose. The medical literature states otherwise. According to Dr. J.E. Wright, the foreskin has a "protective function" (6). Dr. George W. Kaplan states that the foreskin protects the meatus (7). Gairdner states that without the foreskin "the glans becomes susceptible to injury from sodden clothes" (8). The medical literature also refers to increased vulnerability from four types of penile injury: zipper injuries, toilet seat injury, burns, and hair or thread injury (9-12).

There is no controversy that the foreskin contains erogenous tissue. Masters and Johnson write, "The prepuce protects the clitoris in the same manner that the foreskin protects the glans or head of the male penis. The clitoris and prepuce form the most sensitively erotogenic area of the female body" (13). Since the male and female prepuces are identical in their embryological development, cell structure, and nerve systems, it is logical to assume that the male foreskin is also "sensitively erotogenic."

Scandinavian physicians oppose circumcision because it is sexually harmful. According to Dr. William Robertson, "It is their [Scandinavian physicians'] thesis that the foreskin with its exquisite nerve endings can't be spared" (14). Dr. C.J. Falliers is in agreement: "Sensory pleasure of foreskin is . . . lost from circumcision" (15). Paul Tardiff and other males who have been circumcised as adults report significant loss in pleasurable sensation. Mr. Tardiff states, that the sexual differences between a circumcised and uncircumcised penis are

> [like] wearing a glove. . . . Sight without color would be a good analogy. . . . Only being able to see in black and white, for example, rather than seeing in full color would be like experiencing an orgasm with a foreskin and without. There are feelings you'll just never have without a foreskin (16).

The information on pain includes the statement: "However, the procedure is quick—usually lasting less than five minutes." This statement appears to be included to argue against the pain consideration. If so, then as a matter of balance, information arguing against, or at least questioning, other considerations should be included. For example, urinary tract infections are temporary and treatable with antibiotics. Wiswell himself states, "It is unclear at this time whether the increase in incidence of urinary tract infection in uncircumcised infants has any long-term medical significance other than the immediate cost of diagnosis, treatment, and follow-up evaluation of the acute infection" (17). Is amputation of a healthy body part because it may (in less than 1% of cases) cause a future medical problem justified in any case? It seems that all medical arguments strain the limits of rationality.

Another argument that is overlooked is the matter of the individual's right to his own body. Does a parent have the right to authorize the amputation of a normal, functioning body part of a child? If so, then what does that say about amputating other body parts? The first maxim of medical practice is "First, do no harm." Is a doctor who performs circumcisions following this rule of conduct?

In conclusion, there appear to be significant differences between the information sheet provided by the hospital and current knowledge. Specious pro-circumcision arguments are included while significant anti-circumcision arguments are omitted entirely. In addition, since people are likely to interpret data differently about this topic, I suggest that you include more references to exact incidences rather than vague general statements like "may lead to," "less common," "great majority," etc. Then parents can more clearly decide for themselves if the potential benefit is worth the risk.

Sincerely,

RONALD GOLDMAN
Note: In 1995 the same information sheet was being distributed to expectant parents.

NOTES

1. Wiswell, T., "Declining Frequency of Circumcision: Implications for Changes in the Absolute Incidence and Male to Female Sex Ratio of Urinary Tract Infections in Early Infancy," *Pediatrics* 79 (March 1987): 338-342.
2. Altschul, M., "Larger Numbers Needed," *Pediatrics* 80 (November 1987): 763.
3. Cunningham, N., "Circumcision and Urinary Tract Infections." Letter to the editor, *Pediatrics* 77 (February 1986): 267.
4. Kaplan, G., "Complications of Circumcision." *Urologic Clinics of North America* 10 (August 1983): 543-549.

5. Gee, W. & Ansell, J., "Neonatal Circumcision: A Ten Year Overview with Comparison of the Gomco Clamp and the Plastibell Device," *Pediatrics* 58 (1976): 824-827.

6. Wright, J., "Non-Therapeutic Circumcision," *Medical Journal of Australia* 1 (May 27, 1967): 1086.

7. Kaplan, G., "Circumcision: An Overview," *Current Problems in Pediatrics* 7 (March 1977): 23-24.

8. Gairdner, D., "The Fate of the Foreskin," *British Medical Journal* 2 (Dec. 24, 1949): 1434-1435.

9. Mofenson, H. & Greensher, J., "Penile Trauma in Boys," *Medical Aspects of Human Sexuality* 9 (August 1975): 71.

10. Wright, "Non-Therapeutic Circumcision," 1083.

11. Editorial, *Journal of the American Medical Association* 224 (June 4, 1973): 1414.

12. Thomas, A., Reply to a Query, *Medical Aspects of Human Sexuality* 10 (August 1976): 74.

13. Masters, M. & Johnson, V., "Orgasm, Anatomy of the Female," *The Encyclopedia of Sexual Behavior*. (New York: Jason Aronson, 1973), 789.

14. Robertson, W., Comments, *Medical Aspects of Human Sexuality* 8 (January, 1974): 48.

15. Falliers, C., Letter to the editor, *Journal of the American Medical Association* 214 (December 21, 1970): 2194.

16. Tardiff, P., Interview for video medical report by Dean Edell, MD (1984), KGO, San Francisco, CA.

17. Wiswell, T., "Decreased Incidence of Urinary Tract Infections in Circumcised Male Infants." *Pediatrics* 75 (May 1985): 903.

Appendix B

Questionnaire

1. Are you circumcised?
2. Do you feel well-informed about circumcision?
   If not, what aspect(s) are you curious about?

3. Do you have any sons?   Are they circumcised?
   How did you make this decision?

4. If you were to have a son now, would you have him
   circumcised?
   On what grounds would you make this decision?

5. Have you ever seen a circumcision?
   Check if applicable: _____ in person _____ on video
6. My feeling about being circumcised is
   ___ I wish that I were not circumcised
   ___ I do not care that I was circumcised
   ___ I'm glad that I was circumcised
   ___ I'm not circumcised
7. Does the foreskin have any purpose(s)?
   ___ yes ___ no ___ don't know
   If yes, state the purpose(s).

8. About how many square inches is the adult foreskin?
   Guess if you do not know.

Appendix C

Personal Account of FGM

PATIENTS IN ARMS
(ACTIVISTS REFORMING MEDICAL STANDARDS)

Carla Miller, Founder/Director
7480 Gravois, Dittmer, MO 63023
Phone/Fax: (314)274-ARMS

My own nightmare and fight for justice began 14 years ago when I woke up in excruciating pain from what a gynecologic surgeon had told me would be a minor 20-minute operation to repair a hernia (which was asymptomatic and possibly non-existent). He had performed instead a two-hour operation I never consented to *and never would have consented to*. He had cut out my introitus and lengthwise wedge section of my posterior vaginal wall and perineal floor, them sewed me completely shut from my coccyx to my pubic bone. Until I found the doctor who opened my vagina a year later, I could not discharge my menstrual flow, have intercourse, or feel comfortable anywhere except in a bathtub of hot water.

The several other doctors who examined me told me my problems were in my head. They falsified my medical records, told me I needed counseling, and refused to treat me. I realize now that they saw I had been severely mutilated, recognized obvious medical malpractice, didn't want to be involved, and put me off until the two-year statute of limitations had expired.

I finally found a gynecologist who acknowledged that my vagina was completely closed. He said it was the worst case of genital mutilation he had ever seen. In another two-hour operation, he removed massive scar tissue and created a new vaginal space.

But my vulva was still displaced and disconnected from the base of my vagina. My new vaginal orifice was just a slit in my perineal skin, above and behind the arch of my pubic bone. And I was in constant severe pain.

This doctor referred me to Dr. Marshall [a fictitious name for a well-known researcher and physician] with whom he had worked. I told Dr. Marshall that if I pushed my displaced vulvar tissue back behind my pubic bone and around my vaginal orifice, I got instant relief and still had about 95 percent of my ability to experience sexual sensation. Dr. Marshall led me to believe that my vulva, in its entirety, could be pulled back to its original position around my vaginal orifice. Both of these doctors told me they had examined and repaired hundreds of such mutilations. Dr. Marshall said he had seen only three or four as severe as mine.

Dr. Marshall instructed this second surgeon to perform my third operation. This "repair" made my surgically displaced vulva *appear* normal but cut out almost all of my erogenous tissue, severed my sex nerves, robbed me of 95 percent of my ability to experience sexual sensation, left me in chronic pain, turned me into someone no one would want to be, and altered my life and the lives of those closest and dearest to me forever.

I'd have rather been gang raped.

I assumed I was the victim of botched surgery. But I later read in Dr. Marshall's records that *his specific written instructions* were to *separate* my minor labia from my major labia. If he had told me this is what they were going to do, I would have refused. Dr. Marshall *knew* I would never have consented. *And he didn't tell me.*

I've seen almost 20 other doctors since then in my desperation to get help. But I never got help. One doctor, a plastic surgeon, rammed his finger in and out of me and said, "A penis will fit." Another, who described my closed vagina and displaced reconfigured vulva as "grossly anatomically normal," jabbed me in the clitoris and said, "Live with it!"

A psychiatrist I saw said, "First, I want to apologize for all that these medical doctors have done to you. I find this absolutely horrifying. Don't ever let anyone convince you that you have psychiatric problems, because you don't. I compare your trauma to that of a rape victim."

A psychologist who specializes in sexual trauma told me, "You've been sexually abused. It just happens to have been done by doctors."

In early July, 1994, 13 years after I first saw him, Dr. Marshall contacted me about arranging a meeting to discuss my complaints against him. I agreed but told him clearly that it would be just to talk and that *I did not want him to examine me again*. My husband and I met with Dr. Marshall on July 19, 1994. During that meeting, which I audiotaped (with his permission), Dr. Marshall told me he would need "three to four days" to examine me "to check for variance in the surgical result from day to day," even though I had told him I did not want him to examine me again. The Missouri State Board of Registration for the Healing Arts encouraged me, *illegally*, to submit to the four-day pelvic examination Dr. Marshall *illegally* proposed—illegally because *every member of the Board was aware that the eminent Dr. Marshall **had not been licensed to practice medicine in Missouri since January 31, 1994.***

This is typical of the way I've been treated during my four-year run-around with the Missouri State Board of Registration for the Healing Arts, whose "mission is to protect the rights of the citizens of the state." The details of my ongoing ordeal with that organization will be thoroughly documented, along with the rest of my story, at a later date.

During these past 14 years, I've talked with numerous other women with stories similar to mine. I realize now that there are *thousands*, perhaps even millions, of women in this country who have been mutilated by their doctors. One nurse told me, "They do this to women all the time; they just don't tell them about it." One woman told me that she had *18* operations in an unsuccessful attempt to repair her original surgery. One woman's stitches keep falling apart. One has to stand to urinate. Another has to wear diapers. Another can't keep her feces out of her vagina. Doctors performing "repair" operations on several of one surgeon's victims have found hearts and his initials carved on their insides.

Many of these women now live as virtual recluses. I've wondered how many have committed suicide.

I want this surgical destruction of genitals and lives to stop. I cannot live—I cannot die in peace—knowing that doctors are doing to others what they did to me and are getting away with it—without doing everything I can to stop it.

I founded PATIENTS IN ARMS to provide emotional support for victims of this deliberate, premeditated, intentional surgical mutilation of patients by their doctors; to document the physical and psychological damage and suffering it causes; to expose the greed, power lust, contempt, arrogance, indifference, hatred of women and pathological compulsion of the doctors who do it; to expose the collusion/conspiracy between state medical boards and doctors that covers it up and helps perpetuate it; to force state medical boards to do their job by immediately investigating complaints about it and taking swift, firm action against it; to forewarn and forearm the general public by making them aware of it; to help enact laws against it; and to *severely* punish doctors who continue to do it.

I want to know *why* doctors mutilate women. I want to know *why* they mutilate male babies. *I want to know what compels mutilators to mutilate.* It's not just money.

I want to know if the percentage of doctors who cut genitals is higher among doctors whose own genitals have been cut. Is male infant circumcision at the bottom of all this cutting? **Is it?**

I would especially like to contact other women who have been patients of Dr. Marshall, and women who have consulted him about surgical "repair."

I welcome calls, correspondence, questions and comments from anyone who has been the victim of obstetrical or gynecological mutilation or any other kind of mutilation, malpractice, conspiracy or fraud, *including the amputation and trafficking of infant male foreskins.*

I care. I understand. I'll listen. I'll help in any way I can.

Appendix D

Jews and the Circumcision Debate

National Jewish publications have acknowledged a growing debate in the Jewish community about circumcision. Though it is not well known, some Jews do not circumcise their sons. If some Jews can question the ancient ritual of circumcision, then surely Americans can reevaluate the advisability of circumcision as a relatively recent cultural practice.

I hope that the review of American circumcision practice is independent of religious considerations. In particular, I encourage those individuals and groups who may take a position on the issue to do so regardless of how their position may be received by Jews. Though concern for the feelings of Jews is appropriate, Jewish discomfort with this issue is inevitable. However, it is also possible that increased Jewish awareness of the American circumcision debate will encourage more Jews to question the practice. In any case, avoiding discomfort in ourselves or others has served only to perpetuate circumcision.

Although some who are opposed to circumcision may not want to exclude Jewish infants from their concerns, it is preferable if the Jewish community addresses ritual circumcision internally. Those who are not Jews cannot know what it is like to be subject to the kinds of emotional stresses and cultural pressures that Jews must confront when considering the circumcision issue. In addition, like all cultural groups, Jews will be more likely to listen to other Jews rather than to "outsiders." With circumcision of Jewish infants accounting for only about 4 percent of all American infant circumcisions, there are plenty of other Americans to educate.

On the other hand, the Jewish community has a considerable role to play in the national circumcision dialogue. That role, I believe, is to act and speak responsibly. I am concerned that a small but vocal minority of Jews may use reckless charges of anti-Semitism to respond to arguments against circumcision. Thoughtful questioning of circumcision is not anti-Semitic because Jews are also questioning the practice. Furthermore, it is possible to question the actions of a person or group without being categorically opposed to the person or group. In fact, questioning an action that causes harm is more likely to be motivated by concern rather than ill will. I believe that most Jews will not stereotype those opposed to circumcision and impugn their motivation.

Jews have long-held repressed feelings about circumcision. The growing circumcision debate will certainly stir them. In my view, the proper response for Jews is to support each other as we air these feelings within the Jewish community. Of course, those Jews who oppose circumcision may also contribute to the national discussion, while Jews who support circumcision may be perceived as having a religious or ethnic bias.

Those interested in further information and discussion on Jewish circumcision practice may wish to refer to my other book *Questioning Circumcision: A Jewish Perspective.*

Appendix E

Research Considerations

Bias

Research on the psychological effects of circumcision presents a varied set of potential difficulties. Some of them are typical for human subject research, and some are unique to the topic. One of the problems of doing research on circumcision is the usual one of bias. This affects both researcher and subject. The experimenter can hardly claim to be a disinterested observer. Circumcision arouses strong feelings. Some of the current medical research advocating circumcision could be viewed as evidence of the significant impact experimenter bias can have on methodology, results, and conclusions. Perhaps one way of minimizing this bias is for the researcher to examine it in advance. This precaution is suggested not only for researchers, but for those who review work on this subject. Designing the test so that those doing the testing do not know the subjects' circumcision status will also reduce the effects of bias.

Those who may have a bias in support of circumcision include those who are circumcised, have friends or colleagues who are circumcised, practice circumcision, have circumcised sons, know little about circumcision and its effects, and belong to groups who practice circumcision. Those who may have a bias against circumcision may be more likely to be intact or regretful of their own circumcision, be foreign born, have intact friends, colleagues, and sons, and be more knowledgeable about circumcision.

Personal Interview

With proper conditions, interviewing can be a particularly useful and effective way to obtain sensitive material that would otherwise be unavailable, although finding willing participants may be a problem. It is important that the interviewer be understanding and empathetic with the subject to encourage trust. Few people are comfortable talking about circumcision. A hint of judgment, negative response, or discomfort on the part of the interviewer will make disclosure less likely.

A reluctance to disclose may be misinterpreted as a negative response to the question. Therefore, positive responses should be considered particularly significant. If the subject is distressed about the topic, being presented with an opportunity to share confidentially a concealed feeling with an interested listener or to have a possible positive effect on others could provide additional motivation to disclose.

Group Study

When a control group of intact males is studied, it should be matched as closely as possible with the experimental circumcised group. Using American subjects for the intact group, rather than using European subjects, would reduce the effect of demographic and cultural variables on the results. A worthwhile approach might be administering standardized psychological tests and researcher-designed questionnaires to a large group of circumcised men and comparing the results to those from a similar group of intact men. Correlations related to circumcision status could generate hypotheses for further investigation.

Testing a group of violent offenders for circumcision status presents the obvious problem that the large majority of adult males are circumcised. A circumcision rate of 80 or even 90 percent in the group may not be significant. However, if a higher percentage of offenders are circumcised, a connection between circumcision status and violent behavior could be inferred.

Other Approaches

Longitudinal studies of infants and older children might yield very valuable results. However, such studies would be time-consuming and expensive. In addition, since circumcision is the parents' choice, infant subjects could obviously not be assigned at random. Parental attitude toward circumcision might also be related to other parental attitudes that would have an impact on the psychological development of the child, making it hard to isolate the effects of circumcision alone. Parental education and social class might also be intervening variables.

A case study approach is still another method that might reveal some hidden effects of circumcision on infants. It could also suggest the need for further research on larger numbers of subjects. By carefully observing the behavioral responses of a select number of circumcised and intact males, an investigator could help to confirm anecdotal reports that intact male children are more outgoing or responsive. Quantitative and qualitative observations could include both behavioral and physiological variables. As with longitudinal studies, there may be parental factors to consider.

The application of projective tests with circumcised and intact men could yield some interesting results. However, the researcher should consider that these tests may be more vulnerable to criticism from skeptics due to their weaker empirical foundation. Because of the controversial nature of circumcision, researchers should keep in mind the lower credibility of this method.

Certain kinds of laboratory experiments might be useful in identifying possible effects of circumcision on behavior. Circumcised and intact men could participate in a controlled situation, for instance, possibly connected with trust or anger, to test differences between groups.

Participant observation of infants would present the task of gaining access to them in hospitals or homes. Participant observation of adults also has obvious difficulties, particularly when researchers are seeking to link adults' sexual behavior and response to circumcision status. Perhaps a laboratory approach is a feasible option. In either case, the presence of an observer (or camera) might affect behavior.

Prospective studies on infants would have the highest validity if the subjects of control and experimental groups did not experience any other perinatal trauma, birth complications, mother-infant separation, or drug exposure. Otherwise, the presence of these potentially confounding variables should be noted. Breast- or bottle-feeding may also affect results of certain studies.

Potential Research Topics Concerning Effects of Circumcision

To test the possible effects of circumcision, it would be helpful to conduct a number of physiological and psychological tests on male infants, children, and adults (including, in all cases, an intact control group).

Infants: physiological, neurological, and neurochemical changes, immune response, behavioral response (e.g., startle response, irritability, period of alertness and sleep), temperament, excessive crying, attachment, withdrawal, mother-infant interaction, pain response

Older children and/or adults: physiological changes (hormonal, cardiovascular, pupil size, eye movement, electrodermal activity, and facial muscle activity with electromyograph) in response to circumcision-related stimuli, neurological (including magnetic resonance imaging scans of the brain to measure hippocampal volume, see Bremner et al., "MRI-Based Measurement of Hippocampal Volume") and neurochemical changes, blood pressure and respiratory response to electrical stimulation

health problems, immune response, stress response, pain response, arousal level, emotional response, sexual response, sexual response to viewing sexual images containing violence and/or pain, sexual behavior, sadomasochistic behavior, sexual dysfunction, impotence, attitudes (e.g., toward women, female sexuality, rape, pain, parents, infants and children, emotion, authority), body image, self-esteem, shame

history of intimate relationships, relationship satisfaction, social prejudice, conformity, jealousy, loneliness, competitiveness, altruism, trust, empathy, depression, passivity, sensation seeking, ethical behavior, social behavior, attention deficit hyperactivity disorder, aggressiveness, withdrawal, effects of circumcision on parents and circumcisers, circumcision rate after viewing circumcision video

Social studies: violent behavior, criminal behavior, domestic violence, rape, child abuse (victims and perpetrators), child sexual abuse, suicide, sudden infant death syndrome (SIDS), theft, marital status, divorce rate, unnecessary surgery, unprotected sexual behavior

Concluding Thoughts

Investigation of the psychological and social impact of circumcision opens an exciting, valuable new area to researchers. Because much is unknown, experimental designs and the interpretation of results will need to be carefully evaluated. A negative result does not necessarily mean that circumcision has no impact. Instead, there may be limitations in the methodology and the interpretation of data, as has been the case with previous research on infant abilities.

The attitudes of individuals about circumcision can change quickly because of the impact of new information. With widespread exposure to subsequent media reports on circumcision, peoples' attitudes can change to the extent that previous attitude assessments will become outdated. However, greater public awareness of the issue will increase the pool of people willing to participate in certain studies on circumcision.

To date, it has been difficult to obtain adequate funding for research on circumcision effects. However, as the social climate about circumcision changes, interest and available resources will grow. *In the meantime, useful information about the practice can be obtained from studies on other topics by simply including circumcision status as part of the data to be collected.*

The Circumcision Resource Center is interested in assisting researchers and receiving results of their studies.

Glossary

Acute. Of short or sharp course, not chronic.

Affect (noun, accent on first syllable). Feeling, emotion, mood.

Anesthesia. General or local insensibility induced by drugs before surgery and other painful procedures.

Anesthetic. A substance that produces anesthesia.

Carcinoma. Cancer.

Cardiorespiratory. Of or affecting the heart and breathing system.

Chronic. Describes a state which persists over a long period of time or permanently.

Cognitive. Of or pertaining to the process of thinking, encompassing perception, consciousness, learning, and memory.

Contraindicated. Inadvisable.

Correlation. The degree to which two measurements are related. A correlation may not be used to infer causality. ("Association" and "connection" are used similarly.)

Cortisol. Hormone released into the blood in response to stress.

Defense mechanisms. In psychoanalytic theory, unconscious means to deny, falsify, or distort reality.

Denial. A defense mechanism involving refusal to acknowledge certain aspects of reality.

Dissociation. Segregation or "splitting off" from consciousness of any group of mental processes associated with trauma.

Empirical. Based on observation and experiment.

Episiotomy. A surgical incision into the vagina during childbirth.

Etiology. Cause or origin of a disease.

Foreskin. A retractable fold of skin that covers the glans.

Frenum (frenulum). A web of skin on the underside of the glans which helps to hold the foreskin forward to cover the glans.

Glans. The rounded head of the penis.

Hemorrhage. Excessive bleeding.

Hippocampus. A brain structure implicated in emotions and memory.

Hysterectomy. Surgical removal of the uterus.

Indication. A symptom or particular circumstance that shows the advisability or necessity of a specific medical treatment or procedure.

Learned helplessness. An inability to act, acquired by being placed in a situation where no action can help.

Meatotomy. Surgical enlargement of the urinary opening.

Meatus. Opening.

Neonate. Newborn infant.

Neurobiological. Of or pertaining to the anatomy and physiology of the nervous system.

Neurochemical. Of or pertaining to the chemistry of the nervous system, e.g. hormones.

Pathological. Of or pertaining to any deviation from a healthy, normal, or efficient condition.

Perinatal. Occurring during birth or pertaining to the phase surrounding the time of birth.

Phimosis. Nonretractable foreskin after puberty.

Phobia. An anxiety disorder characterized by an intense fear of a specific object or situation. The individual may realize that the fear is irrational but be unable to control it. He or she thus avoids the object or situation.

Prepuce. Foreskin.

Psychobiological. Of or pertaining to the study of the interactions between the body and behavior, especially as exhibited in the nervous system.

Prenatal. Previous to birth or to giving birth.

Projection. The process of attributing to another the ideas or impulses that belong to oneself. A defense mechanism.

Rationalization. The psychoanalytic defense mechanism in which acceptable "reasons" are invented for unacceptable attitudes, beliefs, feelings, and behavior.

Repression. A defense mechanism by which distressing or disagreeable ideas, memories, feelings, or impulses are kept out of conscious awareness.

Sequela (plural: sequelae). A chronic abnormal condition resulting from a previous disease or medical procedure.

Sulcus. The groove around the penis where the glans joins the penile shaft.

Transcutaneous. By way of or through the skin.

Resources

ORGANIZATIONS (send SASE for general information)

**Circumcision Resource
Center** (CRC)
P.O. Box 232
Boston, MA 02133
Tel/Fax: (617) 523-0088
Ronald Goldman, Ph.D.
Information and resources.

**National Organization to Halt
the Abuse and Routine
Mutilation of Males**
(NOHARMM)
P.O. Box 460795
San Francisco, CA 94146
Tel/Fax: (415) 826-9351
Tim Hammond
Activist organization for men.

**National Organization of
Restoring Men** (NORM)
3205 Northwood Dr., #209
Concord, CA 94520-4506
Tel: (510) 827-4077
Fax: (510) 827-4119
R. Wayne Griffiths, M.S.
Support groups on foreskin
restoration.

**Uncircumcising Information
and Resources Center**
(UNCIRC)
P.O. Box 52138
Pacific Grove, CA 93950
Tel/Fax: (408) 375-4326
Jim Bigelow, Ph.D.
Information on foreskin
restoration.

**National Organization of
Circumcision Information
Resource Centers** (NOCIRC)
National Office
P.O. Box 2512
San Anselmo, CA 94979-2512
Tel: (415) 488-9883
Fax: (415) 488-9660
Marilyn Milos, R.N.
Information and resources.

Peaceful Beginnings
13020 Homestead Court
Anchorage, AK 99516
Tel: (907) 345-4813
Rosemary Romberg
Information on circumcision.

**Circumcision Information
Network**
3865 Duncan Place
Palo Alto, CA 94306
Tel: (415) 493-2429
Rich Angell
The Guardian Angell
Newsletter and CompuBulletin
on the Internet.

Lightfoot Associates
5051 N. Sabino Canyon Rd.
#1246
Tucson, AZ 85750
Tel: (520) 529-2029
Fax: (520) 529-9411
Hanny Lightfoot-Klein, M.A.
Information on female genital
mutilation.

Women's International
Network (WIN)
187 Grant St.
Lexington, MA 02173
Tel: (617) 862-9431
Fran Hosken
Information on female genital
mutilation.

Nurses for the Rights
of the Child
369 Montezuma #354
Santa Fe, NM 87501
Tel: (505) 989-7377
Betty Katz Sperlich, R.N.
Information for nurses.

Doctors Opposing
Circumcision
2442 NW Market St., S-42
Seattle, WA 98107
George Denniston, M.D.
Information for physicians.

BOOKS/PUBLICATIONS

Awakenings: A Preliminary
Poll of Circumcised Men
Tim Hammond, 1994
See NOHARMM

Circumcision: The Rest of the
Story, Peggy O'Mara, ed., 1993
Mothering, P.O. Box 1690
Santa Fe, NM 87504

Circumcision: What Every
Parent Should Know
Anne Briggs, 1985
Birth and Parenting
Publications, P.O. Box 128
North Garden, VA 22959

Circumcision: What It Does
Billy Ray Boyd, 1990
C. Olsen, P.O. Box 5100
Santa Cruz, CA 95063

Deeper into Circumcision
John A. Erickson, ed., 1996
John A. Erickson
1664 Beach Blvd. #216
Biloxi, MS 39531

Say No to Circumcision!
Thomas Ritter, M.D. & George
Denniston, M.D., 1996
See CRC or NOCIRC

The Joy of Being a Boy
Elizabeth Noble with Leo
Sorger, M.D., 1994
New Life Images
448 Pleasant Lake Ave.
Harwich, MA 02645

The Joy of Uncircumcising!
Jim Bigelow, Ph.D., 1995
See CRC or UNCIRC

Circumcision: An American
Health Fallacy
Edward Wallerstein, 1980
Springer Publishing, New York
(out of print)

Circumcision: The Painful
Dilemma
Rosemary Romberg, 1985
Bergin & Garvey, S. Hadley,
MA (out of print)

Notes

Introduction: Controversial Questions

[1] Herrera, A., Letter to the Editor, *Pediatrics* 71 (1983): 670.
[2] National Center for Health Statistics, telephone conversation with author, 1995. Rate is for 1993.
[3] Wallerstein, E., "Circumcision: The Uniquely American Medial Enigma," *Urologica Clinics of North America* 12 (February 1985): 123-32.

Chapter 1 Infant Development and Response to Circumcision

[1] Quinn, S., "The Competence of Babies," *The Atlantic Monthly* (January 1982): 54-62.
[2] Spock, B., *The Common Sense Book of Baby and Child Care* (New York: Duell, Sloan, and Pearce, 1946), 146-7.
[3] Hill, S. & Smith, J., "Neonatal Responsiveness as a Function of Maternal Contact and Obstetrical Drugs," *Perceptual and Motor Skills* 58 (1984): 859-66; Brackbill, Y., McManus, K., & Woodward, L., *Medication in Maternity: Infant Exposure and Maternal Information* (Ann Arbor: University of Michigan Press, 1985).
[4] Sepkoski, C. et al.,"The Effects of Maternal Epidural Anesthesia on Neonatal Behavior during the First Month," *Developmental Medicine and Child Neurology* 34 (1992): 1072-80; Brackbill, Y., "Obstetrical Medication and Infant Behavior," in J. Osofsky, ed., *Handbook of Infant Development* (New York: Wiley & Sons, 1979); Jacobson, B. et al., "Obstetric Pain Medication and Eventual Adult Amphetamine Addition in Offspring," *Acta Obstetricia et Gynecologica Scandinavica* 67 (1988): 677-82; Jacobson, B. et al., "Opiate Addition in Adult Offspring through Possible Imprinting after Obstetrical Treatment," *British Medical Journal* 301 (1990): 1067-70.
[5] Bower, T., *The Rational Infant* (New York: Freeman, 1989), 14.
[6] Benedict, R., "Swaddling in Eastern Europe," in I. Al-Issa and W. Dennis, eds., *Cross Cultural Studies of Behavior* (New York: Holt, Rinehart and Winston, 1970), 239.
[7] Stern, D., *The Interpersonal World of the Infant* (New York: Basic Books, 1985), 66.

[8] Montagu, A., *Touching: The Human Significance of the Skin* (New York: Harper & Row, 1971); Solkoff, N. & Matuszak, D., "Tactile Stimulation and Behavioral Development among Low-Birthweight Infants," *Child Psychiatry and Human Development* 6 (1975): 33-7; Field, T., "Alleviating Stress in Newborn Infants in the Intensive Care Unit," *Clinics in Perinatology* 17 (1990): 1-9; Shanberg, S. et al., "Touch: A Biological Regulator of Growth and Development in the Neonate," *Verhaltenstherapie* 3 (Suppl. 1, 1993): 15.

[9] Montagu, *Touching*, 334.

[10] Crudden, C., "Reactions of Newborn Infants to Thermal Stimuli under Constant Tactual Conditions," *Journal of Experimental Psychology* 20 (1937): 350-70.

[11] Werner, L. & Rubel, E., eds., *Developmental Psychoacoustics* (Washington, DC: American Psychological Association, 1992).

[12] Simner, M., "Newborn's Response to the Cry of Another Infant," *Developmental Psychology* 5 (1971): 136-50; Sagi, A. & Hoffman, M., "Empathetic Distress in the Newborn," *Developmental Psychology* 12 (1976): 175-6; Martin, G., & Clark, R., "Distress Crying in Neonates: Species and Peer Specificity," *Developmental Psychology* 18 (1982): 3-9.

[13] Cooper, R., & Aslin, R., "Preference for Infant-Directed Speech in the First Month after Birth," *Child Development* 61 (1990): 1584-95; Clarkson, M. & Berg, W., "Cardiac Orienting and Vowel Discrimination in Newborns: Crucial Stimulus Parameters," *Child Development* 48 (1983): 1666-70.

[14] DeCasper, A. & Fifer, W., "Of Human Bonding: Newborns Prefer Their Mothers' Voices," *Science* 208 (1980): 1174-6.

[15] Verny, T. *The Secret Life of the Unborn Child* (New York: Dell Publishing, 1981), 31.

[16] Slater, A. & Findlay, J., "Binocular Fixation in the Newborn Baby," *Journal of Experimental Child Psychology* 20 (1975): 248-73; Van Hof-Van Duin, J. & G. Mohn., "The Development of Visual Acuity in Normal Fullterm and Preterm Infants," *Vision Research* 26 (1986): 909-16.

[17] Banks, M., "The Development of Visual Accommodation during Early Infancy," *Child Development* 51 (1980): 646-66.

[18] Slater, A. et al., "Pattern Preferences at Birth and Their Interaction with Habituation-Induced Novelty Preferences," *Journal of Experimental Child Psychology* 39 (1985): 37-54; Fantz, R., "Pattern Vision in Newborn Infants," *Science* 140 (1963): 296-7; Slater, A., Rose, D., & Morison, V., "Newborn Infants' Perception of Similarities and Differences between Two- and Three Dimensional Stimuli," *British Journal of Developmental Psychology* 2 (1984): 287-94.

[19] Allik, J. & Valsiner, J., "Visual Development in Ontogenesis: Some Reevaluations," *Advances in Child Development and Behavior* 15 (1980): 2-48.

[20] Goren, C., Sarty, M., & Wu, P., "Visual Following and Pattern Discrimination of Facelike Stimuli by Newborn Infants," *Pediatrics* 56 (1975): 544-9; Vinter, A., De Nobili, G., & Pellegrinetti, G., "Auditory-Visual Coordination: Does It Imply an External World for the Newborn?" *Cahiers de Psychologie Cognitive* 4 (1984): 309-21; Castillo, M & Butterworth, G., "Neonatal Localization of a Sound in Visual Space," *Perception* 10 (1981): 331-8.

[21] Steiner, J., "Human Facial Expressions in Response to Taste and Smell Stimulation," *Advances in Child Development and Behavior* 13 (1979): 257-95.

[22] MacFarlane, A., "Olfaction in the Development of Social Preferences in the Human Neonate," in R. Porter & M. O'Connor, eds., *Parent-Infant Interactions*, Ciba Foundation Symposium 33 (1975): 103-117.

[23] Steiner, J., "Human Facial Expressions in Response to Taste and Smell Stimulation," in H. Reese & L. Lipsitt, eds., *Advances in Child Development and Behavior* 13 (1979): 257-95.

[24] Desor, J., Maller, O., & Andrews, K., "Ingestive Responses of Newborns to Salty, Sour, and Bitter Stimuli," *Journal of Comparative and Physiological Psychology* 89 (1975): 966-70.

[25] Prechtl, H. & O'Brien, M., "Behavioral States of the Fullterm Newborn," in P. Stratton, ed., *Psychobiology of the Newborn* (New York: Wiley, 1982), 52-73.

[26] Hofsten, C. Von, "Eye-Hand Coordination in the Newborn," *Developmental Psychology* 18 (1982): 450-61; Bower, *The Rational Infant*, 15; Butterworth, G. & Hopkins, B., "Hand-Mouth Coordination in the Newborn Baby," *British Journal of Developmental Psychology* 6 (1988): 303-14.

[27] Thelen, E. & Cooke, D., "Relationship between Newborn Stepping and Later Walking: A New Interpretation," *Developmental Medicine and Child Neurology* 29 (1987): 380-93.

[28] Righard, L. & Alade, M., "Effect of Delivery Room Routines on Success of First Breast-Feed," *The Lancet* 336 (1990): 1105-7.

[29] Robertson, S., "Intrinsic Temporal Patterning in the Spontaneous Movement of Awake Neonates," *Child Development* 53 (1982): 1016-21.

[30] Condon, W. & Sander, L., "Synchrony Demonstrated between Movements of the Neonate and Adult Speech," *Child Development* 45 (1974): 456-62.

[31] Trevarthen, C., "The Psychobiology of Speech Development," *Neuroscience Research Progress Bulletin* 12 (1974): 570-85.

[32] Bower, T., Boughton, J., & Moore, M., "Infant Responses to Approaching Objects: An Indicator of Response to Distal Variables," *Perception and Psychophysics* 9 (1970): 193-6.

[33] Johnson, W. et al., "Maternal Perception of Infant Emotion from Birth through 18 Months," *Infant Behavior and Development* 5 (1982): 313-22;

Eisenberg, R. & Marmarou, A., "Behavioral Reactions of Newborns to Speech-Like Sounds and Their Implications for Developmental Studies," *Infant Mental Health Journal* 2 (1981): 129-38.

[34] Bennett, S., "Infant-Caretaker Interactions," *Journal of the American Academy of Child Psychiatry* 10 (1971): 321-35; Papousek, H. & Papousek, M., "Mothering and the Cognitive Head-Start: Psychobiological Considerations," Chapter 4 in H. Schaffer, ed., *Studies in Mother-Infant Interaction* (London: Academic Press, 1977).

[35] Wasz-Hockert, O., Lind, J., & Vuorenkoski, V., "The Infant Cry: A Spectrographic and Auditory Analysis," *Clinical Developmental Medicine* 2 (1968): 9-42; Michelsson, K. et al, "Sound Spectrographic Cry Analysis in Neonate Diagnostics: An Evaluative Study," *Journal of Phonetics* 10 (1982): 79-88; Lester, B. & Boukydis, C., eds., *Infant Crying: Theoretical and Research Perspectives* (New York: Plenum, 1985); Zeskind, P. et al., "Adult Perceptions of Pain and Hunger Cries: A Synchrony of Arousal," *Child Development* 56 (1985): 549-54.

[36] Hunt, J. & Uzgiris, I., "Cathexis from Recognitive Familiarity: An Exploratory Study," (paper presented at the American Psychological Association Convention, Los Angeles, 1964); Siqueland, E. & Lipsett, L., "Conditioned Head-Turning in Human Newborns," *Journal of Experimental Child Psychology* 3 (1966): 356-76; Moon, C. & Fifer, W., "Syllables as Signals for 2-Day-Old Infants," *Infant Behavior and Development* 13 (1990): 377-390.

[37] DeCasper, A. & Carstens, A., "Contingencies of Stimulation: Effects on Learning and Emotion in Neonates," *Infant Behavior and Development* 4 (1981): 19-35.

[38] DeCasper, A. & Prescott, P., "Human Newborns' Perception of Male Voices: Preference, Discrimination, and Reinforcing Value," *Developmental Psychobiology* 17 (1984): 481-91.

[39] Bushnell, I., Sai, F., & Mullin, J., "Neonatal Recognition of the Mother's Face," *British Journal of Developmental Psychology* 7 (1989): 3-15; Cassell, Z. & Sander, L., "Neonatal Recognition Processes and Attachment: The Masking Experiment" (paper presented to the Society for Research in Child Development, Denver, 1975).

[40] Meltzoff, A. & Moore, M., "Newborn Infants Imitate Adult Facial Gestures," *Child Development* 54 (1983): 702-9; Field, T. et al., "Discrimination and Imitation of Facial Expressions by Neonates," *Science* 218 (1982): 179-81.

[41] Klaus, M. & Klaus, P., *The Amazing Newborn* (New York: Addison-Wesley, 1985), 87.

[42] Lipsett, L. & Kaye, H., "Conditioned Sucking in the Human Newborn," *Psychonomic Science* 1 (1964): 29-30; Blass, E., Ganchrow, J., &

Steiner, J., "Classical Conditioning in Newborn Humans 2-48 Hours of Age," *Infant Behavior and Development* 7 (1984): 223-5.
[43] Bower, *The Rational Infant*, 151.
[44] Ibid., 145.
[45] Decasper, A. & Spence, M., "Prenatal Maternal Speech Influences Human Newborn's Auditory Preferences," (paper presented at 3rd Biennial International Conference on Infant Studies, Austin, TX, 1982); Hepper, P., "An Examination of Fetal Learning before and after Birth," *Irish Journal of Psychology* 12 (1991): 95-107.
[46] Berlyne, D., "Curiosity and Exploration," *Science* 153 (1966): 25-33; Slater, A., Morison, V., & Rose, D., "Locus of Habituation in the Human Newborn," *Perception* 12 (1983): 593-8; Brody, L., Zelazo, P., & Chaika, H., "Habituation-Dishabituation to Speech in the Neonate," *Developmental Psychology* 20 (1984): 114-9.
[47] Meltzoff, A. & Borton, R., "Intermodal Matching by Human Neonates," *Nature* 282 (1979): 403-4.
[48] Anand, K. & Hickey, P., "Pain and Its Effects in the Human Neonate and Fetus," *New England Journal of Medicine* 317 (1987): 1326.
[49] Brazelton, T., *Doctor and Child* (New York: Delacorte Press, 1976), 31; Ostwald, P. & Peltzman, P., "The Cry of the Human Infant," *Scientific American* 230 (1974): 85.
[50] Owens, M., & Todt, E., "Pain in Infancy: Neonatal Reaction to a Heel Lance," *Pain* 20 (1984): 77-86; Craig, K. et al., "Pain in the Preterm Neonate: Behavioral and Physiological Indices," *Pain* 52 (1993): 287-99.
[51] Craig, K., Hadjistavropoulos, H., & Grunau, R., "A Comparison of Two Measures of Facial Activity during Pain in the Newborn Child," *Journal of Pediatric Psychology* 19 (1994): 305-18; Grunau, R., Johnston, C., & Craig, K., "Neonatal Facial and Cry Responses to Invasive and Non-Invasive Procedures," *Pain* 42 (1990): 295-305.
[52] Grunau, R. & Craig, K., "Pain Expression in Neonates: Facial Action and Cry," *Pain* 28 (1987): 395-410; Markessinis, J., *The First Week of Life* (Princeton, NJ: Edcom Systems, 1971), 23; Sherman, M. & Sherman, I., "Sensori-Motor Responses in Infants," *Journal of Comparative Psychology* 5 (1925): 53-68.
[53] Gunnar, M. et al., "Adrenocortical Activity and Behavioral Distress in Human Newborns," *Developmental Psychobiology* 21 (1988): 297-310; Malone, S., Gunnar, M., & Fisch, R., "Adrenocortical and Behavioral Responses to Limb Restraint in Human Neonates," *Developmental Psychobiology* 18 (1985): 435-46.
[54] Ryan, C. & Finer, N., "Changing Attitudes and Practices Regarding Local Analgesia for Newborn Circumcision," *Pediatrics* 94 (1994): 232.

[55] Howard, C., Howard, F., & Weitzman, M., "Acetaminophen Analgesis in Neonatal Circumcision: The Effect on Pain," *Pediatrics* 93 (1994): 645.

[56] Benini, F. et al., "Topical Anesthesia during Circumcision in Newborn Infants," *Journal of the American Medical Association* 270 (1993): 850-3.

[57] Gunnar, M. et al., "Coping with Aversive Stimulation in the Neonatal Period: Quiet Sleep and Plasma Cortisol Levels during Recovery from Circumcision," *Child Development* 56 (1985): 824-34.

[58] Williamson, P. & Williamson, M., "Physiologic Stress Reduction by a Local Anesthetic during Newborn Circumcision," *Pediatrics* 71 (1983): 40.

[59] Stang, H. et al., "Local Anesthesia for Neonatal Circumcision," *Journal of the American Medical Association* 259 (1988): 1510.

[60] Porter, F., Miller, R., & Marshall, R., "Neonatal Pain Cries: Effect of Circumcision on Acoustic Features and Perceived Urgency," *Child Development* 57 (1986): 790.

[61] Zeskind, P., & Marshall, T., "The Relation between Variations in Pitch and Maternal Perceptions of Infant Crying," *Child Development* 59 (1988): 193-6.

[62] Connelly, K., Shropshire, L., & Salzberg, A., "Gastric Rupture Associated with Prolonged Crying in a Newborn Undergoing Circumcision," *Clinical Pediatrics* 31 (1992): 560-1.

[63] Gunnar, M., Fisch, R., & Malone, S., "The Effects of a Pacifying Stimulus on Behavioral and Adrenocortical Responses to Circumcision in the Newborn," *Journal of the American Academy of Child Psychiatry* 23 (1984): 34-8.

[64] Milos, M., "Infant Circumcision: 'What I Wish I Had Known,'" *The Truth Seeker* (July/August 1989): 3.

[65] Ryan & Finer, "Changing Attitudes and Practices," 230-3.

[66] Stang et al., "Local Anesthesia for Neonatal Circumcision," 1507-11.

[67] Rabinowitz, R. & Hulbert, W., "Newborn Circumcision Should Not Be Performed without Anesthesia," *Birth* 22 (1995): 45-6.

[68] Schechter, N., "The Undertreatment of Pain in Children: An Overview," *Pediatric Clinics of North America* 36 (1989): 781-94.

[69] Paige, K., "The Ritual of Circumcision," *Human Nature* (May 1978): 42; Anders, T. & Chalemian, R., "The Effects of Circumcision on Sleep-Wake States in Human Neonates," *Psychosomatic Medicine* 36 (1974): 174-9; Brackbill, Y., "Continuous Stimulation and Arousal Level in Infancy: Effects of Stimulus Intensity and Stress," *Child Development* 46 (1975): 364-9.

[70] Marshall, R. et al., "Circumcision: II. Effects upon Mother-Infant Interaction," *Early Human Development* 7 (1982): 367-74.

[71] Howard, C., Howard, F., & Weitzman, M., "Acetaminophen Analgesis in Neonatal Circumcision: The Effect on Pain," *Pediatrics* 93 (1994): 641-6.

[72] Dixon, S. et al., "Behavioral Effects of Circumcision with and without Anesthesia," *Journal of Development and Behavioral Pediatrics* 5 (1984): 246-50.

[73] American Academy of Pediatrics, "Report of the Task Force on Circumcision," *Pediatrics* 84 (1989): 388-91.

[74] Richards, M., Bernal, J., & Brackbill, Y., "Early Behavioral Differences: Gender or Circumcision?" *Developmental Psychobiology* 9 (1976): 89-95.

[75] Marshall, R. et al., "Circumcision: I. Effects upon Newborn Behavior," *Infant Behavior and Development* 3 (1980): 1-14.

[76] Telephone conversation with author, 1994.

[77] Anand & Hickey, "Pain and Its Effects," 1325.

[78] Taddio, A. et al., "The Use of Lidocaine-Prilocaine Cream for Vaccination Pain in Infants," *Journal of Pediatrics* 124 (1994): 643-8; Taddio, A. et al., "Effect of Neonatal Circumcision on Pain Responses during Vaccination of Boys," *The Lancet* 345 (1995): 291-2.

[79] Chamberlain, D., introduction to *Babies Remember Birth* (New York: Ballantine, 1988), xv.

[80] Marchbanks, H., quoted in R. Romberg, *Circumcision: The Painful Dilemma* (South Hadley, MA: Bergin & Garvey, 1985), 133.

[81] Spock, B., letter to the editor, *Moneysworth*, 29 March 1976, 12.

[82] Quoted in Romberg, *Circumcision: The Painful Dilemma*, 321.

[03] Leboyer, F., letter to R. Romberg, in Romberg, *Circumcision: The Painful Dilemma*, vii.

[84] Ibid., 325.

Chapter 2 Why Parents and Physicians Choose to Circumcise Infants

[1] Morgan, W., "The Rape of the Phallus," *Journal of the American Medical Association* 193 (1965): 223.

[2] Lilienfeld, A. & Graham, S., "Validity of Determining Circumcision Status by Questionnaire as Related to Epidemiological Studies of Cancer of the Cervix," *Journal of the National Cancer Institute* 21 (1958): 715.

[3] Terris, M. & Oalmann, A., "Carcinoma of the Cervix," *Journal of the American Medical Association* 174 (1960): 1847-51.

[4] Schlossberger, N., Turner, R., & Irwin, C., "Early Adolescent Knowledge and Attitudes about Circumcision: Methods and Implications for Research," *Journal of Adolescent Health* 13 (1992): 293-7.

[5] Wiswell, T., Smith, F., & Bass, J., "Decreased Incidence of Urinary Tract Infections in Circumcised Male Infants," *Pediatrics* 75 (1985): 901-3; Wiswell, T. et al., "Declining Frequency of Circumcision: Implications for Changes in the Absolute Incidence and Male to Female Sex Ratio of

Urinary Tract Infection in Early Infancy," *Pediatrics* 79 (1987): 338-42.

6 American Academy of Pediatrics, "Task Force on Circumcision," 389.

7 Altschul, M., "Cultural Bias and the Urinary Tract Infection (UTI) Circumcision Controversy," *The Truth Seeker*, July/August 1989, 43-5.

8 Wiswell, Smith, & Bass, "Decreased Incidence," 901-3; Wiswell et al., "Declining Frequency," 338-42.

9 Kaplan, G., "Complications of Circumcision," *Urological Clinics of North America* 10 (1983): 543-9; Gee, W. & Ansell, J., "Neonatal Circumcision: A Ten Year Overview with Comparison of the Gomco Clamp and the Plastibell Device," *Pediatrics* 58 (1976): 824-7.

10 Kaweblum, Y. et al., "Circumcision Using the Mogen Clamp," *Clinical Pediatrics* 23 (1984): 679-82.

11 Ritter, T., *Say No To Circumcision* (Aptos, CA: Hourglass, 1992): 12-1; Richards, Bernal, & Brackbill, "Early Behavioral Differences," 89-95.

12 Denniston, G., "First, Do No Harm," *The Truth Seeker,* July/August 1989, 35-8.

13 Wiswell et al., "Declining Frequency," 338-42.

14 American Academy of Pediatrics, "Task Force on Circumcision," 389.

15 American Academy of Pediatrics, *Newborns: Care of the Uncircumcised Penis* (pamphlet for parents), Elk Grove Village, IL: author, 1992.

16 Wallerstein, E., *Circumcision: An American Health Fallacy* (New York: Springer Publishing, 1980), 128.

17 Spock, B. *The Common Sense Book of Baby and Child Care* (New York: Duell, Sloan, and Pearce, 1946), 18; Spock, B. & Rothenberg, M., *Dr. Spock's Baby and Child Care* (New York: Pocket Books, 1992), 227.

18 Eland, J. & Anderson, J., "The Experience of Pain in Children," in A. Jacox, ed., *Pain: A Source Book for Nurses and Other Health Professionals* (Boston: Little, Brown, 1977), 453-73; Schechter, N., "The Undertreatment of Pain in Children: An Overview," *Pediatric Clinics of North America* 36 (1989): 781-94.

19 Butler, N., "How to Raise Professional Awareness of the Need for Adequate Pain Relief for Infants," *Birth* 15 (March 1988): 39.

20 Schechter, N., "The Undertreatment of Pain in Children: An Overview," *Pediatric Clinics of North America* 36 (1989): 781-94

21 Tilney, F. & Rosett, J., "The Value of Brain Lipoids as an Index of Brain Development," *Bulletin of the Neurological Institute of NY* 1 (1931): 28-71; Katz, J., "The Question of Circumcision," *International Surgery* 62 (1977): 490-2.

22 Schechter, "Undertreatment of Pain," 781-94.

23 Yaster, M., "Pain Relief," *Pediatrics* 95 (1995): 427.

24 Eland, J., "Pain in Children Misunderstood: State of Management 'Shocking,'" *Pediatric News* 20 (August 1986): 1.

[25] Fletcher, A., "Pain in the Neonate" (editorial), *New England Journal of Medicine* 17 (1987): 1347-8.

[26] Anand, K. & Hickey, P., "Pain and Its Effects in the Human Neonate and Fetus," *New England Journal of Medicine* 317 (1987): 1321-9.

[27] Interviewed by author, Boston, 1993.

[28] Kelalis, D., King, L., & Belman, A., *Clinical Pediatric Urology* (Philadelphia: Harcourt Brace Jovanovich, 1992), 2: 1015.

[29] Harris, R., interviewed by Phyllis Levy on WRKO Radio, Boston, April 1995.

[30] NOCIRC Newsletter, Fall 1994, 2

[31] Heath, J., quoted in M. Walsh, "Circumcision: Should You or Shouldn't You?" *The Burlington (VT) Free Press*, 5 February 1995, 1D.

[32] Brazelton, T., *Touchpoints* (New York: Addison-Wesley, 1992), 10-11.

[33] Taylor, J., Lockwood, A., & Taylor, A., "The Prepuce: Specialized Mucosa of the Penis and Its Loss to Circumcision," *British Journal of Urology* 77 (1996): 294.

[34] Ibid., 292, 294.

[35] Ibid., 295.

[36] Ritter, T., *Say No To Circumcision* (Aptos, CA: Hourglass, 1992): 18-1; Morgan, "The Rape of the Phallus," 223-4.

[37] Bigelow, J., *The Joy of Uncircumcising!* (Aptos, CA: Hourglass, 1995), 17; Denniston, G., "Unnecessary Circumcision," *The Female Patient* 17 (1992): 13-14.

[38] Ritter, *Say No To Circumcision*, 11-1.

[39] Gagnon, J. & Simon, W., "The Sexual Scripting of Oral Genital Contacts," *Archives of Sexual Behavior* 16 (1987): 1-25.

[40] Money, J. & Davison, J., "Adult Penile Circumcision: Erotosexual and Cosmetic Sequelae," *Journal of Sex Research* 19 (1983): 291.

[41] Letter to author, 1993.

[42] Telephone conversation with author, 1993.

[43] Milos, M. & Macris, D., "Circumcision: A Medical or a Human Rights Issue?" *Journal of Nurse-Midwifery* 37 (Supplement 1992): 93S.

[44] NOCIRC Newsletter, Fall 1990, 3.

[45] Edell, D., Circumcision report for television news, KGO, San Francisco, 1984.

[46] "The Unkindest Cut of All," letter to the editor, *Playgirl*, July 1979, 108.

[47] Festinger, L. & Carlsmith, J., "Cognitive Consequences of Forced Compliance," *Journal of Abnormal and Social Psychology* 58 (1959): 203-10.

[48] Brehm, J., "Postdecision Changes in the Desirability of Alternatives," *Journal of Abnormal and Social Psychology* 52 (1956): 384-9.

[49] Kumpf, M. & Gotz-Marchand, B., "Reduction of Cognitive Dissonance as a Function of Magnitude of Dissonance, Differentiation, and Self-Esteem," *European Journal of Social Psychology* 3 (1973): 255-70.

50 O Sullivan, C. & Durso, F., "Effect of Schema-Incongruent Information on Memory for Stereotypical Attributes," *Journal of Personality and Social Psychology* 47 (1984): 55-70.

51 Bolande, R., "Ritualistic Surgery: Circumcision and Tonsillectomy," *New England Journal of Medicine* 280 (1969): 591-6; Schwartz, R., Seid, A., & Stool, S., "Tonsillectomy Today: Who Needs It?" *Patient Care* 26 (1992): 173-94.

52 American Academy of Pediatrics, Committee on Fetus and Newborn, *Standards and Recommendations for Hospital Care of Newborn Infants*, 5th ed. (Evanston, IL: AAP, 1971): 71.

53 Stein, M. et al., "Routine Neonatal Circumcision: The Gap between Contemporary Policy and Practice," *Journal of Family Practice* 15 (1982): 47-53.

54 Arkes, H. & Blumer, C., "The Psychology of Sunk Cost," *Organizational Behavior and Human Decision Processes* 35 (1985): 124.

55 Arms, S., *Immaculate Deception* (New York: Bantam Books, 1975), 300.

56 Briggs, A., *Circumcision: What Every Parent Should Know* (Earlysville, VA: Birth and Parenting Publications, 1985), 141.

57 Brown, M. & Brown, C., "Circumcision Decision: Prominence of Social Concerns," *Pediatrics* 80 (1987): 219.

58 Higbee, K., "Fifteen Years of Fear Arousal: Research on Threat Appeals, 1953-1968," *Psychological Bulletin* 72 (1969): 426-44.

59 Koop, C., interviewed on radio station WBZ, Boston, 1993.

60 Dion, S., in S. Werner, television news report on circumcision, WSBK Channel 56, Boston, August 1993.

61 Brodbar-Nemzer, J., Conrad, P., & Tenanbaum, S., "American Circumcision Practices and Social Reality," *Sociology and Social Research* 71 (1987): 275-9.

62 Bolles, R., "Reinforcement, Expectancy, and Learning," *Psychological Review* 79 (1972): 394-409.

63 Ritter, *Say No to Circumcision*, 27-1.

64 Wiswell, T., quoted in B. Lehman, "The Age-Old Question of Circumcision," *Boston Globe,* 22 June 1987, 43.

65 Brodbar-Nemzer, Conrad, & Tenanbaum, "American Circumcision Practices," 275-9.

66 Maslow, A., *Toward a Psychology of Being* (New York: Van Nostrand, 1968), 63.

67 Luchock, J. & McCrosky, J., "The Effect of Quality of Evidence on Attitude Change and Source Credibility," *Southern Speech Communication Journal* 43 (1978): 371-83.

68 Johnson, S. et al., "Teaching the Process of Obtaining Informed Consent to Medical Students," *Academic Medicine* 67 (1992): 598-600.

69 Christensen-Szalanski, J. et al., "Circumcision and Informed Consent: Is More Information Always Better?" *Medical Care* 25 (1987): 856-67.

[70] Herrera, A., letter to the editor, *Pediatrics* 71 (1983): 670.
[71] Harris, R., interviewed by Phyllis Levy on WRKO Radio, Boston, 21 April 1995.
[72] Briggs, *Circumcision: What Every Parent Should Know*, 136.
[73] Ibid., 135.
[74] Patel, H., "The Problem of Routine Circumcision," *Canadian Medical Association Journal* 95 (1966): 578-81.
[75] Gove, P., ed., *Webster's Third International Dictionary* (Springfield, MA: Merriam-Webster, 1981).
[76] Krebs, D., "Empathy and Altruism," *Journal of Personality and Social Psychology* 32 (1975): 1134-46.
[77] Freud, S., *Psychopathology of Everyday Life,* in A. Brill, ed. and trans., *The Basic Writings of Sigmund Freud* (New York: Modern Library, 1938), 101.
[78] Conversation with author, College Park, MD, May 1994.
[79] Romberg, *Circumcision: The Painful Dilemma*, 367.
[80] Raynor, J. & McFarlin, D., "Motivation and the Self-System," in R. Sorrentino & E. Higgins, eds., *Handbook of Motivation and Cognition: Foundations of Social Behavior* (New York: Guilford, 1986); Steele, C. & Liu, T., "Dissonance Processes as Self-Affirmation," *Journal of Personality and Social Psychology* 45 (1983): 5-19.
[81] Walsh, M., "Circumcision: Should You or Shouldn't You?" *Burlington (VT) Free Press,* 5 February 1995, 5D.
[82] Lazarus, R., Kanner, A., & Folkman, S., "Emotions. A Cognitive-Phenomenological Analysis," in R. Plutchick & H. Kellerman, eds., *Emotion: Theory, Research, and Experience,* vol. 1, *Theories of Emotion* (New York: Academic Press, 1980).
[83] Walsh, M., "'Part of Our Tribe': Circumcision and Jewish Identity," *Burlington (VT) Free Press*, 5 February 1995, 1D, 5D; Foley, J., "The Unkindest Cut of All," *Fact,* July 1966, 3; Northrup, C., telephone conversation with author, 1994.
[84] Conversation with author, New York, November 1994.
[85] Felshman, J., "The Foreskin Flap: Is Circumcision Really Worth It?" *Chicago Reader,* 10 March 1995, 17

Chapter 3 Social and Cultural Factors Perpetuating Circumcision in America

[1] Ritter, *Say No to Circumcision*, 16-1.
[2] Wallerstein, *Circumcision: An American Health Fallacy*, 27.
[3] Barker-Benfield, G., *The Horrors of the Half-Known Life* (New York: Harper & Row, 1976); Bella, R. et al., *Habits of the Heart* (New York: Harper & Row, 1985).

[4] Haller, Jr., J. & Haller, R., *The Physician and Sexuality in Victorian America* (New York: Norton, 1974), x.

[5] Graham, S., *A Lecture to Young Men on Chastity, Intended also for the Serious Consideration of Parents and Guardians*, 10th ed. (Boston: C. H. Pierce, 1848).

[6] Kellogg, J., *Plain Facts for Old and Young* (Burlington, IA: F. Segner, 1888).

[7] Editor, "Routine Circumcision at Birth?" *Journal of the American Medical Association* 91 (1928): 201.

[8] Wallerstein, *Circumcision: An American Health Fallacy*, 125, 32-40.

[9] Romberg, *Circumcision: The Painful Dilemma*, 235-76.

[10] Schlereth, T., *Victorian America: Transformations in Everyday Life, 1876-1915* (New York: Harper Collins, 1991), 157.

[11] Ibid., 165.

[12] Barker-Benfield, *The Horrors of the Half-Known Life*, 62.

[13] Romberg, *Circumcision: The Painful Dilemma*, 100-101.

[14] Young, K., "American Conceptions of Infant Development from 1955 to 1984: What the Experts are Telling Parents," *Child Development* 61 (1990): 17-28.

[15] Wallerstein, *Circumcision: An American Health Fallacy*, 28.

[16] Ibid. 30.

[17] Briggs, *Circumcision: What Every Parent Should Know*, 135.

[18] Mansfield, C. & Hueston, W., "Neonatal Circumcision: Associated Factors and Length of Hospital Stay," *Journal of Family Practice* 41 (1995): 370-6.

[19] Letter from an insurance company to inquirer, 1994. Permission has not been granted to disclose names.

[20] Allport, G., *The Nature of Prejudice* (Cambridge, MA: Addison-Wesley, 1954), 29.

[21] Williamson, M & Williamson, P., "Women's Preferences for Penile Circumcision in Sexual Partners," *Journal of Sex Education and Therapy* 14 (1988): 8-12.

[22] Letter to the editor, *Playgirl*, March 1974.

[23] Brown & Brown, "Circumcision Decision," 215-9.

[24] Herrera, A. et al., "Parental Information and Circumcision in Highly Motivated Couples with Higher Education," *Pediatrics* 71 (1983): 234.

[25] Conversation with author, Newton, MA, 1995.

[26] Felshman, "The Foreskin Flap," 17

[27] Wallerstein, *Circumcision: An American Health Fallacy*, 48.

[28] Brodbar-Nemzer, Conrad, & Tenanbaum, "American Circumcision Practices," 275-9.

[29] Wallerstein, *Circumcision: An American Health Fallacy*, 131.

[30] National Center for Health Statistics, telephone conversation with author 1995. Rate is for 1993.

[31] Romberg, R., "Circumcision Feedback" (letter to the editor), *Mensa Bulletin*, May 1993.

[32] Huggins, R., telephone conversation with author, February 1996.

[33] Huggins, M., telephone conversation with author, February 1996.

[34] Asch, S., "Studies of Independence and Conformity: A Minority of One against a Unanimous Majority," *Psychological Monographs* 70 (1956): 9.

[35] Sherif, M., "Conformity-Deviation, Norms, and Group Relations," in I. Berg & B. Bass, eds., *Conformity and Deviation* (New York: Harper, 1961), 59–181; Keating, J. & Brock, T., "Acceptance of Persuasion and the Inhibition of Counterargumentation under Various Distraction Tasks," *Journal of Experimental Social Psychology* 10 (1974): 301-9; Luchins, A., "Focusing on the Object of Judgment in the Social Situation," *Journal of Social Psychology* 60 (1963): 231-49.

[36] Gerald, H., Wilhelm, R., & Conelley, E., "Conformity and Group Size," *Journal of Personality and Social Psychology* 8 (1968): 79-82.

[37] Asch, S., "Effects of Group Pressure upon the Modification and Distortion of Judgements," in H. Guetzkow, ed., *Groups, Leadership, and Men* (Pittsburgh: Carnegie Press, 1951), 177-90.

[38] NOCIRC Newsletter, Spring/Summer 1987, letter to the editor, 3

[39] Latane, B. & Neda, S., "Ten Years of Research on Group Size and Group Helping," *Psychological Bulletin* 89 (1981): 308-24.

[40] Hosken, F., *The Hosken Report* (Lexington, MA: Women's International Network News, 1993), 8, 35; Odujinrin, O., Akitoye, C., & Oyediran, M., "A Study on Female Circumcision in Nigeria," *West Africa Journal of Medicine* 8 (1989): 183-92.

[41] Lightfoot-Klein, H., *Prisoners of Ritual* (Binghamton, NY: Harrington Park Press, 1989), 36.

[42] Lightfoot-Klein, H., *A Woman's Odyssey into Africa: Tracks across a Life* (New York: Haworth Press, 1992), 50.

[43] Hosken, *The Hosken Report*, 33.

[44] Ibid., 35-42.

[45] Lightfoot-Klein, H., "Rites of Purification and Their Effects: Some Psychological Aspects of Female Genital Circumcision and Infibulation in an Afro-Arab Islamic Society," *Journal of Psychology and Human Sexuality* 2 (1989): 79-91.

[46] Ebomoyi, E., "Prevalence of Female Circumcision in Two Nigerian Communities," *Sex Roles* 17 (1987): 139-51.

[47] Lowenstein, L., "Attitudes and Attitude Differences to Female Genital Mutilation in the Sudan: Is There a Change on the Horizon?" *Acta Ethnographica Academiae Scientiarum Hungaricae* 29 (1980): 216-23.

[48] Dirie, M. & Lindmark, G., "Female Circumcision in Somalia and Women's Motives," *Acta Obstetricia Et Gynecologica Scandinavica* 70 (1991): 581-5.

[49] Rushwan, H., "Female Circumcision," *World Health*, April/May 1990, 24.

[50] Lightfoot-Klein, *Prisoners of Ritual*, 42.

[51] Hosken, *The Hosken Report*, 32-39.

[52] Hosken, *The Hosken Report*, 35-42.

[53] Aasen, S., producer, Day One, Report on Female Genital Mutilation, New York: ABC News, 20 September 1993.

[54] Bengston, B. & Baldwin, C., "The International Student: Female Circumcision Issues," *Journal of Multicultural Counseling and Development* 21 (1993): 168-73.

[55] Lightfoot-Klein, *Prisoners of Ritual*, 280.

[56] Toubia, N., "Female Circumcision as a Public Health Issue," *New England Journal of Medicine* 331 (1994) 712-16.

[57] Wallerstein, *Circumcision: An American Health Fallacy*, 48.

[58] Barker-Benfield, *The Horrors of the Half-Known Life*, 120.

[59] Wallerstein, *Circumcision: An American Health Fallacy*, 176; Milos, M., conversation with author, 1993.

[60] Isenberg, S. & Elting, L., "A Guide to Sexual Surgery," *Cosmopolitan* 181 (November 1976): 104-8.

[61] Wallerstein, *Circumcision: An American Health Fallacy*, 183.

[62] Wollman, L., "Female Circumcision," *Journal of the American Society of Psychosomatic Dentistry and Medicine* 20 (1973): 130-1.

[63] Wallerstein, *Circumcision: An American Health Fallacy*, 185.

[64] Wallerstein, *Circumcision: An American Health Fallacy,* 174; Barker-Benfield, *The Horrors of the Half-Known Life*, 89.

[65] Barker-Benfield, *The Horrors of the Half-Known Life*, 121.

[66] Ibid., 131.

[67] Aasen, S., Report on Female Genital Mutilation.

[68] Reich, W., *Character Analysis*, 3rd ed., T. Wolfe, trans., (New York: Farrar, Strauss and Giroux, 1949), 312.

[69] Briggs, *Circumcision: What Every Parent Should Know*, 141.

[70] Kuhn, D., Phelps, E., & Walters, J., "Correlational Reasoning in an Everyday Context," *Journal of Applied Developmental Psychology* 6 (1985): 85-97.

[71] Haire, D. *The Pregnant Patient's Bill of Rights* (pamphlet), Minneapolis, MN: International Childbirth Education Association, 1975.

[72] Davis-Floyd, R., "The Role of Obstetrical Rituals in the Resolution of Cultural Anomaly," *Social Science and Medicine* 31 (1990): 176.

[73] Kleinman, A., *Rethinking Psychiatry* (New York: Free Press, 1988), 144.

[74] Quinn, "The Competence of Babies," 57.

[75] Michael, R. et al., *Sex in America: A Definitive Survey* (Boston: Little Brown, 1994), 11.

[76] Maurer, D. & Maurer, C., *The World of the Newborn* (New York: Basic Books, 1988), 240.

[77] Ibid., 241.
[78] Conversation with author, College Park, MD, May 1994.
[79] Ritter, *Say No To Circumcision*, 26-1.
[80] Taylor, Lockwood, & Taylor, "The Prepuce," 294.
[81] Larsen, G. & Williams, S., "Postneonatal Circumcision: Population Profile," *Pediatrics* 85 (1990): 808-12.
[82] American Academy of Pediatrics, *Newborns: Care of the Uncircumcised Penis.*
[83] Wallerstein, *Circumcision: An American Health Fallacy*, 129.
[84] Goldman, R., letter to the editor, *Pediatrics* 91 (1993): 1215.
[85] Briggs, *Circumcision: What Every Parent Should Know*, 140.
[86] Haas, J. & Shaffir, W., "The Cloak of Competence," in J. Henslin, ed., *Down To Earth Sociology* (New York: Free Press, 1993), 439.
[87] Richardson, L., *The Dynamics of Sex and Gender* (New York: Harper & Row, 1988), 123.
[88] Telephone conversation with author, 1994.
[89] Letter from AAP to author, February 1996.
[90] Schoen, E., "The Relationship between Circumcision and Cancer of the Penis," *Ca—A Cancer Journal for Clinicians* 41 (1991): 306-9.
[91] Holleb, A., editorial comment, *Ca—A Cancer Journal for Clinicians* 39 (1989): 127.
[92] Telephone conversation with author, March 1996.

Chapter 4 Long-Term Psychological Effects of Circumcision: I. Early Trauma and Memory.

[1] Richards, Bernal, & Brackbill, "Early Behavioral Differences," 91.
[2] Ibid., 93.
[3] Marshall, R. et al., "Circumcision: I. Effects upon Newborn Behavior," *Infant Behavior and Development* 3 (1980): 13.
[4] Vaillant, G., "Natural History of Male Psychological Health: II. Some Antecedents of Healthy Adult Adjustment," *Archives of General Psychiatry* 31 (1974): 15-22.
[5] Chamberlain, D., "The Significance of Birth Memories," *Pre and Perinatal Psychology Journal* 2 (1988): 208-226.
[6] Interviewed by author, Boston, MA, 1992.
[7] Freud, S., *Introductory Lectures on Psychoanalysis*, J. Strachey, ed. and trans., (1920; reprint, New York: Norton, 1966), 493.
[8] Ibid., 449.
[9] Rank, O., *The Trauma of Birth*, (1929; reprint, New York: Harper & Row, 1973), 17.

[10] Reber, A., *The Penguin Dictionary of Psychology*, (New York: Penguin Books, 1985), 95.

[11] Leboyer, F., *Birth Without Violence* (New York: Knopf, 1975), 114.

[12] Winnicott, D., "Birth Memories, Birth trauma, and Anxiety," in *Through Paediatrics to Psycho-Analysis*, (New York: Brunner/Mazel, 1992), 183.

[13] McGraw, M., *The Neuromuscular Maturation of the Human Infant* (New York: Columbia University Press, 1943).

[14] Maurer & Maurer, *The World of the Newborn*, 51; Stern, *The Interpersonal World of the Infant*, 23.

[15] Maurer & Maurer, *The World of the Newborn*, 33.

[16] Squire, L., "Mechanisms of Memory," *Science* 232 (1986): 1612-19.

[17] Anand & Hickey, "Pain and Its Effects," 1326.

[18] Ibid., 1325.

[19] Kihlstrom, J., "The Cognitive Unconscious," *Science* 237 (1987): 1445-52; Tulving, E., "How Many Memory Systems Are There?" *American Psychologist* 40 (1985): 385-98.

[20] Menzel, C., "Cognitive Aspects of Foraging in Japanese Monkeys," *Animal Behavior* 41 (1991): 397-402; Gorman, L., Shook, B., & Becker, D., "Traumatic Brain Injury Produces Impairments in Long-Term and Recent Memory," *Brain Research* 614 (1993): 29-36; Rickard, N., Ng, K., & Gibbs, M., "A Nitric Oxide Agonist Stimulates Consolidation of Long-Term Memory in the 1-Day-Old Chick," *Behavioral Neuroscience* 108 (1994) 640-44; Godard, R., "Long-Term Memory of Individual Neighbors in A Migratory Songbird," *Nature* 350 (1991): 228-9; Kandel, E., "Genes, Nerve Cells, and the Remembrance of Things Past," *Journal of Neuropsychiatry and Clinical Neurosciences* 1 (1989): 103-25; Tully, T., Cambiazo, V., & Kruse, L., "Memory through Metamorphosis in Normal and Mutant Drosophila," *Journal of Neuroscience* 14 (1994): 68-74; Errard, C., "Long-Term Memory Involved in Nestmate Recognition in Ants," *Animal Behavior* 48 (1994): 263-71.

[21] Loftus, E. & Loftus, G., "On the Permanence of Stored Information in the Brain," *American Psychologist* 35 (1980): 409-20.

[22] Reich, *Character Analysis*, 343.

[23] Ibid., 364-5.

[24] Anthi, P., "Reconstruction of Preverbal Experiences," *Journal of the American Psychoanalytic Association* 31 (1983): 33-58; Bernstein, A. & Blacher, R., "The Recovery of a Memory from Three Months of Age," *Psychoanalytic Study of the Child* 22 (1967): 156-61; Terr, L., "Children of Chowchilla: A Study of Psychic Trauma," *Psychoanalytic Study of the Child* 34 (1979): 547-623.

[25] Orr, L. & Ray, S., *Rebirthing in the New Age* (Millbrae, CA: Celestial Arts, 1977).

26 Janov, A., *The Primal Scream* (New York: Dell Publishing, 1970); Janov, A., *Imprints: The Lifelong Effects of the Birth Experience* (New York: Coward-McCann, 1983).
27 Weingartner, H., Miller, H., & Murphy, D., "Mood-State Dependent Retrieval of Verbal Associations," *Journal of Abnormal Psychology* 86 (1977): 276-84; Perris, E., Myers, N., & Clifton, R., "Long-Term Memory for a Single Infancy Experience," *Child Development* 61 (1990): 1796-1807; Eich, J., "The Cue Dependent Nature of State Dependent Retrieval," *Memory and Cognition* 8 (1980): 157-68; Bower, G., "Mood and Memory," *American Psychologist* 36 (1981): 129-48.
28 Fodor, N., *The Search for the Beloved* (New York: University Books, 1949).
29 Ibid., 69.
30 Ibid., 19.
31 Janov, A., *The New Primal Scream: Primal Therapy 20 Years On* (Wilmington, DE: Enterprise Publishing, 1991), 63.
32 Ibid., 145-6.
33 Grof, S., *The Adventure of Self-Discovery* (Albany: State University of NY Press, 1988), 4.
34 Ibid., 21.
35 Feher, L., *The Psychology of Birth* (New York: Continuum, 1980), 187-203.
36 Feher, L., "Birth Conditions and the Adult Personality," *Birth Psychology Bulletin* 10 (1989): 108.
37 Verny, *The Secret Life of the Unborn Child*, 101-3.
38 Jacobson, B. et al., "Perinatal Origin of Adult Self Destructive Behavior," *Acta Psychiatrica Scandinavia* 76 (1987): 364-71.
39 Friedman, E. & Neff, R., *Labor and Delivery: Impact on Offspring* (Littleton, MA: PSG Publishing, 1987).
40 Cheek, D., "Maladjustment Patterns Apparently Related to Imprinting at Birth," *American Journal of Clinical Hypnosis* 18 (1975): 75-82; Cheek, D., "Sequential Head and Shoulder Movements Appearing in Age Regression in Hypnosis to Birth," *American Journal of Clinical Hypnosis* 16 (1974): 261-6.
41 Chamberlain, *Babies Remember Birth*, 106.
42 Laibow, R., "Toward a Developmental Nosology Based on Attachment Theory," *Pre and Perinatal Psychology Journal* 3 (1988): 12.
43 Fitzgerald, J., "A Developmental Account of Early Childhood Amnesia," *Journal of Genetic Psychology* 152 (1991): 159-71.
44 Bernstein & Blacher, "Recovery of a Memory," 156-61.
45 Chamberlain, "The Significance of Birth Memories," 208-26.
46 Laibow, R., "Birth Recall: A Clinical Report," *Pre and Perinatal Psychology Journal* 1 (1986): 78-81.

[47] Briggs, *Circumcision: What Every Parent Should Know*, 122.
[48] Chamberlain, D., "Babies Remember Pain," *Pre and Perinatal Psychology Journal* 3 (1989): 304.
[49] Romberg, *Circumcision: The Painful Dilemma*, 82.
[50] Pong, T., "Circumcision: The Pain and the Trauma," autobiographical sketch sent to author, 1993.
[51] Letter to author, 1989; Telephone conversation with author, 1993.
[52] Letter to author, 1989.
[53] Breeding, J., "The Unkindest Cut: Altering Male Genitalia," *Man!*, Winter 1991, 26
[54] Terr, L., "Childhood Traumas: An Outline and Overview," *American Journal of Psychiatry* 148 (1991): 10-20.
[55] American Psychiatric Association, *Diagnostic and Statistical Manual of Mental Disorders*, 4th ed., (Washington, DC: Author, 1994), 424.
[56] Wilson, J., *Trauma, Transformation, and Healing*, (New York: Brunner/Mazel, 1989), 201.
[57] American Psychiatric Association, *Diagnostic and Statistical Manual*, 426.
[58] Terr, L., *Too Scared To Cry* (New York: Harper & Row, 1990); Eth, S. & Pynoos, R., "Developmental Perspective on Psychic Trauma in Childhood," in C. Figley, ed., *Trauma and Its Wake* (New York: Brunner/Mazel, 1985), 36-52.
[59] Green, A., "Dimensions of Psychological Trauma in Abused Children," *Journal of the American Association of Child Psychiatry* 22 (1983): 231-7.
[60] Flannery, R., "From Victim to Survivor: A Stress Management Approach in the Treatment of Learned Helplessness," in B. van der Kolk, *Psychological Trauma* (Washington, DC: American Psychiatric Press, 1987), 217-32; Musty, R., Jordon, M., & Lenox, R., "Criterion for Learned Helplessness in the Rat: A Redefinition," *Pharmacology, Biochemistry and Behavior* 36 (1990): 739-44.
[61] Grof, *The Adventure of Self-Discovery*, 5-6.
[62] Terr, *Too Scared To Cry*, 106.
[63] Cansever, G., "Psychological Effects of Circumcision," *British Journal of Medical Psychology* 38 (1965): 328.
[64] Ozturk, O., "Ritual Circumcision and Castration Anxiety," *Psychiatry* 36 (1973): 55.
[65] Freud, *Introductory Lectures on Psychoanalysis*, 165.
[66] Krupnick, J. & Horowitz, M., "Stress Response Syndromes," *Archives of General Psychiatry* 38 (1981): 428-35.
[67] Lipton, S., "On Psychology of Childhood Tonsillectomy," *Psychoanalytic Study of the Child* 17 (1962): 363-417; Jessner, L., Blom, G., & Waldfogel, S., "Emotional Implications of Tonsillectomy and Adenoidectomy in Children," *Psychoanalytic Study of the Child* 7 (1952): 126-69.

⁶⁸ Levy, D., "Psychic Trauma of Operations in Children," *American Journal of Diseases of Children* 69 (1945): 22.

Chapter 5 Long-Term Psychological Effects of Circumcision:
II. Adult Emotional Impact

¹ Warren, J. et al., "Circumcision of Children," *British Medical Journal* 312 (1996): 377.
² Hammond, T., *Awakenings: A Preliminary Poll of Circumcised Males* (San Francisco: NOHARMM, 1994), A9-A30
³ Terr, L., "What Happens to Early Memories of Trauma?" *Journal of the American Academy of Child and Adolescent Psychiatry* 27 (1988): 96-104; van der Kolk, B., "The Compulsion to Repeat the Trauma: Re-Enactment, Revictimization, and Masochism," *Psychiatric Clinics of North America* 12 (1989): 389-411.
⁴ Terr, "Childhood Traumas," 14.
⁵ Breeding, "The Unkindest Cut," 26.
⁶ Toussieng, P., "Men's Fear of Having Too Small a Penis," *Medical Aspects of Human Sexuality* 11 (1977): 62-70.
⁷ Gagnon, J., ed., *Human Sexuality in Today's World* (Boston: Little, Brown, 1977).
⁸ Toussieng, "Men's Fear," 62-70.
⁹ Jones, D. & Reznikoff, M., "Psychosocial Adjustment to a Mastectomy," *Journal of Nervous and Mental Disease* 177 (1989): 624-31; Margolis, G., Goodman, R., & Rubin, A., "Psychological Effects of Breast-Conserving Cancer Treatment and Mastectomy," *Psychosomatics* 31 (1990): 33-9.
¹⁰ Van Heeringen, C., Van Moffaert, M., & De Cuypere, G., "Depression after Surgery for Breast Cancer: Comparison of Mastectomy and Lumpectomy," *Psychotherapy and Psychosomatics* 51 (1990): 175-9; De Leo, D., Predieri, M., Melodia, C., & Vella, J., "Suicide Attitude in Breast Cancer Patients," *Psychopathology* 24 (1991): 115-9.
¹¹ Hammond, *Awakenings*, 76.
¹² Branden, N., *The Power of Self-Esteem* (Deerfield Beach, FL: Health Communications, 1992), 9.
¹³ Grof, *The Adventure of Self-Discovery*, 83.
¹⁴ Noyes, R., "Depersonalization in Response to Life Threatening Danger," *Comprehensive Psychiatry* 18 (1977): 375-84.
¹⁵ Chu, J. & Dill, D., "Dissociative Symptoms in Relation to Childhood Physical and Sexual Abuse," *American Journal of Psychiatry* 147 (1990): 887-92.

[16] Ciaranello, R., "Neurochemical Aspects of Stress," in N. Garmezy & M. Rutter, eds., *Stress, Coping, and Development* (New York: McGraw Hill, 1983); van der Kolk, B., "The Biological Response to Psychic Trauma: Mechanisms and Treatment of Intrusion and Numbing," *Anxiety Research* 4 (1991): 199-212; Anand, K. & Carr, D., "The Neuroanatomy, Neurophysiology, and Neurochemistry of Pain, Stress, and Analgesia in Newborns and Children," *Pediatric Clinics of North America* 36 (1989): 795-822; Putnam, F., "The Psychophysiological Investigation of Multiple Personality Disorder," *Psychiatric Clinics of North America* 7 (1984): 31-41.

[17] Bower, B., "Child Abuse Leaves Mark on Brain," *Science News* 147 (1995): 340.

[18] Prescott, J., "Genital Pain vs. Genital Pleasure: Why the One and Not the Other?" *The Truth Seeker*, July/August 1989, 15.

[19] Pitman, R., "Animal Models of Compulsive Behavior," *Biological Psychiatry* 26 (1989): 189-98.

[20] Malamuth, N., Heim, M., & Feshback, S., "Sexual Responsiveness of College Students to Rape Depictions: Inhibitory and Disinhibitory Effects," *Journal of Personality and Social Psychology* 38 (1980): 399-408; U.S. Department of Justice, *Attorney General's Commission on Pornography, Final Report* (Washington, DC: July 1986).

[21] Telephone conversation with author, 1994.

[22] American Psychiatric Association, *Diagnostic and Statistical Manual*, 424-429.

[23] Dowling, S., "Dreams and Dreaming in Relation to Trauma in Childhood," *International Journal of Psychoanalysis* 63 (1982): 157-66.

[24] Pong, "Circumcision: The Pain and the Trauma."

[25] Stoller, R., "Consentual Sadomasochistic Perversions," in H. Blum, E. Weinshel, & F. Rodman, eds., *The Psychoanalytic Core* (New York: International Universities Press, 1989).

[26] Leloo, M., "Circumcision: An Unnecessary Trauma?" *Journey,* September 1994, 5.

[27] Verny, *The Secret Life of the Unborn Child*, 119.

[28] Luria, Z., *The Psychology of Human Sexuality* (New York: Wiley, 1979), 332.

[29] Erickson, J., *Making America Safe for Foreskins.* (Biloxi, MS: Author, 1992), 13.

[30] Letter to author, 1996.

[31] Flannery, "From Victim To Survivor," 217.

[32] van der Kolk, "The Compulsion to Repeat the Trauma," 389-411.

[33] American Psychiatric Association, *Diagnostic and Statistical Manual*, 425.

[34] Janov, *Imprints*, 97.

[35] Stinson, J., "Impotence and Adult Circumcision," *Journal of the National Medical Association* 65 (1973): 161.

[36] Feldman, H. et al., "Impotence and Its Medical and Psychosocial Correlates: Results of the Massachusetts Male Aging Study," *Journal of Urology* 151 (1994): 54-61; Cogen, R. & Steinman, W., "Sexual Function and Practice

in Elderly Men of Lower Socioeconomic Status," *Journal of Family Practice* 31 (1990): 162-6.

37 Pietropinto, A., "Male Contributions to Female Sexual Dysfunction," *Medical Aspects of Human Sexuality* 20 (1986): 84.

38 Reiss, I., "Society and Sexuality: A Sociological Theory," in K. McKinney & S. Sprecher, eds., *Human Sexuality: The Societal and Interpersonal Context* (Norwood, NJ: Ablex Publishing, 1989); Rubin, Z. et al., "Self-Disclosure in Dating Couples," *Journal of Marriage and the Family* 42 (1980): 305-18; Reiss, I., "A Sociological Journey into Sexuality," *Journal of Marriage and the Family* 48 (1986): 233-42.

39 Masters, W., Johnson, V., & Kolodny, R., *Sex and Human Loving* (Boston: Little Brown, 1986); Yelsma, P., "Marriage vs. Cohabitation: Couples' Communication Practices and Satisfaction," *Journal of Communication* 36 (1986): 94-107.

40 Klein, C., *Mothers and Sons* (Boston: Houghton Mifflin, 1984), 93.

41 Dosser, D., Balswick, J., & Halverson, C., "Male Inexpressiveness and Relationships," *Journal of Social and Personal Relationships* 3 (1986): 241-58; Ichiyama, M. et al., "Self-Concealment and Correlates of Adjustment in College Students," *Journal of College Student Psychotherapy* 7 (1993): 55-68.

42 Pietropinto, "Male Contributions to Female Sexual Dysfunction," 84.

Chapter 6 Circumcision and the Mother-Child Relationship

1 Bowlby, J., "Grief and Mourning in Infancy and Early Childhood," *Psychoanalytic Study of the Child* 15 (1960): 9-52; Ainsworth, M. & Bell, S., "Mother-Infant Interaction and the Development of Competence," in K. Connelly & J. Bruner, eds., *The Growth of Competence* (New York: Academic Press, 1974); Vandell, D., "Sociability with Peers and Mothers in the First Year," *Developmental Psychology* 16 (1980): 355-61.

2 Arend, R., Gove, F., & Sroufe, L., "Continuity of Individual Adaptation from Infancy to Kindergarten: A Predictive Study of Ego-Resiliency and Curiosity in Preschoolers," *Child Development* 50 (1979): 950-59; Marshall, W., "The Role of Attachments, Intimacy, and Loneliness in the Etiology and Maintenance of Sexual Offending," *Sexual and Marital Therapy* 8 (1993): 109-21; Kestenbaum, R., Farber, E., & Sroufe, L., "Individual Differences in Empathy Among Preschoolers: Relation to Attachment History," *New Directions for Child Development* 44 (1989): 51-64.

3 Donovan, W. & Leavitt, L., "Physiologic Assessment of Mother-Infant Attachment," *Journal of the American Academy of Child Psychiatry* 24 (1985): 65-70; Spangler, G. & Schieche, M., "Biobehavioral Organization

in One-Year-Olds: Quality of Mother-Infant Attachment and Immunological and Adrenocortical Regulation," *Psychologische Beitrage* 36 (1994): 30-5.

[4] Vogt, J. & Levine, S., "Response of Mother and Infant Squirrel Monkeys to Separation and Disturbance," *Physiology and Behavior* 24 (1980): 829-832; Levine, S., Coe, C., & Smotherman, W., "Prolonged Cortisol Elevation in the Infant Squirrel Monkey after Reunion with Mother," *Physiology and Behavior* 20 (1978): 7-10; Levine, S., Wiener, S., & Coe, C., "Temporal and Social Factors Influencing Behavioral and Hormonal Responses to Separation in Mother and Infant Squirrel Monkeys," *Psychoneuroendocrinology* 18 (1993): 297-306; Coe, C. et al., "Mother-Infant Attachment in the Squirrel Monkey: Adrenal Response to Separation," *Behavioral Biology* 22 (1978): 256-63; Hinde, R., "Mother-Infant Separation in Rhesus Monkeys," *Journal of Psychosomatic Research* 16 (1972): 227-8.

[5] Laudenslager, M., "The Psychobiology of Loss: Lessons from Human and Nonhuman Primates," *Journal of Social Issues* 44 (1988): 19-36; Harlow, H., Gluck, J., & Soumi, S., "Generalization of Behavioral Data between Nonhuman and Human Animals," *American Psychologist* 27 (1972): 709-16.

[6] Hollenbeck, A. et al., "Children with Serious Illness: Behavioral Correlates of Separation and Isolation," *Child Psychiatry and Human Development* 11 (1980): 3-11; McCabe, P. & Schneiderman, N., "Psychophysiological Reactions to Stress," in N. Schneiderman & J. Tapp, eds., *Behavioral Medicine: The Biopsychosocial Approach* (Hillsdale, NJ: Erlbaum, 1984).

[7] Youngblade, L. & Belsky, J., "Child Maltreatment, Infant-Parent Attachment Security, and Dysfunctional Peer Relationships in Toddlerhood," *Topics in Early Childhood Special Education* 9 (1989): 1-15; Lyons-Ruth, K. et al., "Infants at Social Risk: Relations among Infant Maltreatment, Maternal Behavior, and Infant Attachment Behavior," *Developmental Psychology* 23 (1987): 223-32; van der Kolk, B., Perry, J., & Herman, J., "Childhood Origins of Self-Destructive Behavior," *American Journal of Psychiatry* 148 (1991): 1665-71; Schmidt, E. & Eldridge, A., "The Attachment Relationship and Child Maltreatment," *Infant Mental Health Journal* 7 (1986): 264-73.

[8] Levy, "Psychic Trauma of Operations in Children," 7-25.

[9] Eth & Pynoos, "Developmental Perspective on Psychic Trauma in Childhood," 36-52.

[10] Marshall et al., "Circumcision: II. Effects upon Mother-Infant Interaction," 367-374; Osofsky, J., "Neonatal Characteristics and Mother-Infant Interaction in Two Observational Situations," *Child Development* 47 (1976): 1138-47.

[11] Calkins, S. & Fox, N., "The Relations among Infant Temperament, Security of Attachment, and Behavioral Inhibition at Twenty-Four Months," *Child Development* 63 (1992): 1456-72.

[12] Bowlby, J., "Attachment Theory and Its Therapeutic Implications," in S.C. Feinstein and P.L. Giovacchini, eds., *Adolescent Psychiatry: Developmental and Clinical Studies* (Chicago: University of Chicago Press, 1978), 5-33; Reite, M. & Capitanio J., "Child Abuse: A Comparative and Psychobiological Perspective" (paper presented at the Conference on Biosocial Perspectives on Child Abuse and Neglect, Social Sciences Research Council, May 1984).

[13] van der Kolk, B., *Psychological Trauma* (Washington, DC: American Psychiatric Press, 1987): 32, 51.

[14] Reite, M. & Capitanio, J., "On the Nature of Social Separation and Social Attachment," in T. Field & M. Reite, eds., *The Psychobiology of Separation and Attachment* (New York: Academic Press, 1985), 223.

[15] Korner, A., Gabby, T., & Kraemer, H., "Relation between Prenatal Maternal Blood Pressure and Infant Irritability," *Early Human Development* 4 (1980): 35-9; Vaughn, B. et al., "Maternal Characteristics Measured Prenatally are Predictive of Ratings of Temperamental 'Difficulty' on the Carey Infant Temperament Questionnaire," *Developmental Psychology* 23 (1987): 152-61.

[16] Simkin, P., "Stress, Pain, and Catecholamines in Labor. II. Stress Associated with Childbirth Events: A Pilot Survey of New Mothers," *Birth Issues in Perinatal Care and Education* 13 (1986): 234-40.

[17] Letter to author, 1991.

[18] Crandon, A., "Maternal Anxiety and Neonatal Wellbeing," *Journal of Psychosomatic Research* 23 (1979): 113-5; McDonald, R., "The Role of Emotional Factors in Obstetrical Complications: A Review," *Psychosomatic Medicine* 30 (1968): 222-37.

[19] Baker, J., Comments at conclusion of presentation by R. Laibow, *Circumcision and Its Relationship to Attachment Impairment,* Second International Symposium on Circumcision, San Francisco, 1991.

[20] Hersher, L., Moore, A., & Richmond, J., "Effect of Post-Partum Separation of Mother and Kid on Maternal Care in the Domestic Goat," *Science* 128 (1958): 1342.

[21] Kennell, J. & Klaus, M., "Early Mother-Infant Contact: Effects on the Mother and the Infant," *Bulletin of the Menninger Clinic* 43 (1979): 69-78; Kennell, J. et al., "Maternal Behavior One Year after Early and Extended Post-Partum Contact," *Developmental Medicine and Child Neurology* 16 (1974): 172-9; Ringler, N. et al., "The Effects of Extra Postpartum Contact and Maternal Speech Patterns on Children's IQ's, Speech and Language Comprehension at Five," *Child Development* 49 (1978): 862-5.

[22] Klein, M. & Stern, L., "Low Birthweight and the Battered Child Syndrome," *American Journal of Diseases of Children* 122 (1971): 15.

[23] Milvich, M., *Circumcision: An American Custom*, Snowmass, CO: Author, 1995, 44.

[24] Howard, Howard, & Weitzman, "Acetaminophen Analgesis in Neonatal Circumcision," 641-6.

[25] Anholm, P., "Breastfeeding: A Preventive Approach to Health Care in Infancy," *Issues in Comprehensive Pediatric Nursing* 9 (1986): 1-10; Temboury, M. et al., "Influence of Breastfeeding on the Infant's Intellectual Development," *Journal of Pediatric Gastroenterology and Nutrition* 18 (1994): 32-6; Fitzsimmons, S. et al., "Immunoglobulin A Subclasses in Infants' Saliva and in Saliva and Milk from Their Mothers," *Journal of Pediatrics* 124 (1994): 566-73; Polluck, J., "Long-Term Associations with Infant Feeding in a Clinically Advantaged Population of Babies," *Developmental Medicine and Child Neurology* 36 (1994): 429-40.

[26] Solter, A., "Why Do Babies Cry?" *Pre and Perinatal Psychology Journal* 10 (1995): 21-43; Emerson, W., "Psychotherapy with Infants and Children," *Pre and Perinatal Psychology Journal* 3 (1989): 190-217.

[27] Hoffman, M., "Developmental Synthesis of Affect and Cognition and Its Implications for Altruistic Motivation," *Developmental Psychology* 11 (1975): 607-22.

[28] Donovan, W., "Maternal Learned Helplessness and Physiologic Response to Infant Crying," *Journal of Personality and Social Psychology* 40 (1981): 919-26; Campbell, S., "Mother-Infant Interaction as a Function of Maternal Ratings of Temperament," *Child Psychiatry and Human Development* 10 (1979): 67-76.

[29] Field, T., "Models for Reactive and Chronic Depression in Infancy," *New Directions for Child Development* 34 (1986): 47-60.

[30] Ainsworth, M. & Wittig, B., "Attachment and Exploratory Behavior of One-Year-Olds in a Strange Situation," in B. Foss, ed., *Determinants of Infant Behavior IV* (London: Methuen, 1969).

[31] Bell, S. & Ainsworth, M., "Infant Crying and Maternal Responsiveness," *Child Development* 43 (1972): 1171-90; Ainsworth, M. et al., *Patterns of Attachment: A Psychological Study of the Strange Situation* (Hillsdale, NJ: Erlbaum, 1978); Beckwith, L. et al., "Caregiver-Infant Interaction and Early Cognitive Development in Preterm Infants," *Child Development* 47 (1976): 576-87.

[32] Izard, C. et al., "Emotional Determinants of Infant-Mother Attachment," *Child Development* 62 (1991): 906-17.

[33] Bell & Ainsworth, "Infant Crying and Maternal Responsiveness," 1171-90.

[34] Devore, I. & Konner, M., "Infancy in a Hunter-Gatherer Life: An Ethological Perspective," in N. White, ed., *Ethology and Psychiatry* (Toronto: University of Toronto Press, 1974).

[35] Ainsworth, M., "Attachment and Child Abuse," in G. Gerbner, C. Ross, & E. Zigler, eds., *Child Abuse: An Agenda for Action* (New York: Oxford University Press, 1980).

[36] Sherrod, K. et al., "Child Health and Maltreatment," *Child Development* 55 (1984): 1174-83; Field, T., "Attachment as Psychobiological Attunement: Being on the Same Wavelength," in T. Field and M. Reite, eds., *The Psychobiology of Attachment and Separation* (Academic Press: Orlando, FL, 1985), 415-54.

[37] Erikson, E., *Childhood and Society* (New York: Norton, 1963), 249.

[38] Laibow, R., "Circumcision and Its Relationship to Attachment Impairment," in *Syllabus of Abstracts*, the Second International Symposium on Circumcision, San Francisco, 1991, 14.

[39] van der Kolk, *Psychological Trauma*, 35.

[40] Hartman, C. & Burgess, A., "Information Processing of Trauma," *Child Abuse and Neglect* 17 (1993): 47-58.

[41] Kennedy, H., "Trauma in Childhood: Signs and Sequelae as Seen in the Analysis of an Adolescent," *Psychoanalytic Study of the Child* 41 (1986): 209-19.

[42] Cansever, "Psychological Effects of Circumcision," 328.

[43] Bigelow, *The Joy of Uncircumcising!*, 116.

[44] Frodi, A. & Lamb, M., "Sex Differences in Responsiveness to Infants: A Developmental Study of Psychophysical and Behavioral Responses," *Child Development* 49 (1978): 1182-8.

[45] O'Mara, P., ed., *Circumcision: The Rest of the Story* (Santa Fe, NM: Mothering, 1993), 75-6.

[46] Telephone conversation with author, 1995.

[47] Friederich, L., letter in O'Mara, *Circumcision: The Rest of the Story*, 79.

[48] Pollack, M., "Jewish Feminist Perspective" (paper presented at the Third International Symposium on Circumcision, College Park, MD, May 1994; Conversation with author, College Park, MD, May 1994.

[49] Interviewed by author, Needham, MA, 1994.

[50] Romberg, *Circumcision: The Painful Dilemma*, 78-84.

[51] Sexty, L., letter in O'Mara, *Circumcision: The Rest of the Story*, 84.

[52] Cohen, N., interviewed by author, Needham, MA, 1994.

[53] Northrup, C., telephone conversation with author, 1994.

[54] Raisbeck, B., "Circumcision: A Wound Which Lasts a Lifetime," *Healing Currents*, 1993, 21.

[55] Dion, J., telephone conversation with author, 1995.

[56] Miller, C., telephone conversation with author, 1995.

[57] Letter to author, 1994.

[58] American Psychiatric Association, *Diagnostic and Statistical Manual*, 424.

[59] Parsons, M., "The Beginning," Ashbury (NJ) Park Press, 3 February 1996, B1.

Chapter 7 The Impact of Circumcision on American Society

[1] Terr, *Too Scared To Cry*, 26, 317.

[2] Ibid., 331.

[3] Feher, "Birth Conditions and the Adult Personality."

[4] Major, B., Sciacchitano, A., & Crocker, J., "In-Group versus Out-Group Comparisons and Self-Esteem," *Personality and Social Psychology Bulletin* 19 (1993): 711-21; Stimson, A., Stimson, J., & Dougherty, W., "Female and Male Sexuality and Self-Esteem," *Journal of Social Psychology* 112 (1980): 157-8.

[5] Allport, *The Nature of Prejudice*, 388.

[6] Nelson, E., Hill-Barlow, D., & Benedict, J., "Addiction versus Intimacy as Related to Sexual Involvement in a Relationship," *Journal of Sex and Marital Therapy* 20 (1994): 35-45; Antonucci, T., Peggs, J., & Marquez, J., "The Relationship between Self-Esteem and Physical Health in a Family Practice Population," *Family Practice Research Journal* 9 (1989): 65-72; Santee, R. & Maslach, C., "To Agree or Not to Agree: Personal Dissent Amid Social Pressure to Conform," *Journal of Personality and Social Psychology* 42 (1982): 690-700; Butler, A., Hokanson, J., & Flynn, H., "A Comparison of Self-Esteem Lability and Low Trait Self-Esteem as Vulnerability Factors for Depression," *Journal of Personality and Social Psychology* 66 (1994): 166-77; Cookson, H., "Personality Variables Associated with Alcohol Use in Young Offenders," *Personality and Individual Differences* 16 (1994): 179-82; Jackson, J. & Cochran, S., "Loneliness and Psychological Distress," *Journal of Psychology* 125 (1991): 257-62.

[7] Robinson, R. & Frank, D., "The Relation between Self-Esteem, Sexual Activity, and Pregnancy," *Adolescence* 29 (1994): 27-35.

[8] Goodman, E., "Targeting the Men Who Prey on Teen-Age Girls," *Boston Globe*, 8 February 1996, 17.

[9] Allport, *The Nature of Prejudice*, 372.

[10] Duff, C. & Wells, K., "Forget Cars, Sports or Sex: Guys Today Want to Talk PCs, *Wall Street Journal*, 28 January 1994, 1.

[11] Ibid., 1.

[12] Rutherford, E. & Mussen, P., "Generosity in Nursery School Boys," *Child Development* 39 (1968): 755-65; Kagan, S. & Masden, M., "Rivalry in Anglo-American and Mexican Children of Two Ages," *Journal of Personality and Social Psychology* 24 (1972): 214-20.

[13] Walsh, A., "Self-Esteem and Sexual Behavior: Exploring Gender Differences," *Sex Roles* 25 (1991): 441-50.

[14] Lightfoot-Klein, *Prisoners of Ritual*, 40-41.

[15] Herman, J., *Trauma and Recovery* (New York: Basic Books, 1992), 52.

[16] Kulka, R., Schlenger, W., & Fairbank, J., *National Vietnam Veteran Readjustment Study*, executive summary (Research Triangle Park, NC: Research Triangle Institute, 1988).

[17] Hite, S., *Women and Love: A Cultural Revolution in Progress* (New York: Knopf, 1987), 804.

[18] Ibid., 459.

[19] Gottman, J., *What Predicts Divorce? The Relationship between Marital Processes and Marital Outcomes* (Hillsdale, NJ: Lawrence Erlbaum Associates, 1994), 6.

[20] Gottman, J. & Levenson, R., "The Social Psychophysiology of Marriage," in P. Noller & M. Fitzpatrick, eds., *Perspectives on Marital Interaction* (Clevedon, England: Multilingual Matters Ltd., 1988), 182-200.

[21] Rubin, J., Provenzano, F., & Luria, Z., "The Eye of the Beholder: Parents' Views on Sex of Newborns," *American Journal of Orthopsychiatry* 44 (1974): 512-9; Clarke-Stewart, K. & Hevey, C., "Longitudinal Relations in Repeated Observations of Mother-Child Interaction from One to Two and One-Half Years," *Developmental Psychology* 17 (1981): 127-45; Messer, S. & Lewis, M., "Social Class and Sex Difference in the Attachment and Play Behavior of the Year-Old Infant," *Merrill-Palmer Quarterly* 18 (1972): 295-306.

[22] See note 16, Chapter 5.

[23] Glover, H. "Emotional Numbing: A Possible Endorphin-Mediated Phenomenon Associated with Post-Traumatic Stress Disorders and Other Allied Psychopathologic States." *Journal of Traumatic Stress* 5 (1992): 643-75.

[24] U.S. Department of Commerce, *Statistical Abstract of the U.S.* (Lanham, MD: Bernan Press, 1994), 55, 103

[25] United Nations, *1993 Demographic Yearbook*, (New York: Author, 1995), 557-9.

[26] Postman, N., *Technopoly: The Surrender of Culture to Technology*, (New York: Knopf, 1992), 105; Foreman, J., "It Helps to Prepare for Surgery," Boston Globe, 29 April 1996, 26.

[27] Ibid., 94.

[28] Mendelsohn, R., *Confessions of a Medical Heretic*, (Chicago: Contemporary Books, 1979), 55.

[29] Ibid., 60.

[30] Manfield & Hueston, "Neonatal Circumcision: Associated Factors," 370-6.

[31] Friedmann, L., *The Psychological Rehabilitation of the Amputee* (Springfield, IL: Charles C. Thomas, 1978), 18-20.

[32] Bhojak, M. & Nathawat, S., "Body Image, Hopelessness and Personality Dimensions in Lower Limb Amputees," *Indian Journal of Psychiatry* 30 (1988): 161-5.

[33] Friedmann, *The Psychological Rehabilitation of the Amputee*, 53-56.

[34] Barker-Benfield, *The Horrors of the Half-Known Life*, 125.

[35] Scully, D. & Bart, P., "A Funny Thing Happened on the Way to the Orifice: Women in Gynecology Textbooks," in J. Huber, ed., *Changing Women in a Changing Society* (Chicago: University of Chicago Press, 1973), 283-8.

[36] Astrachan, A., *How Men Feel: Their Responses to Women's Demands for Equality and Power* (Garden City, NY: Anchor Press/Doubleday, 1986), 272.

[37] Delaney, L., "When To Say 'Wait' When Your Doctor Says 'Cut,'" *Prevention* 43 (September 1991): 44.

[38] Klein, M. et al., "Physicians' Beliefs and Behavior during a Randomized Controlled Trial of Episiotomy: Consequences for Women in Their Care," *Canadian Medical Association Journal* 153 (1995): 769-79; Fernando, B. et al., "Audit of the Relationship between Episiotomy and Risk of Major Perineal Laceration during Childbirth," *British Journal of Clinical Practitioners* 49 (1995): 40-1.

[39] Bickell, N. et al., "Gynecologists' Sex, Clinical Beliefs, and Hysterectomy Rates," *American Journal of Public Health* 84 (1994): 1649-52; Behnegar, A., "Hysterectomy Report," *American Health*, September 1992.

[40] Cowley, G. "The Hunt for a Breast Cancer Gene," *Newsweek*, 6 December 1993, 46-52.

[41] Levin, T., "'Unspeakable Atrocities': The Psycho-Sexual Etiology of Female Genital Mutilation," *Journal of Mind and Behavior* 1 (1980): 197-210.

[42] Sargent, C., "Between Death and Shame: Dimensions of Pain in Bariba Culture," *Social Science and Medicine* 19 (1984): 1299-304.

[43] Gilmore, D., *Manhood in the Making: Cultural Concepts of Masculinity* (New Haven, CT: Yale University Press, 1990), 135.

[44] Schechter, "The Undertreatment of Pain in Children," 781-94.

[45] Brende, J., "Electrodermal Responses in Post-Traumatic Syndromes," *Journal of Nervous and Mental Disease* 170 (1982): 352-61.

[46] Kellaris, J. & Rice, R., "The Influence of Tempo, Loudness, and Gender of Listener on Responses to Music," *Psychology and Marketing* 10 (1993): 15-29; Toney, G. & Weaver, J., "Effects of Gender and Gender Roles Self-Perceptions on Affective Reactions to Rock Music Videos," *Sex Roles* 30 (1994): 567-83; Arnett, J., "The Soundtrack of Recklessness: Musical Preferences and Reckless Behavior among Adolescents," *Journal of Adolescent Research* 7 (1992): 313-31.

[47] Marshall et al., "Circumcision: I. Effects upon Newborn Behavior."

[48] Cansever, "Psychological Effects of Circumcision."

[49] Flannery, "From Victim to Survivor," 217-32.

[50] Peterson, C. & Seligman, M., "Learned Helplessness and Victimization," *Journal of Social Issues* 39 (1983): 103-16.

[51] Alloy, L. & Seligman, M., "On the Cognitive Component of Learned Helplessness and Depression," *The Psychology of Learning and Motivation* 13 (1979): 219-76.

[52] Glenn, N., "Television Watching, Newspaper Reading, and Cohort Differences in Verbal Ability," *Sociology of Education* 67 (1994): 216-30.

[53] Hoffman, M., "Is Altruism Part of Human Nature?" *Journal of Personality and Social Psychology* 40 (1981) 121-37; Sagi & Hoffman, "Empathetic Distress in the Newborn," 175-6.

[54] Summit, R. & Kryso, J., "Sexual Abuse of Children: A Clinical Spectrum," *American Journal of Orthopsychiatry* 48 (1978): 237-51.

[55] Gold, S. et al., "Vicarious Emotional Responses of Macho College Males," *Journal of Interpersonal Violence* 7 (1992): 165-74.

[56] Bryant, B., "An Index of Empathy for Children and Adolescents," *Child Development* 53 (1982): 413-25; Richardson, D., Hammock, G., & Smith, S., "Empathy as a Cogitive Inhibitor of Interpersonal Aggression," *Aggressive Behavior* 20 (1994): 275-89.

[57] Glover, "Emotional Numbing."

[58] Main, M & George, C., "Responses of Abused and Disadvantaged Toddlers to Distress in Agemates: A Study in the Daycare Setting," *Developmental Psychology* 21 (1985): 407-12.

[59] United Nations, *Human Development Report* (New York: Oxford University Press, 1994), 186; Federal Bureau of Investigation, U.S. Department of Justice, *Crime in the United States: Uniform Crime Reports 1993* (Washington, DC, 1994), 4; Maguire, K. & Pastore, A., eds., *Sourcebook of Criminal Justice Statistics, 1994* (Washington, DC: U.S. Department of Justice, Bureau of Justice Statistics, 1995), 231.

[60] Rothbart, M., Ahadi, S., & Hershey, K., "Temperament and Social Behavior in Childhood," *Merrill Palmer Quarterly* 40 (1994): 21-39.

[61] Campbell, S. et al., "Correlates and Predictors of Hyperactivity and Aggression: A Longitudinal Study of Parent-Referred Problem Preschoolers," *Journal of Abnormal Child Psychology* 14 (1986): 217-34.

[62] Kagan, J. & Moss, H., *Birth To Maturity* (New York: Wiley, 1962), 87.

[63] Ibid., 276

[64] Huesmann, L., Eron, L., & Lefkowitz, M., "Stability of Aggression over Time and Generations," *Developmental Psychology* 20 (1984): 1120-34.

[65] Bass, A., "A Touch for Evil," *Boston Globe Magazine*, 7 July 1991, 12.

[66] Carmen, E., Ricker, P., & Mills, T., "Victims of Violence and Psychiatric Illness," *American Journal of Psychiatry* 141 (1984): 378-83.

[67] Widom, C. & Ames, M., "Criminal Consequences of Childhood Sexual Victimization," *Child Abuse and Neglect* 18 (1994): 303-18.

[68] van der Kolk, "The Compulsion to Repeat the Trauma," 389-411.

[69] Raine, A., Brennan, P., & Mednick, S., "Birth Complications Combined with Early Maternal Rejection at Age 1 Predispose to Violent Crime at Age 18 Years," *Archives of General Psychiatry* 51 (1994): 984.

[70] Reiss, Jr., A. & Roth, J., eds., National Research Council, *Understanding and Preventing Violence* (Washington, DC: Jossey-Bass, 1993), 364.

[71] Kandel, E. & Mednick, S., "Perinatal Complications Predict Violent Offending," *Criminology* 29 (1991): 519-29; Mungas, D., "An Empirical Analysis of Specific Syndromes of Violent Behavior," *Journal of Nervous and Mental Disease* 171 (1983): 354-61.

[72] Ulrich, R., "Pain as a Cause of Aggression," *American Zoologist* 6 (1966): 643-62; Berkowitz, L., "Pain and Aggression: Some Findings and Implications," *Motivation and Emotion* 17 (1993): 277-93.

[73] Ditman, J., "Circumcision Plight," letter to the editor, *Mensa Bulletin*, March 1993.

[74] Hammond, *Awakenings*, 76.

[75] Lowenstein, L., "Homicide: A Review of Recent Research (1975-1985)," *Criminologist* 13 (1989): 74-89.

[76] Hsieh, C. & Pugh, M., "Poverty, Income Inequality, and Violent Crime: A Meta-Analysis of Recent Aggregate Data Studies," *Criminal Justice Review* 18 (1993): 182-202.

[77] Giller, B. "All in the Family: Violence in the Jewish Home." *Women & Therapy* 10 (1990): 101-9.

[78] Moss, M., Gidycz, C., & Wisniewski, N., "The Scope of Rape: Incidence and Prevalence of Sexual Aggression and Victimization in a Natural Sample of Higher Education Students," *Journal of Consulting and Clinical Psychology* 55 (1987): 162-70; White, J. & Koss, M., "Courtship Violence: Incidence in a National Sample of Higher Education Student," *Violence and Victims* 6 (1991): 247-56.

[79] Raine, A., Venables, P., & Williams, M., "Autonomic Orienting Responses in 15-Year-Old Male Subjects and Criminal Behavior at Age 24," *American Journal of Psychiatry* 147 (1990): 933-7.

[80] Raine, A. & Venables, P., "Evoked Potential Augmenting-Reducing in Psychopaths and Criminals with Impaired Smooth-Pursuit Eye Movements," *Psychiatry Research* 31 (1990): 85-98.

[81] Glover, "Emotional Numbing."

[82] Maguire & Pastore, *Sourcebook,* 305.

[83] Federal Bureau of Investigation, U.S. Department of Justice, *Crime in the United States: Uniform Crime Reports 1993* (Washington, DC, 1994), 286.

[84] Straus, M., Gelles, R. & Steinmetz, S., *Behind Closed Doors: Violence in the American Family* (Garden City, NY: Anchor/Doubleday, 1980).

[85] White, J. & Koss, M., "Courtship Violence: Incidence in a National Sample of Higher Education Students," *Violence and Victims* 6 (1991): 247-56.

[86] Federal Bureau of Investigation, *Crime in the United States*, 17.

[87] Tellis-Nayak, V. & Donoghue, G., "Conjugal Egalitarianism and Violence across Cultures," *Journal of Comparative Family Studies* 13 (1982): 277-90.

[88] Bicehouse, T. & Hawker, L., "Degrees of Games: An Application to the Understanding of Domestic Violence," *Transactional Analysis Journal* 23 (1993): 195-200; Goody, E., "Why Must Might Be Right? Observations on Sexual Herrshaft," *Quarterly Newsletter of the Laboratory of Comparative Human Cognition* 9 (1987): 55-76.

[89] Stewart, R. & Beatty, M., "Jealousy and Self-Esteem," *Perceptual and Motor Skills* 60 (1985): 153-4; Melamed, T., "Individual Differences in Romantic Jealousy: The Moderating Effect of Relationship Characteristics," *European Journal of Social Psychology* 21 (1991): 455-61.

[90] Laner, M., "Violence or Its Precipitators: Which is More Likely to Be Identified as a Dating Problem?" *Deviant Behavior* 11 (1990): 319-29; Adams, D., "Identifying the Assaultive Husband in Court: You Be the Judge," *Response to the Victimization of Women and Children* 13 (1990): 13-6.

[91] Prince, J. & Arias, I., "The Role of Perceived Control and the Desirability of Control among Abusive and Nonabusive Husbands," *American Journal of Family Therapy* 22 (1994): 126-34; Murphy, C., Meyer, S., & O'Leary, K., "Dependency Characteristics of Partner Assaultive Men," *Journal of Abnormal Psychology* 103 (1994): 729-35.

[92] Else, L., Wonderlich, S., & Beatty, W., "Personality Characteristics of Men Who Physically Abuse Women," *Hospital and Community Psychiatry* 44 (1993): 54-8.

[93] van der Kolk, "The Compulsion to Repeat the Trauma," 389-411.

[94] Hammond, *Awakenings*, 92.

[95] Pong, "Circumcision: The Pain and the Trauma."

[96] Scully, D. & Marolla, J., "'Riding the Bull at Gilley's,'" in J. Henslin, ed., *Down to Earth Sociology* (New York: Free Press, 1993), 53, 58 (all statements of rapists).

[97] Groth, N., *Men Who Rape* (New York: Plenum Press, 1979); Griffin, S., *Rape: The All-American Crime* (Andover, MA: Warner Modular Publications, 1973).

[98] U.S. Senate Committee on the Judiciary, "Violence against Women: The Increase of Rape in America 1990," *Response to the Victimization of Women and Children* 14 (1991): 20-3.

[99] Rapaport, K. & Burkhart, B., "Personality and Attitudinal Correlates of Sexual Coercive College Males," *Journal of Abnormal Personality* 93 (1984): 216-21.

[100] Russell, D., *Rape in Marriage* (New York: Macmillan, 1982).

[101] Malamuth, N. "Rape Proclivity among Males," *Journal of Social Issues* 37 (1981): 138-57.

[102] Russell, D. & Howell, N., "The Prevalence of Rape in the U.S. Revisited," *Signs* 8 (1983): 688-95.

[103] United Nations, *Human Development Report*, 186.

[104] Stolbach, D., *If Someone You Care About Has Been Raped*, pamphlet, Cambridge, MA: Boston Area Rape Crisis Center, 1986, 1.

[105] Morgan, "The Rape of the Phallus," 223-224.

[106] Bass, A., "Domestic Violence: Roots Go Deep," *Boston Globe*, 30 September 1991, 1.

[107] Braswell, L., *Quest for Respect: A Healing Guide for Survivors of Rape* (Ventura, CA: Pathfinder Publishing, 1989), 21.

[108] Ibid., 8, 10, 16, 33.

[109] Hanson, R., "The Psychological Impact of Sexual Assault on Women and Children: A Review," *Annals of Sex Research* 3 (1990): 187-232; Braswell, *Quest for Respect*, 9-11; Rose, D., "'Worse Than Death': Psychodynamics of Rape Victims and the Need for Psychotherapy," *American Journal of Psychiatry* 143 (1986): 817-24.

[110] Mosher, D. & Anderson, R., "Macho Personality, Sexual Aggression and Reactions to Guided Imagery of Realistic Rape," *Journal of Research in Personality* 20 (1986): 77-94.

[111] Reiss, I., "A Sociological Journey into Sexuality," *Journal of Marriage and the Family* 48 (1986): 233-42; Scully, D. & Marolla, J., "Convicted Rapists' Vocabulary of Motive: Excuses and Justifications," *Social Problems* 31 (1984): 530-44.

[112] Sanday, P., "The Socio-Cultural Context of Rape: A Cross-Cultural Study," *Journal of Social Issues* 37 (1981): 5-27.

[113] Alder, C., "An Exploration of Self-Reported Sexually Aggressive Behavior," *Crime and Delinquency* 31 (1985): 306-31.

[114] Scully & Marolla, "'Riding the Bull at Gilley's,'" 46-61.

[115] Kempe, R. & Kempe, C., *The Common Secret: Sexual Abuse of Children and Adolescents* (New York: W.H. Freeman, 1984); Russell, D., "The Incidence and Prevalence of Intrafamilial and Extrafamilial Sexual Abuse of Female Children," *Child Abuse and Neglect* 7 (1983): 133-46.

[116] Wyatt, G., "The Sexual Abuse of Afro-American and White Women in Childhood," *Child Abuse and Neglect* 9 (1985): 507-19.

[117] deMause L., "The Universality of Incest," *Journal of Psychohistory* 19 (1991): 123-64.

[118] Finkelhor, D., *Child Sexual Abuse: New Theory and Research* (New York: Free Press, 1984).

[119] Briere, J. & Runtz, M., "Childhood Sexual Abuse: Long-Term Sequelae and Implications for Psychological Assessment," *Journal of Interpersonal Violence* 8 (1993): 312-30; Glod, C., "Long-Term Consequences of Childhood Physical and Sexual Abuse," *Archives of Psychiatric Nursing* 7 (1993): 163-73.

120 Rowan, A. & Foy, D., "Post-Traumatic Stress Disorder in Child Sexual Abuse: A Literature Review," *Journal of Traumatic Stress* 6 (1993): 3-20; Kiser, L., Ackerman, B., & Brown, E., "Post-Traumatic Stress Disorder in Young Children: A Reaction to Purported Sexual Abuse," *Journal of the American Academy of Child and Adolescent Psychiatry* 27 (1988): 645-9.

121 Green, A., "Dimensions of Psychological Trauma in Abused Children," *Journal of the American Association of Child Psychiatry* 22 (1983): 231-7.

122 Finkelhor, D. & Browne, A., "The Traumatic Impact of Child Sexual Abuse: A Conceptualization," *American Journal of Orthopsychiatry* 55 (1985): 530-41.

123 Koverola, C., "Psychological Effects of Child Sexual Abuse," in A. Heger and S. Emans, *Evaluation of the Sexually Abused Child* (New York: Oxford University Press, 1992), 19; Engel, B., introduction to *The Right to Innocence* (Los Angeles: J.P. Tarcher, 1989), xvi.

124 Finkelhor, D., *A Sourcebook on Child Sexual Abuse: New Theory and Research* (Beverly Hills, CA: Sage, 1986).

125 Bagley, C. & Ramsay, R., "Sexual Abuse in Childhood: Psychosocial Outcomes and Implications for Social Work Practice," *Journal of Social Work and Human Sexuality* 4 (1986): 33-47; Gold, E., "Long-Term Effects of Sexual Victimization in Childhood: An Attributional Approach," *Journal of Consulting and Clinical Psychology* 54 (1986): 471-5.

126 DeYoung, M., *The Sexual Victimization of Children* (Jefferson, NC: McFarland, 1982); Courtois, C., "The Incest Experience and Its Aftermath," *Victimology: An International Journal* 4 (1979): 337-47.

127 Browne, A. & Finkelhor, D., "Impact of Child Sexual Abuse: A Review of the Research," *Psychological Bulletin* 99 (1986): 66-77.

128 Loss, P. & Glancy, E., "Men Who Sexually Abuse Their Children," *Medical Aspects of Human Sexuality* 17 (1983): 328-9.

129 Gillespie, W., "The Psycho-Analytic Theory of Sexual Deviation with Special Reference to Fetishism," in I. Rosen, ed., *The Psychology and Treatment of Sexual Deviation* (New York: Oxford University Press, 1964); Hammer, E. & Glueck, B., Jr., "Psychodynamic Patterns in Sex Offense: A Four-Factor Theory," *Psychiatric Quarterly* 3 (1957): 325-45.

130 Seghorn, T., Prentky, R., & Boucher, R., "Childhood Sexual Abuse in the Lives of Sexually Aggressive Offenders," *Journal of the American Academy of Child and Adolescent Psychiatry* 26 (1987): 262-7.

131 van der Kolk, "The Compulsion to Repeat the Trauma," 389-411.

132 Herman, *Trauma and Recovery*, 49.

133 Maguire, K. & Pastore, A., eds., *Sourcebook of Criminal Justice Statistics, 1993* (Washington, DC: U.S. Department of Justice, Bureau of Justice Statistics, 1994), 391.

[134] Canetto, S., "Gender Issues in the Treatment of Suicidal Individuals," *Death Studies* 18 (1994): 513-27; Smith, D. & Hackathorn, L., "Some Social and Psychological Factors Related to Suicide in Primitive Societies: A Cross-Cultural Comparative Study," *Suicide and Life Threatening Behavior* 12 (1982): 195-211.
[135] National SIDS Resource Center, Information Exchange, Vienna, VA: Author, January, 1990.
[136] Court, C. et al., "Cot Deaths (Global Survey)," *British Medical Journal* 310 (1995): 7.
[137] U.S. Department of Justice, *Criminal Victimization in the U.S., 1992* (Rockville, MD: Bureau of Justice Statistics Clearinghouse, 1994), 3; Federal Bureau of Investigation, *Crime in the United States*, 4.
[138] Sheline, J., Skipper, B., & Broadhead, W., "Risk Factors for Violent Behavior in Elementary School Boys: Have You Hugged Your Child Today?" *American Journal of Public Health* 84 (1994): 661-3.
[139] Gelles, R., "Poverty and Violence toward Children," *American Behavioral Scientist* 35 (1992): 258-74; Hsieh & Pugh, "Poverty, Income Inequality, and Violent Crime;" Gelles, R., "Child Abuse and Violence in Single-Parent Families: Parent Absence and Economic Deprivation," *American Journal of Orthopsychiatry* 59 (1989): 492-501.
[140] Lester, D. & Abe, K., "The Regional Variation of Divorce Rates in Japan and the United States," *Journal of Divorce and Remarriage* 21 (1993): 227-30.

Chapter 8 The Lesson of Circumcision

[1] Stephan, W., Ageyev, V., & Coates-Shrider, L., "On the Relationship between Stereotypes and Prejudice: An International Study," *Personality and Social Psychology Bulletin* 20 (1994): 277-84.
[2] Quinn, "The Competence of Babies," 62.
[3] Chamberlain, "The Significance of Birth Memories," 208-26.
[4] Blurton Jones, N., "Comparative Aspects of Mother-Child Contact," in N. Blurton Jones, ed., *Ethological Studies of Child Behavior* (New York: Cambridge University Press, 1972), 315-28; Fishbein, H., *Evolution, Development, and Children's Learning* (Santa Monica: Goodyear, 1976); Hinde, R., *Towards Understanding Relationships* (London: Academic Press, 1979).
[5] Clarke-Stewart, K., "Infant Day Care: Maligned or Malignant?" *American Psychologist* 44 (1989): 266-73.
[6] Konner, M., "Maternal Care, Infant Behavior, and Development among the !Kung," in R. Lee & I. Devores, eds., *Kalahari Hunter Gathers* (Cambridge, MA: Harvard University Press, 1976), 218-45.

[7] Belsky, J., "Infant Day Care and Socioemotional Development: The United States," *Journal of Child Psychology and Psychiatry and Allied Disciplines* 29 (1988): 397-406.

[8] May, R., *Love and Will* (New York: Norton, 1969), 165.

[9] Erikson, E., *Childhood and Society* (New York: Norton, 1963), 404.

[10] Ganiats, T. et al., "Routine Neonatal Circumcision: A Cost-Utility Analysis," *Medical Decision Making* 11 (1991): 282-93.

[11] Hayward, J. & Varela, F., eds., *Gentle Bridges: Conversations with the Dalai Lama on the Sciences of Mind* (Boston: Shambhala, 1992), 20.

[12] Benini et al., "Topical Anesthesia During Circumcision," 850-3.

[13] Walco, G., Cassidy, R., & Schechter, N., "Pain, Hurt, and Harm: The Ethics of Pain Control in Infants and Children," *New England Journal of Medicine* 331 (1994): 543.

[14] DHHS, Publication NIH 85-23, *Guide for the Care and Use of Laboratory Animals*, 1985.

[15] *Academic American Encyclopedia*, s.v. "Hippocratic Oath," 1993.

[16] Kohlberg, L., *The Psychology of Moral Development* (San Francisco: Harper & Row, 1984), 174.

[17] Romberg, *Circumcision: The Painful Dilemma*, 353.

[18] Milgram, S., "Behavior Study of Obedience," *Journal of Abnormal and Social Psychology* 67 (1963): 371-8.

[19] Milgram, S., "Group Pressure and Action against a Person," *Journal of Abnormal and Social Psychology* 69 (1964): 137-43.

[20] Breslan, N. & Davis, G., "Post-Traumatic Stress Disorder: The Etiologic Specificity of Wartime Stressors," *American Journal of Psychiatry* 144 (1987): 578-83.

[21] Fleiss, P., "Circumcision," letter to the editor, *The Lancet* 345 (1995): 927.

[22] British Medical Association, *Medicine Betrayed* (London: Zed Books, 1992), 33.

[23] Ibid., 35-40.

[24] Bloche, M., *Uruguay's Military Physicians: Cogs in A System of State Terror* (Washington: AAAS, 1987), 40.

[25] Denniston, G., letter to the editor, *The Female Patient* 17 (1992): 10.

[26] Toubia, "Female Circumcision," 712-6.

[27] Kluge, E., "Female Circumcision: When Medical Ethics Confronts Cultural Values," *Canadian Medical Association Journal* 148 (1993): 288-9.

[28] Ibid., 289.

[29] Hansson, R. & Jones, W., "Loneliness, Cooperation, and Conformity among American Undergraduates," *Journal of Social Psychology* 115 (1981): 103-8.

[30] Bagley, C., "Is the Prevalence of Child Sexual Abuse Decreasing? Evidence From a Random Sample of 750 Young Adult Women," *Psychological Reports* 66 (1990): 1037-8.

[31] Burgess, A. & Holmstrom, L., "Adaptive Strategies and Recovery from Rape," *American Journal of Psychiatry* 136 (1979): 1278-82.

[32] Eagly, A. & Telaak, K., "Width of the Latitude of Acceptance as a Determinant of Attitude Change," *Journal of Personal and Social Psychology* 23 (1972): 388-97.

[33] Bochner, S. & Insko, C., "Communicator Discrepancy, Source Credibility, and Influence," *Journal of Personality and Social Psychology* 4 (1966): 614-21.

[34] Freedman, J., "Involvement, Discrepancy, and Change," *Journal of Abnormal and Social Psychology* 64 (1964): 290-5.

Bibliography

Aasen, S., producer. *Day One*, Report on Female Genital Mutilation. New York: ABC News, 20 September 1993.

Adams, D. "Identifying the Assaultive Husband in Court: You Be the Judge." *Response to the Victimization of Women and Children* 13 (1990): 13-6.

Ainsworth, M. "Attachment and Child Abuse." In G. Gerbner, C. Ross, & E. Zigler, eds., *Child Abuse: An Agenda for Action*. New York: Oxford University Press, 1980.

Ainsworth, M. & Bell, S. "Mother-Infant Interaction and the Development of Competence." In K. Connelly & J. Bruner, eds., *The Growth of Competence*. New York: Academic Press, 1974.

Ainsworth, M., Blehar, M., Waters, E., & Wall, S. *Patterns of Attachment: a Psychological Study of the Strange Situation*. Hillsdale, NJ: Erlbaum, 1978.

Ainsworth, M. & Wittig, B. "Attachment and Exploratory Behavior of One-Year-Olds in a Strange Situation." In B. Foss, ed., *Determinants of Infant Behavior IV*. London: Methuen, 1969.

Alder, C. "An Exploration of Self-Reported Sexually Aggressive Behavior." *Crime and Delinquency* 31 (1985): 306-31.

Allik, J. & Valsiner, J. "Visual Development in Ontogenesis: Some Reevaluations." *Advances in Child Development and Behavior* 15 (1980): 2-48.

Alloy, L. & Seligman, M. "On the Cognitive Component of Learned Helplessness and Depression." *The Psychology of Learning and Motivation* 13 (1979): 219-76.

Allport, G. *The Nature of Prejudice*. Cambridge, MA: Addison-Wesley, 1954.

Altschul, M. "Cultural Bias and the Urinary Tract Infection (UTI) Circumcision Controversy." *The Truth Seeker*, July/August 1989, 43-5.

American Academy of Pediatrics, Committee on Fetus and Newborn. *Standards and Recommendations for Hospital Care of Newborn Infants*, 5th ed. Evanston, IL: author, 1971.

American Academy of Pediatrics. "Report of the Task Force on Circumcision." *Pediatrics* 84 (1989): 388-91.

American Academy of Pediatrics. *Newborns: Care of the Uncircumcised Penis*, pamphlet for parents. Elk Grove Village, IL: author, 1992.

American Academy of Pediatrics. *Circumcision: Pros and Cons*, pamphlet for parents. Elk Grove, IL: author, 1995.

American Psychiatric Association. *Diagnostic and Statistical Manual of Mental Disorders*, 4th ed. Washington, DC: author, 1994.

Anand, K. & Carr, D. "The Neuroanatomy, Neurophysiology, and Neurochemistry of Pain, Stress, and Analgesia in Newborns and Children." *Pediatric Clinics of North America* 36 (1989): 795-822.

Anand, K. & Hickey, P. "Pain and Its Effects in the Human Neonate and Fetus." *New England Journal of Medicine* 317 (1987): 1321-9.

Anders, T. & Chalemian, R. "The Effects of Circumcision on Sleep-Wake States in Human Neonates." *Psychosomatic Medicine* 36 (1974): 174-9.

Anholm, P. "Breastfeeding: A Preventive Approach to Health Care in Infancy." *Issues in Comprehensive Pediatric Nursing* 9 (1986): 1-10.

Anthi, P. "Reconstruction of Preverbal Experiences." *Journal of the American Psychoanalytic Association* 31 (1983): 33-58.

Antonucci, T., Peggs, J., & Marquez, J. "The Relationship between Self-Esteem and Physical Health in a Family Practice Population." *Family Practice Research Journal* 9 (1989): 65-72.

Arend, R., Gove, F., & Sroufe, L. "Continuity of Individual Adaptation from Infancy to Kindergarten: A Predictive Study of Ego-Resiliency and Curiosity in Preschoolers." *Child Development* 50 (1979): 950-9.

Arkes, H. & Blumer, C. "The Psychology of Sunk Cost. *Organizational Behavior and Human Decision Processes* 35 (1985): 124.

Arms, S. *Immaculate Deception*. New York: Bantam Books, 1975.

Arnett, J. "The Soundtrack of Recklessness: Musical Preferences and Reckless Behavior among Adolescents." *Journal of Adolescent Research* 7 (1992): 313-31.

Asch, S. "Effects of Group Pressure upon the Modification and Distortion of Judgments." In H. Guetzkow, ed., *Groups, Leadership, and Men*. Pittsburgh: Carnegie Press, 1951, 177-90.

Asch, S. "Studies of Independence and Conformity: A Minority of One against a Unanimous Majority. *Psychological Monographs* 70 (1956): 9.

Astrachan, A. *How Men Feel: Their Responses to Women's Demands for Equality and Power*. Garden City, NY: Anchor Press/Doubleday, 1986.

Bacon, M., Child, I., & Barry, H. "A Cross-Cultural Study of Correlates of Crime." In I. Al-Issa and W. Dennis, eds., *Cross Cultural Studies of Behavior*. New York: Holt, Rinehart and Winston, 1970.

Bagley, C. "Is the Prevalence of Child Sexual Abuse Decreasing? Evidence from a Random Sample of 750 Young Adult Women." *Psychological Reports* 66 (1990): 1037-8.

Bagley, C. & Ramsay, R. "Sexual Abuse in Childhood: Psychosocial Outcomes and Implications for Social Work Practice." *Journal of Social Work and Human Sexuality* 4 (1986): 33-47.

Baker, J. Comments at conclusion of presentation by R. Laibow, *Circumcision and Its Relationship to Attachment Impairment*. Second International Symposium on Circumcision. San Francisco, CA, 1991.

Banks, M. "The Development of Visual Accommodation during Early Infancy." *Child Development* 51 (1980): 646-66.

Barker-Benfield, G. *The Horrors of the Half-Known Life*. New York: Harper & Row, 1976.

Bass, A. "A Touch for Evil." *Boston Globe Magazine*, 7 July 1991, 12.

Bass, A. "Domestic Violence: Roots Go Deep." *Boston Globe*, 30 September 1991, 1.

Beckwith, L., Cohen, S., Kopp, C., Parmelee, A., & Marcy, T. "Caregiver-Infant Interaction and Early Cognitive Development in Preterm Infants." *Child Development* 47 (1976): 576-87.

Behnegar, A. "Hysterectomy Report." *American Health*, September 1992.

Bell, S. & Ainsworth, M. "Infant Crying and Maternal Responsiveness." *Child Development* 43 (1972): 1171-90.

Bella, R., Madsen, R., Sullivan, W., Swidler, A., & Tipton, S. *Habits of the Heart.* New York: Harper & Row, 1985.

Belsky, J. "Child Maltreatment: An Ecological Integration." *American Psychologist* 35 (1980): 320-35.

Belsky, J. "Infant Day Care and Socioemotional Development: The United States." *Journal of Child Psychology and Psychiatry and Allied Disciplines* 29 (1988): 397-406.

Benedict, R. "Swaddling in Eastern Europe." In I. Al-Issa and W. Dennis, eds., *Cross Cultural Studies of Behavior.* New York: Holt, Rinehart and Winston, 1970.

Bengston, B. & Baldwin, C. "The International Student: Female Circumcision Issues." *Journal of Multicultural Counseling and Development* 21 (1993): 168-73.

Benini, F., Johnson, C., Faucher, D., & Aranda, J. "Topical Anesthesia during Circumcision in Newborn Infants." *Journal of the American Medical Association* 270 (1993): 850-3.

Bennett, S. "Infant-Caretaker Interactions." *Journal of the American Academy of Child Psychiatry* 10 (1971): 321-35.

Berkowitz, L. "Pain and Aggression: Some Findings and Implications." *Motivation and Emotion* 17 (1993): 277-93.

Berlyne, D. "Curiosity and Exploration." *Science* 153 (1966): 25-33.

Bernstein, A. & Blacher, R. "The Recovery of a Memory from Three Months of Age." *Psychoanalytic Study of the Child* 22 (1967): 156-61.

Bhojak, M. & Nathawat, S. "Body Image, Hopelessness and Personality Dimensions in Lower Limb Amputees." *Indian Journal of Psychiatry* 30 (1988): 161-5.

Bicehouse, T. & Hawker, L. "Degrees of Games: An Application to the Understanding of Domestic Violence." *Transactional Analysis Journal* 23 (1993): 195-200.

Bickell, N., Earp, J., Garrett, J., & Evans, A. "Gynecologists' Sex, Clinical Beliefs, and Hysterectomy Rates." *American Journal of Public Health* 84 (1994): 1649-52.

Bigelow, J. *The Joy of Uncircumcising!* Aptos, CA: Hourglass, 1995.

Blass, E., Ganchrow, J., & Steiner, J. "Classical Conditioning in Newborn Humans 2-48 Hours of Age." *Infant Behavior and Development* 7 (1984): 223-35.

Bleier, R. "Bias in Biological and Human Sciences: Some Comments." *Signs* 4 (1978): 159-63.

Bloche, M. *Uruguay's Military Physicians: Cogs in a System of State Terror.* Washington: AAAS, 1987.

Blurton Jones, N. "Comparative Aspects of Mother-Child Contact." In N. Blurton Jones, ed., *Ethological Studies of Child Behavior*. New York: Cambridge University Press, 1972, 315-28.

Bochner, S. & Insko, C. "Communicator Discrepancy, Source Credibility, and Influence." *Journal of Personality and Social Psychology* 4 (1966): 614-21.

Bolande, R. "Ritualistic Surgery: Circumcision and Tonsillectomy." *New England Journal of Medicine* 280 (1969): 591-6.

Bolles, R. "Reinforcement, Expectancy, and Learning." *Psychological Review* 79 (1972): 394-409.

Bower, B. "Child Abuse Leaves Mark on Brain." *Science News* 147 (1995): 340.

Bower, G. "Mood and Memory." *American Psychologist* 36 (1981): 129-48.

Bower, T. *The Rational Infant*. New York: Freeman, 1989.

Bower, T., Boughton, J., & Moore, M. "Infant Responses to Approaching Objects: An Indicator of Response to Distal Variables." *Perception and Psychophysics* 9 (1970): 193-6.

Bowlby, J. "Grief and Mourning in Infancy and Early Childhood." *Psychoanalytic Study of the Child* 15 (1960): 9-52.

Bowlby, J. "Attachment Theory and Its Therapeutic Implications." In S.C. Feinstein and P.L. Giovacchini, eds., *Adolescent Psychiatry: Developmental and Clinical Studies*. Chicago: University of Chicago Press, 1978, 5-33

Brackbill, Y. "Continuous Stimulation and Arousal Level in Infancy: Effects of Stimulus Intensity and Stress." *Child Development* 46 (1975): 364-9.

Brackbill, Y. "Obstetrical Medication and Infant Behavior." In J. Osofsky, ed., *Handbook of Infant Development*. New York: Wiley & Sons, 1979.

Brackbill, Y., McManus, K., & Woodward, L. *Medication in Maternity: Infant Exposure and Maternal Information*. Ann Arbor: University of Michigan Press, 1985.

Branden, N. *The Power of Self-Esteem*. Deerfield Beach, FL: Health Communications, 1992.

Braswell, L. *Quest for Respect: A Healing Guide for Survivors of Rape*. Ventura, CA: Pathfinder Publishing, 1989.

Brazelton, T. *Doctor and Child*. New York: Delacorte Press, 1976.

Brazelton, T. *Touchpoints*. New York: Addison-Wesley, 1992.

Breeding, J. "The Unkindest Cut: Altering Male Genitalia." *Man!*, Winter 1991, 25.

Brehm, J. "Postdecision Changes in the Desirability of Alternatives." *Journal of Abnormal and Social Psychology* 52 (1956): 384-9.

Bremner, J., Randall, P., Scott, T., Bronen, R., Seibyl, J., Southwick, S. Delaney, R., McCarthy, G., Charney, D., & Innis, R. "MRI-Based Measurement of Hippocampal Volume in Patients with Combat-Related Posttraumatic Stress Disorder." *American Journal of Psychiatry* 152 (1995): 973-81.

Brende, J. "Electrodermal Responses in Post-Traumatic Syndromes." *Journal of Nervous and Mental Disease* 170 (1982): 352-361.

Breslan, N. & Davis, G. "Post-Traumatic Stress Disorder: The Etiologic Specificity of Wartime Stressors. *American Journal of Psychiatry* 144 (1987): 578-83.

Briere, J. & Runtz, M. "Childhood Sexual Abuse: Long-Term Sequelae and Implications for Psychological Assessment." *Journal of Interpersonal Violence* 8 (1993): 312-30.
Briggs, A. *Circumcision: What Every Parent Should Know.* Earlysville, VA: Birth and Parenting Publications, 1985.
British Medical Association. *Medicine Betrayed.* London: Zed Books, 1992.
Brodbar-Nemzer, J., Conrad, P., & Tenanbaum, S. "American Circumcision Practices and Social Reality." *Sociology and Social Research* 71 (1987): 275-9.
Brody, L., Zelazo, P., & Chaika, H. "Habituation-Dishabituation to Speech in the Neonate." *Developmental Psychology* 20 (1984): 114-9.
Brooks, T. Quoted in R. Romberg, *Circumcision: the Painful Dilemma.* South Hadley, MA: Bergin & Garvey, 1985.
Brown, M. & Brown, C. "Circumcision Decision: Prominence of Social Concerns." *Pediatrics* 80 (1987): 215-9.
Browne, A. & Finkelhor, D. "Impact of Child Sexual Abuse: A Review of the Research." *Psychological Bulletin* 99 (1986): 66-77.
Bryant, B. "An Index of Empathy for Children and Adolescents." *Child Development* 53 (1982): 413-25.
Burgess, A. & Holmstrom, L. "Adaptive Strategies and Recovery from Rape." *American Journal of Psychiatry* 136 (1979): 1278-82.
Bushnell, I., Sai, F., & Mullin, J. "Neonatal Recognition of the Mother's Face." *British Journal of Developmental Psychology* 7 (1989): 3-15.
Butler, A., Hokanson, J., & Flynn, H. "A Comparison of Self-Esteem Lability and Low Trait Self-Esteem as Vulnerability Factors for Depression." *Journal of Personality and Social Psychology* 66 (1994): 166-77.
Butler, N. "How to Raise Professional Awareness of the Need for Adequate Pain Relief for Infants." *Birth* 15 (March 1988): 39.
Butterworth, G. & Hopkins, B. "Hand-Mouth Coordination in the Newborn Baby." *British Journal of Developmental Psychology* 6 (1988): 303-14.
Calkins, S. & Fox, N. "The Relations among Infant Temperament, Security of Attachment, and Behavioral Inhibition at Twenty-Four Months." *Child Development* 63 (1992): 1456-72.
Campbell, S. "Mother-Infant Interaction as a Function of Maternal Ratings of Temperament." *Child Psychiatry and Human Development* 10 (1979): 67-76.
Campbell, S., Breaux, A., Ewing, L., & Szumowski, E. "Correlates and Predictors of Hyperactivity and Aggression: A Longitudinal Study of Parent-Referred Problem Preschoolers." *Journal of Abnormal Child Psychology* 14 (1986): 217-34.
Canetto, S. "Gender Issues in the Treatment of Suicidal Individuals." *Death Studies* 18 (1994): 513-27.
Cansever, G. "Psychological Effects of Circumcision." *British Journal of Medical Psychology* 38 (1965): 321-31.
Carmen, E., Ricker, P., & Mills, T. "Victims of Violence and Psychiatric Illness." *American Journal of Psychiatry* 141 (1984): 378-83.

Cassell, Z. & Sander, L. "Neonatal Recognition Processes and Attachment: The Masking Experiment." Paper presented to the Society for Research in Child Development, Denver, CO, 1975.

Castillo, M & Butterworth, G. "Neonatal Localization of a Sound in Visual Space." *Perception* 10 (1981): 331-8.

Chamberlain, D. "The Significance of Birth Memories." *Pre and Perinatal Psychology Journal* 2 (1988): 208-26.

Chamberlain, D. *Babies Remember Birth.* New York: Ballantine, 1988.

Chamberlain, D. "Babies Remember Pain." *Pre and Perinatal Psychology Journal* 3 (1989): 297-310.

Cheek, D. "Sequential Head and Shoulder Movements Appearing in Age Regression in Hypnosis to Birth." *American Journal of Clinical Hypnosis* 16 (1974): 261-6.

Cheek, D. "Maladjustment Patterns Apparently Related to Imprinting at Birth." *American Journal of Clinical Hypnosis* 18 (1975): 75-82.

Christensen-Szalanski, J., Boyce, W., Harrell, H., & Gardner, M. "Circumcision and Informed Consent: Is More Information Always Better?" *Medical Care* 25 (1987): 856-67.

Chu, J. & Dill, D. "Dissociative Symptoms in Relation to Childhood Physical and Sexual Abuse." *American Journal of Psychiatry* 147 (1990): 887-92.

Ciaranello, R. "Neurochemical Aspects of Stress." In N. Garmezy & M. Rutter, eds., *Stress, Coping, and Development.* New York: McGraw Hill, 1983.

Clarke-Stewart, K. "Infant Day Care: Maligned or Malignant?" *American Psychologist* 44 (1989): 266-73.

Clarke-Stewart, K. & Hevey, C. "Longitudinal Relations in Repeated Observations of Mother-Child Interaction from One to Two and One-Half Years." *Developmental Psychology* 17 (1981): 127-45.

Clarkson, M. & Berg, W. "Cardiac Orienting and Vowel Discrimination in Newborns: Crucial Stimulus Parameters." *Child Development* 48 (1983): 1666-70.

Coe, C., Mendoza, S., Smotherman, W., & Levine, S. "Mother-Infant Attachment in the Squirrel Monkey: Adrenal Response to Separation." *Behavioral Biology* 22 (1978): 256-263.

Cogen, R. & Steinman, W. "Sexual Function and Practice in Elderly Men of Lower Socioeconomic Status." *Journal of Family Practice* 31 (1990): 162-6.

Condon, W. & Sander, L. "Synchrony Demonstrated between Movements of the Neonate and Adult Speech." *Child Development* 45 (1974): 456-62.

Connelly, K., Shropshire, L., & Salzberg, A. "Gastric Rupture Associated with Prolonged Crying in a Newborn Undergoing Circumcision." *Clinical Pediatrics* 31 (1992): 560-1.

Cookson, H. "Personality Variables Associated with Alcohol Use in Young Offenders." *Personality and Individual Differences* 16 (1994): 179-82.

Cooper, R., & Aslin, R. "Preference for Infant-Directed Speech in the First Month after Birth. *Child Development* 61 (1990): 1584-95.

Court, C., Roberts, J., Essex, C., Mudur, M., Dorozynski, A., Wilcox, E., & Siegel-Itzkovich. "Cot Deaths (Global Survey)." *British Medical Journal* 310 (1995): 7.

Courtois, C. "The Incest Experience and Its Aftermath." *Victimology: An International Journal* 4 (1979): 337-47.

Cowley, G. "The Hunt for a Breast Cancer Gene." *Newsweek,* 6 December 1993, 46-52.

Craig, K., Hadjistavropoulos, H., & Grunau, R. "A Comparison of Two Measures of Facial Activity during Pain in the Newborn Child." *Journal of Pediatric Psychology* 19 (1994): 305-18.

Craig, K., Whitfield, M., Grunau, R., & Linton, J. "Pain in the Preterm Neonate: Behavioral and Physiological Indices." *Pain* 52 (1993): 287-99.

Crandon, A. "Maternal Anxiety and Neonatal Wellbeing." *Journal of Psychosomatic Research* 23 (1979): 113-5.

Crudden, C. "Reactions of Newborn Infants to Thermal Stimuli under Constant Tactual Conditions." *Journal of Experimental Psychology* 20 (1937): 350-70.

Davis-Floyd, R. "The Role of Obstetrical Rituals in the Resolution of Cultural Anomaly." *Social Science and Medicine* 31 (1990): 175-89.

DeCasper, A. & Carstens, A. "Contingencies of Stimulation: Effects on Learning and Emotion in Neonates." *Infant Behavior and Development* 4 (1981): 19-35.

DeCasper, A. & Fifer, W. "Of Human Bonding: Newborns Prefer Their Mothers' Voices." *Science* 208 (1980): 1174-6.

DeCasper, A. & Prescott, P. "Human Newborns' Perception of Male Voices: Preference, Discrimination, and Reinforcing Value." *Developmental Psychobiology* 17 (1984): 481-91.

DeCasper, A. & Spence, M. "Prenatal Maternal Speech Influences Human Newborn's Auditory Preferences." Paper presented at 3rd Biennial International Conference on Infant Studies, Austin, TX, 1982.

Delaney, L. "When to Say 'Wait' When Your Doctor Says 'Cut.'" *Prevention 43* (September 1991): 44.

de Leo, D., Predieri, M., Melodia, C., & Vella, J. "Suicide Attitude in Breast Cancer Patients." *Psychopathology* 24 (1991): 115-9.

deMause L. "The Universality of Incest." *Journal of Psychohistory* 19 (1991): 123-64.

DeMeo, J. "The Geography of Genital Mutilations." *The Truth Seeker,* July/August 1989, 9-13.

Denniston, G. "First, Do No Harm." *The Truth Seeker,* July/August 1989, 35-8.

Denniston, G. Letter to the editor on circumcision. *The Female Patient* 17 (1992): 10.

Denniston, G. "Unnecessary Circumcision." *The Female Patient* 17 (1992): 13-4.

Desor, J., Maller, O., & Andrews, K. "Ingestive Responses of Newborns to Salty, Sour, and Bitter Stimuli." *Journal of Comparative and Physiological Psychology* 89 (1975): 966-70.

Devore, I. & Konner, M. "Infancy in a Hunter-Gatherer Life: An Ethological Perspective." In N. White, ed., *Ethology and Psychiatry*. Toronto, Canada: University of Toronto Press, 1974.

DeYoung, M. *The Sexual Victimization of Children.* Jefferson, NC: McFarland, 1982.

DHHS. Publication NIH 85-23, *Guide for the Care and Use of Laboratory Animals,* 1985.

Dirie, M. & Lindmark, G. "Female Circumcision in Somalia and Women's Motives." *Acta Obstetricia Et Gynecologica Scandinavica* 70 (1991): 581-5.

Ditman, J. "Circumcision Plight," letter to the editor. *Mensa Bulletin,* March 1993.

Dixon, S., Snyder, J., Holve, R., & Bromberger, P. "Behavioral Effects of Circumcision with and without Anesthesia." *Journal of Development and Behavioral Pediatrics* 5 (1984): 246-50.

Donovan, W. "Maternal Learned Helplessness and Physiologic Response to Infant Crying." *Journal of Personality and Social Psychology* 40 (1981): 919-26.

Donovan, W. & Leavitt, L. "Physiologic Assessment of Mother-Infant Attachment." *Journal of the American Academy of Child Psychiatry* 24 (1985): 65-70.

Dosser, D., Balswick, J., & Halverson, C. "Male Inexpressiveness and Relationships." *Journal of Social and Personal Relationships* 3 (1986): 241-58.

Dowling, S. "Dreams and Dreaming in Relation to Trauma in Childhood." *International Journal of Psychoanalysis* 63 (1982): 157-66.

Duff, C. & Wells, K. "Forget Cars, Sports or Sex: Guys Today Want to Talk PCs." *Wall Street Journal,* 28 January 1994.

Eagly, A. & Telaak, K. "Width of the Latitude of Acceptance as a Determinant of Attitude Change." *Journal of Personal and Social Psychology* 23 (1972): 388-97.

Ebomoyi, E. "Prevalence of Female Circumcision in Two Nigerian Communities." *Sex Roles* 17 (1987): 139-51.

Edell, D. Television news report on circumcision. KGO, San Francisco, 1984.

Editor, "Routine Circumcision at Birth?" *Journal of the American Medical Association* 91 (1928): 201.

Eich, J. "The Cue Dependent Nature of State Dependent Retrieval." *Memory and Cognition* 8 (1980): 157-68.

Eisenberg, R. & Marmarou, A. "Behavioral Reactions of Newborns to Speech-Like Sounds and Their Implications for Developmental Studies." *Infant Mental Health Journal* 2 (1981): 129-38.

Eland, J. "Pain in Children Misunderstood: State of Management 'Shocking.'" *Pediatric News* 20 (August 1986): 1.

Eland, J. & Anderson, J. "The Experience of Pain in Children." In A. Jacox, ed., *Pain: A Source Book for Nurses and Other Health Professionals.* Boston: Little, Brown, 1977, 453-73.

Else, L., Wonderlich, S., & Beatty, W. "Personality Characteristics of Men Who Physically Abuse Women." *Hospital and Community Psychiatry* 44 (1993): 54-8.

Emerson, W. "Psychotherapy with Infants and Children." *Pre and Perinatal Psychology Journal* 3 (1989): 190-217.

Engel, B. *The Right to Innocence*. Los Angeles: J.P. Tarcher, 1989.

Erickson, J. *Making America Safe for Foreskins*, 1992. (Available from author, 1664 Beach Blvd. #216, Biloxi, MS 39531)

Erikson, E. *Childhood and Society*. New York: Norton, 1963.

Errard, C. "Long-Term Memory Involved in Nestmate Recognition in Ants." *Animal Behavior* 48 (1994): 263-71.

Fantz, R. "Pattern Vision in Newborn Infants." *Science* 140 (1963): 296-7.

Federal Bureau of Investigation, U.S. Department of Justice, *Crime in the United States: Uniform Crime Reports 1993*. Washington, DC, 1994.

Feher, L. *The Psychology of Birth*. New York: Continuum, 1980.

Feher, L. "Birth Conditions and the Adult Personality." *Birth Psychology Bulletin* 10 (1989): 108.

Feldman, H., Goldstein, I., Hatzichristou, D., Krane, R., & McKinlay, J. "Impotence and Its Medical and Psychosocial Correlates: Results of the Massachusetts Male Aging Study." *Journal of Urology* 151 (1994): 54-61.

Felshman, J. "The Foreskin Flap: Is Circumcision Really Worth It?" *Chicago Reader*, 10 March 1995, 17.

Fernando, B., Leeves, L., Greenacre, J., & Roberts, G. "Audit of the Relationship between Episiotomy and Risk of Major Perineal Laceration during Childbirth." *British Journal of Clinical Practitioners* 49 (1995): 40-1.

Festinger, L. & Carlsmith, J. "Cognitive Consequences of Forced Compliance." *Journal of Abnormal and Social Psychology* 58 (1959): 203-10.

Field, T. "Attachment as Psychobiological Attunement: Being on the Same Wavelength." In T. Field & M. Reite, eds., *The Psychobiology of Attachment and Separation*. Academic Press: Orlando, FL, 1985.

Field, T. "Models for Reactive and Chronic Depression in Infancy." *New Directions for Child Development* 34 (1986): 47-60.

Field, T. "Alleviating Stress in Newborn Infants in the Intensive Care Unit." *Clinics in Perinatology* 17 (1990): 1-9.

Field, T., Woodson, R., Greenberg, R., & Cohen, D. "Discrimination and Imitation of Facial Expressions by Neonates." *Science* 218 (1982): 179-81.

Finkelhor, D. *Child Sexual Abuse: New Theory and Research*. New York: Free Press, 1984.

Finkelhor, D. *A Sourcebook on Child Sexual Abuse: New Theory and Research*. Beverly Hills, CA: Sage, 1986.

Finkelhor, D. & Browne, A. "The Traumatic Impact of Child Sexual Abuse: A Conceptualization." *American Journal of Orthopsychiatry* 55 (1985): 530-41.

Fishbein, H. *Evolution, Development, and Children's Learning*. Santa Monica, CA: Goodyear, 1976.

Fitzgerald, J. "A Developmental Account of Early Childhood Amnesia." *Journal of Genetic Psychology* 152 (1991): 159-71.

Fitzsimmons, S., Evans, M., Pearce, C., Sheridan, M., Wientzen, R., & Cole, M. "Immunoglobulin A Subclasses in Infants' Saliva and in Saliva and Milk from Their Mothers." *Journal of Pediatrics* 124 (1994): 566-73.

Flannery, R. "From Victim to Survivor: A Stress Management Approach in the Treatment of Learned Helplessness." In B. van der Kolk, *Psychological Trauma.* Washington, DC: American Psychiatric Press, 1987.

Fleiss, P. "Circumcision," letter to the editor. *The Lancet* 345 (1995): 927.

Fletcher, A. "Pain in the Neonate," editorial. *New England Journal of Medicine* 17 (1987): 1347-8.

Fodor, N. *The Search for the Beloved.* New York: University Books, 1949.

Foley, J. "The Unkindest Cut of All." *Fact,* July 1966.

Foreman, J. "It Helps to Prepare for Surgery." *Boston Globe,* 29 April 1996, 25.

Freedman, J. "Involvement, Discrepancy, and Change." *Journal of Abnormal and Social Psychology* 64 (1964): 290-5.

Freud, S. *Psychopathology of Everyday Life.* In A. Brill, ed. and trans., *The Basic Writings of Sigmund Freud.* New York: Modern Library, 1938.

Freud, S. *Introductory Lectures on Psychoanalysis.* J. Strachey, ed. and trans. 1920. Reprint, New York: Norton, 1966.

Friedman, E. & Neff, R. *Labor and Delivery: Impact on Offspring.* Littleton, MA: PSG Publishing, 1987.

Friedmann, L. *The Psychological Rehabilitation of the Amputee.* Springfield, IL: Charles C. Thomas, 1978.

Frodi, A. & Lamb, M. "Sex Differences in Responsiveness to Infants: A Developmental Study of Psychophysical and Behavioral Responses." *Child Development* 49 (1978): 1182-8.

Gagnon, J., ed. *Human Sexuality in Today's World.* Boston: Little, Brown, 1977.

Gagnon, J. & Simon, W. "The Sexual Scripting of Oral Genital Contacts." *Archives of Sexual Behavior* 16 (1987): 1-25.

Ganiats, T., Humphrey, J., Taras, H., & Kaplan, R. "Routine Neonatal Circumcision: A Cost-Utility Analysis." *Medical Decision Making* 11 (1991): 282-93.

Gee, W. & Ansell, J. "Neonatal Circumcision: A Ten Year Overview with Comparison of the Gomco Clamp and the Plastibell Device." *Pediatrics* 58 (1976): 824-7.

Gelles, R. "Family Violence." *Annual Review of Sociology* 11 (1985): 347-67.

Gelles, R. "Child Abuse and Violence in Single-Parent Families: Parent Absence and Economic Deprivation." *American Journal of Orthopsychiatry* 59 (1989): 492-501.

Gelles, R. "Poverty and Violence toward Children." *American Behavioral Scientist* 35 (1992): 258-74.

Gerald, H., Wilhelm, R., & Conolley, E. "Conformity and Group Size." *Journal of Personality and Social Psychology* 8 (1968): 79-82.

Giller, B. "All in the Family: Violence in the Jewish Home." *Women & Therapy* 10 (1990): 101-9.

Gillespie, W. "The Psycho-Analytic Theory of Sexual Deviation with Special Reference to Fetishism." In I. Rosen, ed., *The Psychology and Treatment of Sexual Deviation.* New York: Oxford University Press, 1964.

Gilmore, D. *Manhood in the Making: Cultural Concepts of Masculinity.* New Haven, CT: Yale University Press, 1990.

Glenn, N. "Television Watching, Newspaper Reading, and Cohort Differences in Verbal Ability." *Sociology of Education* 67 (1994): 216-30.

Glod, C. "Long-Term Consequences of Childhood Physical and Sexual Abuse." *Archives of Psychiatric Nursing* 7 (1993): 163-73.

Glover, H. "Emotional Numbing: A Possible Endorphin-Mediated Phenomenon Associated with Post-Traumatic Stress Disorders and Other Allied Psychopathologic States." *Journal of Traumatic Stress* 5 (1992): 643-75.

Godard, R. "Long-Term Memory of Individual Neighbors in a Migratory Songbird." *Nature* 350 (1991): 228-9.

Gold, E. "Long-Term Effects of Sexual Victimization in Childhood: An Attributional Approach." *Journal of Consulting and Clinical Psychology* 54 (1986): 471-5.

Gold, S., Fultz, J., Burke, C., & Prisco, A. "Vicarious Emotional Responses of Macho College Males." *Journal of Interpersonal Violence* 7 (1992): 165-74.

Goldman, R. Letter to the editor. *Pediatrics* 91 (1993): 1215.

Goleman, D. *Vital Lies, Simple Truths.* New York: Simon & Schuster, 1985.

Goody, E. "Why Must Might Be Right? Observations on Sexual Herrshaft." *Quarterly Newsletter of the Laboratory of Comparative Human Cognition* 9 (1987): 55-76.

Goren, C., Sarty, M., & Wu, P. "Visual Following and Pattern Discrimination of Facelike Stimuli by Newborn Infants." *Pediatrics* 56 (1975): 544-9.

Gorman, L., Shook, B., & Becker, D. "Traumatic Brain Injury Produces Impairments in Long-Term and Recent Memory." *Brain Research* 614 (1993): 29-36.

Gottman, J. *What Predicts Divorce? The Relationship between Marital Processes and Marital Outcomes.* Hillsdale, NJ: Lawrence Erlbaum Associates, 1994.

Gottman, J. & Levenson, R. "The Social Psychophysiology of Marriage." In P. Noller & M. Fitzpatrick, eds., *Perspectives on Marital Interaction.* Clevedon, England: Multilingual Matters Ltd., 1988.

Graham, S. *A Lecture to Young Men on Chastity, Intended also for the Serious Consideration of Parents and Guardians.* 10th ed. Boston: C. H. Pierce, 1848.

Graham, S., Catanzarite, V., & Bernstein, J. "A Comparison of Attitudes and Practices of Episiotomy among Obstetrical Practitioners in New Mexico." *Social Science and Medicine* 31 (1990): 191-201.

Green, A. "Dimensions of Psychological Trauma in Abused Children." *Journal of the American Association of Child Psychiatry* 22 (1983): 231-7.

Griffin, S. *Rape: The All-American Crime.* Andover, MA: Warner Modular Publications, 1973.

Grof, S. *The Adventure of Self-Discovery.* Albany: State University of NY Press, 1988.

Groth, N. *Men Who Rape.* New York: Plenum Press, 1979.

Grunau, R. & Craig, K. "Pain Expression in Neonates: Facial Action and Cry." *Pain* 28 (1987): 395-410.

Grunau, R., Johnston, C., & Craig, K. "Neonatal Facial and Cry Responses to Invasive and Non-Invasive Procedures." *Pain* 42 (1990): 295-305.

278   *Bibliography*

Gunnar, M., Connors, J., Isensee, J., & Wall, L. "Adrenocortical Activity and Behavioral Distress in Human Newborns." *Developmental Psychobiology* 21 (1988): 297-310.

Gunnar, M., Fisch, R., & Malone, S. "The Effects of a Pacifying Stimulus on Behavioral and Adrenocortical Responses to Circumcision in the Newborn." *Journal of the American Academy of Child Psychiatry* 23 (1984): 34-8.

Gunnar, M., Malone, S., Vance, G., & Fisch, R. "Coping with Aversive Stimulation in the Neonatal Period: Quiet Sleep and Plasma Cortisol Levels during Recovery from Circumcision." *Child Development* 56 (1985): 824-34.

Haire, D. *The Pregnant Patient's Bill of Rights*, pamphlet. Minneapolis, MN: International Childbirth Education Association, 1975.

Haller, Jr., J. & Haller, R. *The Physician and Sexuality in Victorian America.* New York: Norton, 1974.

Hamilton, M. & Yee, J. "Rape Knowledge and Propensity to Rape." *Journal of Research in Personality* 24 (1990): 111-22.

Hammer, E. & Glueck, B., Jr. "Psychodynamic Patterns in Sex Offense: A Four-Factor Theory." *Psychiatric Quarterly* 3 (1957): 325-45.

Hammond, T. *Awakenings: A Preliminary Poll of Circumcised Males*, 1994. (Available from National Organization to Halt the Abuse and Routine Mutilation of Males, P.O. Box 460795, San Francisco, CA 94146)

Hanson, R. "The Psychological Impact of Sexual Assault on Women and Children: A Review." *Annals of Sex Research* 3 (1990): 187-232.

Hansson, R. & Jones, W. "Loneliness, Cooperation, and Conformity among American Undergraduates." *Journal of Social Psychology* 115 (1981): 103-8.

Harlow, H., Gluck, J., & Soumi, S. "Generalization of Behavioral Data between Nonhuman and Human Animals," *American Psychologist* 27 (1972): 709-16.

Hartman, C. & Burgess, A. "Information Processing of Trauma." *Child Abuse and Neglect* 17 (1993): 47-58.

Haas, J. & Shaffir, W. "The Cloak of Competence." In J. Henslin, ed., *Down to Earth Sociology*. New York: Free Press, 1993, 432-41.

Hayward, J. & Varela, F., eds. *Gentle Bridges: Conversations with the Dalai Lama on the Sciences of Mind.* Boston: Shambhala, 1992.

Hepper, P. "An Examination of Fetal Learning Before and after Birth." *Irish Journal of Psychology* 12 (1991): 95-107.

Herman, J. *Trauma and Recovery*. New York: Basic Books, 1992.

Herrera, A. Letter to the editor. *Pediatrics* 71 (1983): 670.

Herrera, A., Cochran, B., Herrera, A., & Wallace, B. "Parental Information and Circumcision in Highly Motivated Couples with Higher Education." *Pediatrics* 71 (1983): 233-4.

Hersher, L., Moore, A., & Richmond, J. "Effect of Post-Partum Separation of Mother and Kid on Maternal Care in the Domestic Goat." *Science* 128 (1958): 1342.

Higbee, K. "Fifteen Years of Fear Arousal: Research on Threat Appeals, 1953-1968." *Psychological Bulletin* 72 (1969): 426-44.

Hill, S. & Smith, J. "Neonatal Responsiveness as a Function of Maternal Contact and Obstetrical Drugs." *Perceptual and Motor Skills* 58 (1984): 859-66.

Hinde, R. "Mother-Infant Separation in Rhesus Monkeys." *Journal of Psychosomatic Research* 16 (1972): 227-8.

Hinde, R. *Towards Understanding Relationships*. London: Academic Press, 1979.

Hite, S. *Women and Love: A Cultural Revolution in Progress*. New York: Knopf, 1987.

Hoffman, M. "Developmental Synthesis of Affect and Cognition and Its Implications for Altruistic Motivation." *Developmental Psychology* 11 (1975): 607-22.

Hoffman, M. "Is Altruism Part of Human Nature?" *Journal of Personality and Social Psychology* 40 (1981): 121-37.

Hofsten, C. Von. "Eye-Hand Coordination in the Newborn." *Developmental Psychology* 18 (1982): 450-61.

Holleb, A. Editorial comment. *Ca—A Cancer Journal for Clinicians* 39 (1989): 127.

Hollenbeck, A., Susman, E., Nannis, E., Strope, B., Hersh, S., Levine, A., & Pizzo, P. "Children with Serious Illness: Behavioral Correlates of Separation and Isolation." *Child Psychiatry and Human Development* 11 (1980): 3-11.

Hosken, F. *The Hosken Report*. Lexington, MA: Women's International Network News, 1993.

Howard, C., Howard, F., & Weitzman, M. "Acetaminophen Analgesis in Neonatal Circumcision: The Effect on Pain." *Pediatrics* 93 (1994): 641-6.

Hsieh, C. & Pugh, M. "Poverty, Income Inequality, and Violent Crime: A Meta-Analysis of Recent Aggregate Data Studies." *Criminal Justice Review* 18 (1993): 182-202.

Huesmann, L., Eron, L., & Lefkowitz, M. "Stability of Aggression over Time and Generations." *Developmental Psychology* 20 (1984): 1120-34.

Hunt, J. & Uzgiris, I. "Cathexis from Recognitive Familiarity: An Exploratory Study." Paper presented at the American Psychological Association Convention, Los Angeles, CA, 1964.

Ichiyama, M., Colbert, D., Laramore, H., & Heim, M. "Self-Concealment and Correlates of Adjustment in College Students." *Journal of College Student Psychotherapy* 7 (1993): 55-68.

Isenberg, S. & Elting, L. "A Guide to Sexual Surgery." *Cosmopolitan* 181 (November 1976): 104-8.

Izard, C., Haynes, O., Chisholm, G., & Baak, K. "Emotional Determinants of Infant-Mother Attachment." *Child Development* 62 (1991): 906-17.

Jackson, J. & Cochran, S. "Loneliness and Psychological Distress." *Journal of Psychology* 125 (1991): 257-62.

Jacobson, B., Eklund, G., Hamberger, L., & Linnarsson, D. "Perinatal Origin of Adult Self Destructive Behavior." *Acta Psychiatrica Scandinavia* 76 (1987): 364-71.

Jacobson, B., Nyberg, K., Eklund, G., et al. "Obstetric Pain Medication and Eventual Adult Amphetamine Addition in Offspring." *Acta Obstetricia et Gynecologica Scandinavica* 67 (1988): 677-82.

Jacobson, B., Nyberg, K., Gronbladh, L., et al. "Opiate Addition in Adult
    Offspring through Possible Imprinting after Obstetrical Treatment." *British
    Medical Journal* 301 (1990): 1067-70.
Janov, A. *The Primal Scream.* New York: Dell Publishing, 1970.
Janov, A. *Imprints: The Lifelong Effects of the Birth Experience.* New York:
    Coward-McCann, 1983.
Janov, A. *The New Primal Scream: Primal Therapy 20 Years On.* Wilmington,
    DE: Enterprise Publishing, 1991.
Jessner, L., Blom, G., & Waldfogel, S. "Emotional Implications of Tonsillectomy
    and Adenoidectomy in Children." *Psychoanalytic Study of the Child* 7
    (1952): 126-69.
Johnson, S., Kurtz, M., Tomlinson, T., & Fleck, L. "Teaching the Process of
    Obtaining Informed Consent to Medical Students." *Academic Medicine* 67
    (1992): 598-600.
Johnson, W., Emde, R., Pannabecker, B. Stenborg, C., & Davis, M. "Maternal
    Perception of Infant Emotion from Birth Through 18 Months." *Infant
    Behavior and Development* 5 (1982): 313-22.
Jones, D. & Reznikoff, M. "Psychosocial Adjustment to a Mastectomy." *Journal
    of Nervous and Mental Disease* 177 (1989): 624-31.
Jones, E. & Nisbett, R. *The Actor and the Observer: Divergent Perceptions of the
    Causes of Behavior.* Morristown, NJ: General Learning, 1971.
Kagan, J. & Moss, H. *Birth to Maturity.* New York: Wiley, 1962.
Kagan, S. & Masden, M. "Rivalry in Anglo-American and Mexican Children of
    Two Ages." *Journal of Personality and Social Psychology* 24 (1972): 214-20.
Kalmuss, D. "The Intergenerational Transmission of Marital Aggression."
    Journal of Marriage and the Family 46 (1984): 11-9.
Kandel, E. "Genes, Nerve Cells, and the Remembrance of Things Past." *Journal
    of Neuropsychiatry and Clinical Neurosciences* 1 (1989): 103-25.
Kandel, E. & Mednick, S. "Perinatal Complications Predict Violent Offending."
    Criminology 29 (1991): 519-29.
Kaplan, G. "Complications of Circumcision." *Urological Clinics of North
    America* 10 (1983): 543-9.
Katz, J. "The Question of Circumcision." *International Surgery* 62 (1977): 490-2.
Kaweblum, Y., Press, S., Kogan, L., Levine, M., & Kaweblum, M. "Circumcision
    Using the Mogen Clamp." *Clinical Pediatrics* 23 (1984): 679-82.
Keating, J. & Brock, T. "Acceptance of Persuasion and the Inhibition of
    Counterargumentation under Various Distraction Tasks." *Journal of
    Experimental Social Psychology* 10 (1974): 301-9.
Kelalis, D., King, L., & Belman, A. *Clinical Pediatric Urology.* Vol. 2.
    Philadelphia: Harcourt Brace Jovanovich, 1992.
Kellaris, J. & Rice, R. "The Influence of Tempo, Loudness, and Gender of
    Listener on Responses to Music." *Psychology and Marketing* 10 (1993): 15-29.
Kellogg, J. *Plain Facts for Old and Young.* Burlington, IA: F. Segner, 1888.
Kempe, R. & Kempe, C. *The Common Secret: Sexual Abuse of Children and
    Adolescents.* New York: W. H. Freeman, 1984.

Kennedy, H. "Trauma in Childhood: Signs and Sequelae as Seen in the Analysis of an Adolescent." *Psychoanalytic Study of the Child* 41 (1986): 209-19.

Kennell, J., Jerauld, R., Wolfe, H., Chesler, D., Kreger, N., McAlpine, W, Steffa, M., & Klaus, M. "Maternal Behavior One Year After Early and Extended Post-Partum Contact." *Developmental Medicine and Child Neurology* 16 (1974): 172-9.

Kennell, J. & Klaus, M. "Early Mother-Infant Contact: Effects on the Mother and the Infant." *Bulletin of the Menninger Clinic* 43 (1979): 69-78.

Kestenbaum, R., Farber, E., & Sroufe, L. "Individual Differences in Empathy among Preschoolers: Relation to Attachment History." *New Directions for Child Development* 44 (1989): 51-64.

Kihlstrom, J. "The Cognitive Unconscious." *Science* 237 (1987): 1445-52.

Kiser, L., Ackerman, B., & Brown, E. "Post-Traumatic Stress Disorder in Young Children: A Reaction to Purported Sexual Abuse." *Journal of the American Academy of Child and Adolescent Psychiatry* 27 (1988): 645-9.

Klein, M. & Stern, L. "Low Birthweight and the Battered Child Syndrome." *American Journal of Diseases of Children* 122 (1971): 15.

Klaus, M. & Klaus, P. *The Amazing Newborn.* New York: Addison-Wesley, 1985.

Klein, C. *Mothers and Sons.* Boston: Houghton Mifflin, 1984.

Klein, M., Kaczorowski, J., Robbins, J., Gauthier, R., Jorgensen, S., & Joshi, A. "Physicians' Beliefs and Behavior during a Randomized Controlled Trial of Episiotomy: Consequences for Women in Their Care." *Canadian Medical Association Journal* 153 (1995): 769-79.

Kleinman, A. *Rethinking Psychiatry.* New York: Free Press, 1988.

Kluge, E. "Female Circumcision: When Medical Ethics Confronts Cultural Values." *Canadian Medical Association Journal* 148 (1993): 288-9.

Kohlberg, L. *The Psychology of Moral Development.* San Francisco: Harper & Row, 1984.

Konner, M. "Maternal Care, Infant Behavior, and Development among the !Kung." in R. Lee & I. Devores, eds., *Kalahari Hunter Gathers.* Cambridge, MA: Harvard University Press, 1976, 218-45.

Korner, A., Gabby, T., & Kraemer, H. "Relation between Prenatal Maternal Blood Pressure and Infant Irritability. *Early Human Development* 4 (1980): 35-9.

Koverola, C. "Psychological Effects of Child Sexual Abuse." In A. Heger & S. Emans, *Evaluation of the Sexually Abused Child.* New York: Oxford University Press, 1992.

Krebs, D. "Empathy and Altruism." *Journal of Personality and Social Psychology* 32 (1975): 1134-46.

Krugman, S. "Trauma in the Family: Perspectives on the Intergenerational Transmission of Violence." In B. van der Kolk, *Psychological Trauma.* Washington, DC: American Psychiatric Press, 1987.

Krupnick, J. & Horowitz, M. "Stress Response Syndromes." *Archives of General Psychiatry* 38 (1981): 428-35.

Kuhn, D., Phelps, E., & Walters, J. "Correlational Reasoning in an Everyday Context." *Journal of Applied Developmental Psychology* 6 (1985): 85-97.

Kulka, R., Schlenger, W., & Fairbank, J. *National Vietnam Veteran Readjustment Study*, executive summary. Research Triangle Park, NC: Research Triangle Institute, 1988.

Kumpf, M. & Gotz-Marchand, B. "Reduction of Cognitive Dissonance as a Function of Magnitude of Dissonance, Differentiation, and Self-Esteem." *European Journal of Social Psychology* 3 (1973): 255-70.

Laibow, R. "Birth Recall: A Clinical Report." *Pre and Perinatal Psychology Journal* 1 (1986): 78-81.

Laibow, R. "Toward a Developmental Nosology Based on Attachment Theory." *Pre and Perinatal Psychology Journal* 3 (1988): 5-24.

Laibow, R. "Circumcision and Its Relationship to Attachment Impairment." In *Syllabus of Abstracts*, the Second International Symposium on Circumcision, 1991.(Available from NOCIRC, P.O. Box 2512, San Anselmo, CA 94960)

Laner, M. "Violence or Its Precipitators: Which Is More Likely to Be Identified as a Dating Problem?" *Deviant Behavior* 11 (1990): 319-29.

Lanzetta, J. & Englis, B. "Expectations of Cooperation and Their Effects on Observers' Vicarious Emotional Responses." *Journal of Personality and Social Psychology* 56 (1989): 543-54.

Larsen, G. & Williams, S. "Postneonatal Circumcision: Population Profile." *Pediatrics* 85 (1990): 808-12.

Latane, B. & Neda, S. "Ten Years of Research on Group Size and Group Helping." *Psychological Bulletin* 89 (1981): 308-24.

Laudenslager, M. "The Psychobiology of Loss: Lessons from Human and Nonhuman Primates." *Journal of Social Issues* 44 (1988): 19-36.

Lazarus, R., Kanner, A., & Folkman, S. "Emotions: A Cognitive-Phenomenological Analysis." In R. Plutchick & H. Kellerman, eds., *Emotion: Theory, Research, and Experience: Vol. 1. Theories of Emotion*. New York: Academic Press, 1980.

Leboyer, F. *Birth Without Violence*. New York: Knopf, 1975.

Lefkowitz, M., Eron, L., Walder, L., & Huesman, L. *Growing Up to Be Violent*. New York: Pergamon, 1977.

Lehman, B. "The Age-Old Question of Circumcision." *Boston Globe*, 22 June 1987, 41.

Leloo, M. "Circumcision: An Unnecessary Trauma?" *Journey*, September 1994, 5.

Lepowsky, M. "Women, Men, and Aggression in an Egalitarian Society." *Sex Roles* 30 (1994): 199-211.

Lester, B. & Boukydis, C., eds., *Infant Crying: Theoretical and Research Perspectives*. New York: Plenum, 1985.

Lester, D. & Abe, K. "The Regional Variation of Divorce Rates in Japan and the United States." *Journal of Divorce and Remarriage* 21 (1993): 227-30.

Letter to the editor, *Playgirl*, March 1974.

Levin, T. "'Unspeakable Atrocities': The Psycho-Sexual Etiology of Female Genital Mutilation." *Journal of Mind and Behavior* 1 (1980): 197-210.

Levine, S., Coe, C., & Smotherman, W. "Prolonged Cortisol Elevation in the Infant Squirrel Monkey after Reunion with Mother." *Physiology and Behavior* 20 (1978): 7-10.

Levine, S., Wiener, S., & Coe, C. "Temporal and Social Factors Influencing Behavioral and Hormonal Responses to Separation in Mother and Infant Squirrel Monkeys." *Psychoneuroendocrinology* 18 (1993): 297-306.

Levy, D. "Psychic Trauma of Operations in Children." *American Journal of Diseases of Children* 69 (1945): 7-25.

Lightfoot-Klein, H. *Prisoners of Ritual.* Binghamton, NY: Harrington Park Press, 1989.

Lightfoot-Klein, H. Rites of Purification and Their Effects: Some Psychological Aspects of Female Genital Circumcision and Infibulation in an Afro-Arab Islamic Society." *Journal of Psychology and Human Sexuality* 2 (1989): 79-91.

Lilienfeld, A. & Graham, S. "Validity of Determining Circumcision Status by Questionnaire as Related to Epidemiological Studies of Cancer of the Cervix." *Journal of the National Cancer Institute* 21 (1958): 715.

Lipsett, L. & Kaye, H. "Conditioned Sucking in the Human Newborn." *Psychonomic Science* 1 (1964): 29-30.

Lipton, S. "On Psychology of Childhood Tonsillectomy." *Psychoanalytic Study of the Child* 17 (1962): 363-417.

Loftus, E. & Loftus, G. "On the Permanence of Stored Information in the Brain." *American Psychologist* 35 (1980): 409-20.

Loss, P. & Glancy, E. "Men Who Sexually Abuse Their Children." *Medical Aspects of Human Sexuality* 17 (1983): 328-9.

Lowenstein, L. "Attitudes and Attitude Differences to Female Genital Mutilation in the Sudan: Is There a Change on the Horizon?" *Acta Ethnographica Academiae Scientiarum Hungaricae* 29 (1980): 216-23.

Lowenstein, L. "Homicide: A Review of Recent Research (1975-1985)." *Criminologist* 13 (1989): 74-89.

Luchins, A. "Focusing on the Object of Judgment in the Social Situation." *Journal of Social Psychology* 60 (1963): 231-49.

Luchock, J. & McCrosky, J. "The Effect of Quality of Evidence on Attitude Change and Source Credibility." *Southern Speech Communication Journal* 43 (1978): 371-83.

Luria, Z. *The Psychology of Human Sexuality.* New York: Wiley, 1979.

Lyons-Ruth, K., Connell, D., Zoll, D., & Stahl, J. "Infants at Social Risk: Relations among Infant Maltreatment, Maternal Behavior, and Infant Attachment Behavior." *Developmental Psychology* 23 (1987): 223-32.

MacFarlane, A. "Olfaction in the Development of Social Preferences in the Human Neonate." In R. Porter & M. O'Connor, eds., *Parent-Infant Interactions,* Ciba Foundation Symposium, 33, (1975): 103-17.

Maguire, K. & Pastore, A., eds., *Sourcebook of Criminal Justice Statistics, 1993.* Washington, DC: U.S. Department of Justice, Bureau of Justice Statistics, 1994.

Maguire, K. & Pastore, A., eds. *Sourcebook of Criminal Justice Statistics, 1994.* Washington, DC: U.S. Department of Justice, Bureau of Justice Statistics, 1995.

Main, M & George, C. "Responses of Abused and Disadvantaged Toddlers to Distress in Agemates: A Study in the Daycare Setting." *Developmental Psychology* 21 (1985): 407-12.

Major, B., Sciacchitano, A., & Crocker, J. "In-Group versus Out-Group Comparisons and Self-Esteem." *Personality and Social Psychology Bulletin* 19 (1993): 711-21.

Malamuth, N. "Rape Proclivity among Males." *Journal of Social Issues* 37 (1981): 138-57.

Malamuth, N., Heim, M., & Feshback, S. "Sexual Responsiveness of College Students to Rape Depictions: Inhibitory and Disinhibitory Effects." *Journal of Personality and Social Psychology* 38 (1980): 399-408.

Malone, S., Gunnar, M., & Fisch, R. "Adrenocortical and Behavioral Responses to Limb Restraint in Human Neonates." *Developmental Psychobiology* 18 (1985): 435-46.

Mansfield, C. & Hueston, W. "Neonatal Circumcision: Associated Factors and Length of Hospital Stay." *Journal of Family Practice* 41 (1995): 370-6.

Margolis, G., Goodman, R., & Rubin, A. "Psychological Effects of Breast-Conserving Cancer Treatment and Mastectomy." *Psychosomatics* 31 (1990): 33-9.

Markessinis, J. *The First Week of Life*. Princeton, NJ: Edcom Systems, 1971.

Marshall, W. "The Role of Attachments, Intimacy, and Loneliness in the Etiology and Maintenance of Sexual Offending." *Sexual and Marital Therapy* 8 (1993): 109-21.

Marshall, R., Stratton, W., Moore, J., & Boxerman, S. "Circumcision: I. Effects upon Newborn Behavior." *Infant Behavior and Development* 3 (1980): 1-14.

Marshall, R., Porter, F., Rogers, A., Moore, J., Anderson, B., & Boxerman, S. "Circumcision: II. Effects upon Mother-Infant Interaction." *Early Human Development* 7 (1982): 367-74.

Martin, G., & Clark, R. "Distress Crying in Neonates: Species and Peer Specificity." *Developmental Psychology* 18 (1982): 3-9.

Maslow, A. *Toward a Psychology of Being*. New York: Van Nostrand, 1968.

Masters, W., Johnson, V., & Kolodny, R. *Sex and Human Loving*. Boston: Little Brown, 1986.

Maurer, D. & Maurer, C. *The World of the Newborn*. New York: Basic Books, 1988.

May, R. *Love and Will*. New York: Norton, 1969.

McCabe, P. & Schneiderman, N. "Psychophysiological Reactions to Stress." In N. Schneiderman & J. Tapp, eds., *Behavioral Medicine: The Biopsychosocial Approach*. Hillsdale, NJ: Erlbaum, 1984.

McDonald, R. "The Role of Emotional Factors in Obstetrical Complications: A Review." *Psychosomatic Medicine* 30 (1968): 222-37.

McGraw, M. *The Neuromuscular Maturation of the Human Infant*. New York: Columbia University Press, 1943.

Melamed, T. "Individual Differences in Romantic Jealousy: The Moderating Effect of Relationship Characteristics." *European Journal of Social Psychology* 21 (1991): 455-61.

Meltzoff, A. & Borton, R. "Intermodal Matching by Human Neonates." *Nature* 282 (1979): 403-4.

Meltzoff, A. & Moore, M. "Newborn Infants Imitate Adult Facial Gestures." *Child Development* 54 (1983): 702-9.

Mendelsohn, R. *Confessions of a Medical Heretic*. Chicago: Contemporary Books, 1979.

Menzel, C. "Cognitive Aspects of Foraging in Japanese Monkeys." *Animal Behavior* 41 (1991): 397-402.

Messer, S. & Lewis, M. "Social Class and Sex Difference in the Attachment and Play Behavior of the Year-Old Infant." *Merrill-Palmer Quarterly* 18 (1972): 295-306.

Michael, R., Gagnon, J., Laumann, E., & Kolata, G. *Sex in America: A Definitive Survey*. Boston: Little Brown, 1994.

Michelsson, K., Raes, J., Thoden, C., & Wasz-Hockert, O. "Sound Spectrographic Cry Analysis in Neonate Diagnostics: An Evaluative Study." *Journal of Phonetics* 10 (1982): 79-88.

Milgram, S. "Behavior Study of Obedience." *Journal of Abnormal and Social Psychology* 67 (1963): 371-8.

Milgram, S. "Group Pressure and Action against a Person." *Journal of Abnormal and Social Psychology* 69 (1964): 137-43.

Milos, M. "Infant Circumcision: 'What I Wish I Had Known.'" *The Truth Seeker,* July/August 1989, 3.

Milos, M. & Macris, D. "Circumcision: A Medical or a Human Rights Issue?" *Journal of Nurse-Midwifery* 37 (Supplement, 1992): 87S-96S.

Milvich, M. *Circumcision: An American Custom*. Snowmass, CO: Author, 1995.

Money, J. & Davison, J. "Adult Penile Circumcision: Erotosexual and Cosmetic Sequelae." *Journal of Sex Research* 19 (1983): 289-92.

Montagu, A. *Sex, Man, and Society*. New York: G. P. Putnam's Sons, 1969.

Montagu, A. *Touching: The Human Significance of the Skin*. New York: Harper & Row, 1971.

Moon, C. & Fifer, W. "Syllables as Signals for 2-Day-Old Infants." *Infant Behavior and Development* 13 (1990): 377-90.

Morgan, W. "The Rape of the Phallus." *Journal of the American Medical Association* 193 (1965): 223-4.

Mosher, D. & Anderson, R. "Macho Personality, Sexual Aggression and Reactions to Guided Imagery of Realistic Rape." *Journal of Research in Personality* 20 (1986): 77-94.

Moss, M., Gidycz, C., & Wisniewski, N. "The Scope of Rape: Incidence and Prevalence of Sexual Aggression and Victimization in a Natural Sample of Higher Education Students." *Journal of Consulting and Clinical Psychology* 55 (1987): 162-70.

Mungas, D. "An Empirical Analysis of Specific Syndromes of Violent Behavior." *Journal of Nervous and Mental Disease* 171 (1983): 354-61.

Murphy, C., Meyer, S., & O'Leary, K. "Dependency Characteristics of Partner Assaultive Men." *Journal of Abnormal Psychology* 103 (1994): 729-35.

Musty, R., Jordon, M., & Lenox, R. "Criterion for Learned Helplessness in the Rat: A Redefinition." *Pharmacology, Biochemistry and Behavior* 36 (1990): 739-44.

National Center for Health Statistics. 6525 Belcrest Rd., Hyattsville, MD 20782 (301)436-8500.

286   *Bibliography*

National Committee for Prevention of Child Abuse. "Think You Know Something about Child Abuse?" brochure. Chicago: Author, 1990.

National SIDS Resource Center. Information Exchange. Vienna, VA: Author, January 1990.

Nelson, E., Hill-Barlow, D., & Benedict, J. "Addiction versus Intimacy as Related to Sexual Involvement in a Relationship." *Journal of Sex and Marital Therapy* 20 (1994): 35-45.

NIH. *Guide for the Care and Use of Laboratory Animals*, Publication 8523. U.S. Dept. of Health and Human Services, 1985.

NOCIRC Newsletter. Letter to the editor. Spring/Summer 1987. (Available from NOCIRC, P.O. Box 2512, San Anselmo, CA 94960)

NOCIRC Newsletter. Fall 1990.

NOCIRC Newsletter. Fall 1994.

Noyes, R. "Depersonalization in Response to Life Threatening Danger." *Comprehensive Psychiatry* 18 (1977): 375-84.

Odujinrin, O., Akitoye, C., & Oyediran, M. "A Study on Female Circumcision in Nigeria." *West Africa Journal of Medicine* 8 (1989): 183-92.

O'Mara, P. *Circumcision: The Rest of the Story.* 1993. (Available from *Mothering*, P.O. Box 1690, Santa Fe, NM 87504)

Orr, L. & Ray, S. *Rebirthing in the New Age.* Millbrae, CA: Celestial Arts, 1977.

Osofsky, J. "Neonatal Characteristics and Mother-Infant Interaction in Two Observational Situations." *Child Development* 47 (1976): 1138-47.

O'Sullivan, C. & Durso, F. "Effect of Schema-Incongruent Information on Memory for Stereotypical Attributes." *Journal of Personality and Social Psychology* 47 (1984): 55-70

Ostwald, P. & Peltzman, P. "The Cry of the Human Infant." *Scientific American* 230 (1974): 85.

Owens, M., & Todt, E. "Pain in Infancy: Neonatal Reaction to a Heel Lance." *Pain* 20 (1984): 77-86.

Ozturk, O. "Ritual Circumcision and Castration Anxiety." *Psychiatry* 36 (1973): 49-60.

Paige, K. "The Ritual of Circumcision." *Human Nature*, May 1978, 42.

Papousek, H. & Papousek, M. "Mothering and the Cognitive Head-Start: Psychobiological Considerations." In H. Schaffer, ed., *Studies in Mother-Infant Interaction* (Chapter 4). London: Academic Press, 1977.

Parsons, M. "The Beginning." Ashbury (NJ) Park Press, 3 February 1996, B1.

Patel, H. "The Problem of Routine Circumcision." *Canadian Medical Association Journal* 95 (1966): 578-81.

Perris, E., Myers, N., & Clifton, R. "Long-Term Memory for a Single Infancy Experience." *Child Development* 61 (1990): 1796-1807.

Peterson, C. & Seligman, M. "Learned Helplessness and Victimization." *Journal of Social Issues* 39 (1983): 103-16.

Pickard-Ginsburg. M. "Jesse's Circumcision." letter, *Mothering*, Spring 1979, 80.

Pietropinto, A. "Male Contributions to Female Sexual Dysfunction." *Medical Aspects of Human Sexuality* 20 (1986): 84-91.

Pitman, R. "Animal Models of Compulsive Behavior." *Biological Psychiatry* 26 (1989): 189-98.

Pollack, M. "Jewish Feminist Perspective." Presentation at the Third International Symposium on Circumcision, College Park, MD, May 1994.

Polluck, J. "Long-Term Associations with Infant Feeding in a Clinically Advantaged Population of Babies." *Developmental Medicine and Child Neurology* 36 (1994): 429-40.

Porter, F., Miller, R., & Marshall, R. "Neonatal Pain Cries: Effect of Circumcision on Acoustic Features and Perceived Urgency." *Child Development* 57 (1986): 790-802.

Postman, N. *Technopoly: The Surrender of Culture to Technology.* New York: Knopf, 1992.

Prechtl, H. & O'Brien, M. "Behavioral States of the Fullterm Newborn." In P. Stratton, ed., *Psychobiology of the Newborn.* New York: Wiley, 1982, 52-73.

Prescott, J. "Genital Pain vs. Genital Pleasure: Why the One and Not the Other?" *The Truth Seeker,* July/August 1989, 14-21.

Prince, J. & Arias, I. "The Role of Perceived Control and the Desirability of Control among Abusive and Nonabusive Husbands." *American Journal of Family Therapy* 22 (1994): 126-34.

Putnam, F. "The Psychophysiologial Investigation of Multiple Personality Disorder." *Psychiatic Clinics of North America* 7 (1984): 31-41.

Pynoos, R. & Eth, S. "Developmental Perspective on Psychic Trauma in Childhood." In C. Figley, ed., *Trauma and Its Wake.* New York: Brunner/Mazel, 1985.

Quinn, S. "The Competence of Babies." *The Atlantic Monthly,* January 1982, 54-62.

Rabinowitz, R. & Hulbert, W. "Newborn Circumcision Should Not Be Performed without Anesthesia." *Birth* 22 (1995): 45-6.

Raine, A., Brennan, P., & Mednick, S. "Birth Complications Combined with Early Maternal Rejection at Age 1 Predispose to Violent Crime at Age 18 Years." *Archives of General Psychiatry* 51 (1994): 984-8.

Raine, A. & Venables, P. "Evoked Potential Augmenting-Reducing in Psychopaths and Criminals with Impaired Smooth-Pursuit Eye Movements." *Psychiatry Research* 31 (1990): 85-98.

Raine, A., Venables, P., & Williams, M. "Autonomic Orienting Responses in 15-Year-Old Male Subjects and Criminal Behavior at Age 24." *American Journal of Psychiatry* 147 (1990): 933-7.

Raisbeck, B. "Circumcision: A Wound Which Lasts a Lifetime." *Healing Currents,* 1993.

Rank, O. *The Trauma of Birth.* 1929. Reprint, New York: Harper & Row, 1973.

Rapaport, K. & Burkhart, B. "Personality and Attitudinal Correlates of Sexual Coercive College Males." *Journal of Abnormal Personality* 93 (1984): 216-21.

Raynor, J. & McFarlin, D. "Motivation and the Self-System." In R. Sorrentino & E. Higgins, eds., *Handbook of Motivation and Cognition: Foundations of Social Behavior.* New York: Guilford, 1986.

Reber, A. *The Penguin Dictionary of Psychology.* New York: Penguin Books, 1985.

Reich, W. *Character Analysis*. 3rd ed. T. Wolfe, trans. New York: Farrar, Strauss and Giroux, 1949.

Reiss, I. "A Sociological Journey into Sexuality." *Journal of Marriage and the Family* 48 (1986): 233-42.

Reiss, I. "Society and Sexuality: A Sociological Theory." In K. McKinney & S. Sprecher, eds., *Human Sexuality: The Societal and Interpersonal Context.* Norwood, NJ: Ablex Publishing, 1989.

Reiss, Jr., A. & Roth, J., eds. National Research Council. *Understanding and Preventing Violence.* Washington, DC: Jossey-Bass, 1993.

Reite, M. & Capitanio J. "Child Abuse: A Comparative and Psychobiological Perspective." Paper presented at the Conference on Biosocial Perspectives on Child Abuse and Neglect, Social Sciences Research Council, May 1984.

Reite, M. & Capitanio, J. "On the Nature of Social Separation and Social Attachment." In T. Field & M. Reite, eds., *The Psychobiology of Separation and Attachment.* New York: Academic Press, 1985.

Richards, M., Bernal, J., & Brackbill, Y. "Early Behavioral Differences: Gender or Circumcision?" *Developmental Psychobiology* 9 (1976): 89-95.

Richardson, D., Hammock, G., & Smith, S. "Empathy as a Cogitive Inhibitor of Interpersonal Aggression." *Aggressive Behavior* 20 (1994): 275-89.

Richardson, L. *The Dynamics of Sex and Gender.* New York: Harper & Row, 1988.

Rickard, N., Ng, K., & Gibbs, M. "A Nitric Oxide Agonist Stimulates Consolidation of Long-Term Memory in the 1-Day-Old Chick." *Behavioral Neuroscience* 108 (1994): 640-4.

Righard, L. & Alade, M. "Effect of Delivery Room Routines on Success of First Breast-Feed." *The Lancet* 336 (1990): 1105-7.

Ringler, N., Trause, M., Klaus, M., & Kennell, J. "The Effects of Extra Postpartum Contact and Maternal Speech Patterns on Children's IQ's, Speech and Language Comprehension at Five." *Child Development* 49 (1978): 862-5.

Ritter, T. *Say No to Circumcision.* Aptos, CA: Hourglass, 1992.

Robertson, S. "Intrinsic Temporal Patterning in the Spontaneous Movement of Awake Neonates." *Child Development* 53 (1982): 1016-21.

Robinson, R. & Frank, D. "The Relation between Self-Esteem, Sexual Activity, and Pregnancy." *Adolescence* 29 (1994): 27-35.

Romberg, R. *Circumcision: The Painful Dilemma.* South Hadley, MA: Bergin & Garvey, 1985.

Romberg, R. "Circumcision Feedback," letter to the editor. *Mensa Bulletin,* May 1993.

Rose, D. "'Worse Than Death': Psychodynamics of Rape Victims and the Need for Psychotherapy." *American Journal of Psychiatry* 143 (1986): 817-24.

Rothbart, M., Ahadi, S., & Hershey, K. "Temperament and Social Behavior in Childhood." *Merrill Palmer Quarterly* 40 (1994): 21-39.

Rowan, A. & Foy, D. "Post-Traumatic Stress Disorder in Child Sexual Abuse: A Literature Review." *Journal of Traumatic Stress* 6 (1993): 3-20.

Rubin, J., Provenzano, F., & Luria, Z. "The Eye of the Beholder: Parents' Views on Sex of Newborns." *American Journal of Orthopsychiatry* 44 (1974): 512-9.

Rubin, Z., Hill, C., Peplau, L., & Dunkel-Schetter, C. "Self-Disclosure in Dating Couples." *Journal of Marriage and the Family* 42 (1980): 305-18.

Rushwan, H. "Female Circumcision." *World Health,* April/May 1990, 24.

Russell, D. *Rape in Marriage.* New York: Macmillan, 1982.

Russell, D. "The Incidence and Prevalence of Intrafamilial and Extrafamilial Sexual Abuse of Female Children." *Child Abuse and Neglect* 7 (1983): 133-46.

Russell, D. & Howell, N. "The Prevalence of Rape in the U.S. Revisited." *Signs* 8 (1983): 688-95.

Rutherford, E. & Mussen, P. "Generosity in Nursery School Boys." *Child Development* 39 (1968): 755-65.

Ryan, C. & Finer, N. "Changing Attitudes and Practices Regarding Local Analgesia for Newborn Circumcision." *Pediatrics* 94 (1994): 230-3.

Sagi, A. & Hoffman, M. "Empathetic Distress in the Newborn." *Developmental Psychology* 12 (1976): 175-6.

Sanday, P. "The Socio-Cultural Context of Rape: A Cross-Cultural Study." *Journal of Social Issues* 37 (1981): 5-27.

Santee, R. & Maslach, C. "To Agree or Not to Agree: Personal Dissent Amid Social Pressure to Conform." *Journal of Personality and Social Psychology* 42 (1982): 690-700.

Sargent, C. "Between Death and Shame: Dimensions of Pain in Bariba Culture." *Social Science and Medicine* 19 (1984): 1299-304.

Schechter, N. "The Undertreatment of Pain in Children: An Overview." *Pediatric Clinics of North America* 36 (1989): 781-94.

Schlereth, T. *Victorian America: Transformations in Everyday Life, 1876-1915.* New York: Harper Collins, 1991.

Schlossberger, N., Turner, R., & Irwin, C. "Early Adolescent Knowledge and Attitudes about Circumcision: Methods and Implications for Research." *Journal of Adolescent Health* 13 (1992): 293-7.

Schmidt, E. & Eldridge, A. "The Attachment Relationship and Child Maltreatment. *Infant Mental Health Journal* 7 (1986): 264-73.

Schoen, E. "The Relationship between Circumcision and Cancer of the Penis." *Ca—A Cancer Journal for Clinicians* 41 (1991): 306-9.

Schwartz, R., Seid, a., & Stool, S. "Tonsillectomy Today: Who Needs It?" *Patient Care* 26 (1992): 173-94.

Scully, D. & Bart, P. "A Funny Thing Happened on the Way to the Orifice: Women in Gynecology Textbooks." In J. Huber, ed., *Changing Women in a Changing Society.* Chicago: University of Chicago Press, 1973, 283-8

Scully, D. & Marolla, J. "Convicted Rapists' Vocabulary of Motive: Excuses and Justifications." *Social Problems* 31 (1984): 530-44.

Scully, D. & Marolla, J. "'Riding the Bull at Gilley's.'" In J. Henslin, ed., *Down to Earth Sociology.* New York: Free Press, 1993.

Seghorn, T., Prentky, R., & Boucher, R. "Childhood Sexual Abuse in the Lives of Sexually Aggressive Offenders." *Journal of the American Academy of Child and Adolescent Psychiatry* 26 (1987): 262-7.

Sepkoski, C., Lester, B., Ostheimer, G., & Brazelton, T. "The Effects of Maternal Epidural Anesthesia on Neonatal Behavior during the First Month." *Developmental Medicine and Child Neurology* 34 (1992): 1072-80.

Shabad, P. "Repetition and Incomplete Mourning: The Intergenerational Transmission of Traumatic Themes." *Psychoanalytic Psychology* 10 (1993): 61-75.

Shahidullah, S. & Hepper, P. "Hearing in the Fetus: Prenatal Detection of Deafness." *International Journal of Prenatal and Perinatal Studies* 4 (1992): 235-40.

Shanberg, S., Field, T., Kuhn, C., & Bartolome, J. "Touch: A Biological Regulator of Growth and Development in the Neonate." *Verhaltenstherapie,* 3(Suppl. 1, 1993): 15.

Sheline, J., Skipper, B., & Broadhead, W. "Risk Factors for Violent Behavior in Elementary School Boys: Have You Hugged Your Child Today?" *American Journal of Public Health* 84 (1994): 661-3.

Sherif, M. "Conformity-Deviation, Norms, and Group Relations." In I. Berg & B. Bass, eds., *Conformity and Deviation.* New York: Harper, 1961, 59-181.

Sherman, M. & Sherman, I. "Sensori-Motor Responses in Infants." *Journal of Comparative Psychology* 5 (1925): 53-68.

Sherrod, K., O'Connor S., Vietze, P., & Altemeier, W. "Child Health and Maltreatment." *Child Development* 55 (1984): 1174-83.

Simkin, P. "Stress, Pain, and Catecholamines in Labor: II. Stress Associated with Childbirth Events: A Pilot Survey of New Mothers." *Birth Issues in Perinatal Care and Education* 13 (1986): 234-40.

Simner, M. "Newborn's Response to the Cry of Another Infant." *Developmental Psychology* 5 (1971): 136-50.

Siqueland, E. & Lipsett, L. "Conditioned Head-Turning in Human Newborns." *Journal of Experimental Child Psychology* 3 (1966): 356-76.

Slater, A., Earle, D., Morison, V., & Rose. "Pattern Preferences at Birth and Their Interaction with Habituation-Induced Novelty Preferences." *Journal of Experimental Child Psychology* 39 (1985): 37-54.

Slater, A. & Findlay, J. "Binocular Fixation in the Newborn Baby." *Journal of Experimental Child Psychology* 20 (1975): 248-73.

Slater, A., Morison, V., & Rose, D. "Locus of Habituation in the Human Newborn." *Perception* 12 (1983): 593-8.

Slater, A., Rose, D., & Morison, V. "Newborn Infants' Perception of Similarities and Differences between Two- and Three Dimensional Stimuli." *British Journal of Developmental Psychology* 2 (1984): 287-94.

Smith, D. & Hackathorn, L. "Some Social and Psychological Factors Related to Suicide in Primitive Societies: A Cross-Cultural Comparative Study." *Suicide and Life Threatening Behavior* 12 (1982): 195-211.

Solkoff, N. & Matuszak, D. "Tactile Stimulation and Behavioral Development among Low-Birthweight Infants." *Child Psychiatry and Human Development* 6 (1975): 33-7.

Solter, A. "Why Do Babies Cry?" *Pre and Perinatal Psychology Journal* 10 (1995): 21-43.

Spangler, G. & Schieche, M. "Biobehavioral Organization in One-Year-Olds: Quality of Mother-Infant Attachment and Immunological and Adrenocortical Regulation." *Psychologische Beitrage* 36 (1994): 30-5.

Spock, B. *The Common Sense Book of Baby and Child Care*. New York: Duell, Sloan, & Pearce, 1946.

Spock, B. Letter to the editor. *Moneysworth*, 29 March 1976, 12.

Spock, B. & Rothenberg, M. *Dr. Spock's Baby and Child Care*. New York: Pocket Books, 1992.

Squire, L. "Mechanisms of Memory." *Science* 232 (1986): 1612-9.

Stang, H., Gunnar, M., Snellman, L., Condon, L., & Kestenbaum, R. "Local Anesthesia for Neonatal Circumcision." *Journal of the American Medical Association* 259 (1988): 1507-11.

Steele, C. & Liu, T. "Dissonance Processes as Self-Affirmation." *Journal of Personality and Social Psychology* 45 (1983): 5-19.

Stein, M., Marx, M., Taggert, S., & Bass, R. "Routine Neonatal Circumcision: The Gap between Contemporary Policy and Practice." *Journal of Family Practice* 15 (1982): 47-53.

Steiner, J. "Human Facial Expressions in Response to Taste and Smell Stimulation." *Advances in Child Development and Behavior* 13 (1979): 257-95.

Stephan, W., Ageyev, V., Coates-Shrider, L. "On the Relationship between Stereotypes and Prejudice: An International Study." *Personality and Social Psychology Bulletin* 20 (1994): 277-84.

Stern, D. *The Interpersonal World of the Infant*. New York: Basic Books, 1985.

Stewart, R. & Beatty, M. "Jealousy and Self-Esteem." *Perceptual and Motor Skills* 60 (1985): 153-4.

Stimson, A., Stimson, J., & Dougherty, W. "Female and Male Sexuality and Self-Esteem." *Journal of Social Psychology* 112 (1980): 157-8.

Stinson, J. "Impotence and Adult Circumcision." *Journal of the National Medical Association* 65 (1973): 161.

Stolbach, D. *If Someone You Care About Has Been Raped*, pamphlet. Cambridge, MA: Boston Area Rape Crisis Center, 1986.

Stoller, R. "Consentual Sadomasochistic Perversions." In H. Blum, E. Weinshel, & F. Rodman, eds., *The Psychoanalytic Core*. New York: International Universities Press, 1989.

Straus, M., Gelles, R. & Steinmetz, S. *Behind Closed Doors: Violence in the American Family*. Garden City, NY: Anchor/Doubleday, 1980.

Summit, R. & Kryso, J. "Sexual Abuse of Children: A Clinical Spectrum." *American Journal of Orthopsychiatry* 48 (1978): 237-51.

Taddio, A., Goldbach, M., Ipp, M., Stevens, B., & Koren, G. "Effect of Neonatal Circumcision on Pain Responses During Vaccination of Boys." *The Lancet* 345 (1995): 291-2.

Taddio, A., Nulman, I., Goldbach, M., Ipp, M., & Koren, G. "The Use of Lidocaine-Prilocaine Cream for Vaccination Pain in Infants." *Journal of Pediatrics* 124 (1994): 643-8.

292 *Bibliography*

Taylor, J., Lockwood, A., & Taylor, A. "The Prepuce: Specialized Mucosa of the Penis and Its Loss to Circumcision." *British Journal of Urology* 77 (1996): 291-95.

Tellis-Nayak, V. & Donoghue, G. "Conjugal Egalitarianism and Violence across Cultures." *Journal of Comparative Family Studies* 13 (1982): 277-90.

Temboury, M., Otero, A., Polanco, I., & Arribas, E. "Influence of Breastfeeding on the Infant's Intellectual Development." *Journal of Pediatric Gastroenterology and Nutrition* 18 (1994): 32-6.

Terr, L. "Children of Chowchilla: A Study of Psychic Trauma." *Psychoanalytic Study of the Child* 34 (1979): 547-623.

Terr, L. "What Happens to Early Memories of Trauma?" *Journal of the American Academy of Child and Adolescent Psychiatry* 27 (1988): 96-104.

Terr, L. *Too Scared to Cry.* New York: Harper & Row, 1990.

Terr, L. "Childhood Traumas: An Outline and Overview." *American Journal of Psychiatry* 148 (1991): 10-20.

Terris, M. & Oalmann, A. "Carcinoma of the Cervix." *Journal of the American Medical Association* 174 (1960): 1847-51.

Thelen, E. & Cooke, D. "Relationship between Newborn Stepping and Later Walking: A New Interpretation." *Developmental Medicine and Child Neurology* 29 (1987): 380-93.

Tilney, F. & Rosett, J. "The Value of Brain Lipoids as an Index of Brain Development." *Bulletin of the Neurological Institute of NY* 1 (1931): 28-71.

Toney, G. & Weaver, J. "Effects of Gender and Gender Roles Self-Perceptions on Affective Reactions to Rock Music Videos." *Sex Roles* 30 (1994): 567-83.

Toubia, N. "Female Circumcision as a Public Health Issue." *New England Journal of Medicine* 331 (1994): 712-6.

Toussieng, P. "Men's Fear of Having Too Small a Penis." *Medical Aspects of Human Sexuality* 11 (1977): 62-70.

Trevarthen, C. "The Psychobiology of Speech Development." *Neuroscience Research Progress Bulletin* 12 (1974): 570-85.

Tully, T., Cambiazo, V., & Kruse, L. "Memory through Metamorphosis in Normal and Mutant Drosophila." *Journal of Neuroscience* 14 (1994): 68-74.

Tulving, E. "How Many Memory Systems Are There?" *American Psychologist* 40 (1985): 385-98.

Ulrich, R. "Pain as a Cause of Aggression." *American Zoologist* 6 (1966): 643-62.

United Nations. *Human Development Report.* New York: Oxford University Press, 1994.

United Nations. *1993 Demographic Yearbook.* New York: Author, 1995.

Unkindest Cut of All, letter to the editor. *Playgirl,* July 1979, 108.

U.S. Department of Commerce. *Statistical Abstract of the U.S.* Lanham, MD: Bernan Press, 1994.

U.S. Department of Justice. *Attorney General's Commission on Pornography, Final Report.* Washington, DC: July 1986.

U.S. Senate Committee on the Judiciary. "Violence against Women: The Increase of Rape in America 1990." *Response to the Victimization of Women and Children* 14 (1991): 20-3.

Vaillant, G. "Natural History of Male Psychological Health: II. Some Antecedents of Healthy Adult Adjustment." *Archives of General Psychiatry* 31 (1974): 15-22.

Vandell, D. "Sociability with Peers and Mothers in the First Year." *Developmental Psychology* 16 (1980): 355-61.

van der Kolk, B. *Psychological Trauma.* Washington, DC: American Psychiatric Press, 1987.

van der Kolk, B. "The Compulsion to Repeat the Trauma: Re-Enactment, Revictimization, and Masochism." *Psychiatric Clinics of North America 12* (1989): 389-411.

van der Kolk, B. "The Biological Response to Psychic Trauma: Mechanisms and Treatment of Intrusion and Numbing." *Anxiety Research* 4 (1991): 199-212.

van der Kolk, B., Perry, J., & Herman, J. "Childhood Origins of Self-Destructive Behavior." *American Journal of Psychiatry* 148 (1991): 1665-71.

Van Heeringen, C., Van Moffaert, M., & De Cuypere, G. "Depression after Surgery for Breast Cancer: Comparison of Mastectomy and Lumpectomy." *Psychotherapy and Psychosomatics* 51 (1990): 175-9.

Van Hof-Van Duin, J. & G. Mohn. "The Development of Visual Acuity in Normal Fullterm and Preterm Infants." *Vision Research* 26 (1986): 909-16.

Vaughn, B., Bradley, C., Joffe, L., Seifer, R., & Barglow, P. "Maternal Characteristics Measured Prenatally Are Predictive of Ratings of Temperamental 'Difficulty' on the Carey Infant Temperament Questionnaire." *Developmental Psychology* 23 (1987): 152-61.

Verny, T. *The Secret Life of the Unborn Child.* New York: Dell Publishing, 1981.

Vinter, A., De Nobili, G., & Pellegrinetti, G. "Auditory-Visual Coordination: Does It Imply an External World for the Newborn?" *Cahiers De Psychologie Cognitive* 4 (1984): 309-21.

Vogt, J. & Levine, S. "Response of Mother and Infant Squirrel Monkeys to Separation and Disturbance." *Physiology and Behavior* 24 (1980): 829-32.

Walco, G., Cassidy, R., & Schechter, N. "Pain, Hurt, and Harm: The Ethics of Pain Control in Infants and Children." *New England Journal of Medicine* 331 (1994): 541-4.

Wallerstein, E. *Circumcision: An American Health Fallacy.* New York: Springer Publishing, 1980.

Wallerstein, E. "Circumcision: The Unique American Medical Enigma." *Urologic Clinics of North America* 12 (1985): 123-32.

Walsh, A. "Self-Esteem and Sexual Behavior: Exploring Gender Differences." *Sex Roles* 25 (1991): 441-50.

Walsh, M. "Circumcision: Should You or Shouldn't You?" *Burlington (VT) Free Press,* 5 February 1995, 1D, 5D.

Walsh, M. "'Part of Our Tribe': Circumcision and Jewish Identity." *Burlington (VT) Free Press,* 5 February 1995, 1D, 5D.

Warren, J. et al., "Circumcision of Children," *British Medical Journal* 312 (1996): 377.

Wasz-Hockert, O., Lind, J., & Vuorenkoski, V. "The Infant Cry: A
    Spectrographic and Auditory Analysis." *Clinical Developmental Medicine* 2
    (1968): 9-42.
Weingartner, H., Miller, H., & Murphy, D. "Mood-State Dependent Retrieval of
    Verbal Associations." *Journal of Abnormal Psychology* 86 (1977): 276-84.
Werner, S. Television news report on circumcision. WSBK Channel 56, Boston,
    MA, August 1993.
Werner, L. & Rubel, E., eds., *Developmental Psychoacoustics*. Washington, DC:
    American Psychological Association, 1992.
White, J. & Koss, M. "Courtship Violence: Incidence in a National Sample of
    Higher Education Students." *Violence and Victims* 6 (1991): 247-56.
Widom, C. & Ames, M. "Criminal Consequences of Childhood Sexual
    Victimization." *Child Abuse and Neglect* 18 (1994): 303-18.
Williamson, M & Williamson, P. "Women's Preferences for Penile Circumcision
    in Sexual Partners." *Journal of Sex Education and Therapy* 14 (1988): 8-12.
Williamson, P. & Williamson, M. "Physiologic Stress Reduction by a Local
    Anesthetic during Newborn Circumcision. *Pediatrics* 71 (1983): 36-40.
Wilson, J. *Trauma, Transformation, and Healing.* New York: Brunner/Mazel, 1989.
Winnicott, D. "Birth Memories, Birth trauma, and Anxiety." In *Through
    Paediatrics to Psycho-Analysis.* New York: Brunner/Mazel, 1992.
Wiswell, T., Smith, F., & Bass, J. "Decreased Incidence of Urinary Tract
    Infections in Circumcised Male Infants." *Pediatrics* 75 (1985): 901-3.
Wiswell, T., Enzenauer, R., Holton, M., Cornish, J., & Hankins, C. "Declining
    Frequency of Circumcision: Implications for Changes in the Absolute
    Incidence and Male to Female Sex Ratio of Urinary Tract Infection in Early
    Infancy." *Pediatrics* 79 (1987): 338-42.
Wollman, L. "Female Circumcision." *Journal of the American Society of
    Psychosomatic Dentistry and Medicine* 20 (1973): 130-1.
Wyatt, G. "The Sexual Abuse of Afro-American and White Women in
    Childhood." *Child Abuse and Neglect* 9 (1985): 507-19.
Yaster, M. "Pain Relief." *Pediatrics* 95 (1995): 427.
Yelsma, P. "Marriage vs. Cohabitation: Couples' Communication Practices and
    Satisfaction." *Journal of Communication* 36 (1986): 94-107.
Young, K. "American Conceptions of Infant Development from 1955 to 1984:
    What the Experts Are Telling Parents." *Child Development* 61 (1990): 17-28.
Youngblade, L. & Belsky, J. "Child Maltreatment, Infant-Parent Attachment
    Security, and Dysfunctional Peer Relationships in Toddlerhood." *Topics in
    Early Childhood Special Education* 9 (1989): 1-15.
Zeskind, P., Sale, J., Maio, M., Huntington, L., & Weiseman, J. "Adult
    Perceptions of Pain and Hunger Cries: A Synchrony of Arousal." *Child
    Development* 56 (1985): 549-54.
Zeskind, P., & Marshall, T. "The Relation between Variations in Pitch and
    Maternal Perceptions of Infant Crying." *Child Development* 59 (1988): 193-6.

Index

child sexual abuse and problems
with, 170
disclosure and, 121
trust and, 132

—**J**—

James, William, 188
Janov, Arthur, 88–90
Jewish circumcision
circumcision debate and, 220–21
observed by other children, 54–
55
*Journal of the American Medical
Association*, 59, 77
Journeymen, 66

—**K**—

Kellogg, John Harvey, 58
King, Stephen, 139, 151
knowledge
circumcised men's lack of (*see*
circumcision decision,
male attitudes toward)
parents' lack of, 29–30
physicians lack of (*see* infants,
physicians' beliefs about
pain of; foreskin, beliefs
about)
Kohlberg, Lawrence, 190
Konia, Charles, 97
Koop, C. Everett, 43

—**L**—

Laibow, Rima, 92, 131
language factors supporting
circumcision, 51–52
learned helplessness. *See* trauma
Leboyer, Frederick, 28
Lewis, Dorothy Otnow, 158
Lightfoot-Klein, Hanny, 71

—**M**—

Marchbanks, Howard, 27
Maslow, Abraham, 46
Massachusetts Men's Gathering,
44, 103
mastectomy, 108, 152
masturbation
circumcision as preventive cure
for, 59
as compulsive behavior, 120
female genital mutilation and, 73
history of, 58–59
use of foreskin during, 39
maternal anxiety, effects on birth,
127–28
maternal responsiveness to infant,
130
Maurer, Charles and Daphne, 77
May, Rollo, 185
McClintock, Barbara, 189
media reports, 3
medical community
lack of open debate in, 188
principles of conduct, 189
as reflection of larger society, 81
medical education, 78, 79
memory, long-term
in infants (*see* perinatal memory)
in other species, 87
Mendelsohn, Robert, 149
Milgram, Stanley, 191
Milos, Marilyn, 23
Money, John, 39
moral reasoning and development,
190–91
Morgan, William, 29
mother-child relationship
interaction in, 128–31, 138
primary importance of, 124
separation and effect on, 125–
26, 128
See also child rearing

ORDER FORM

[ ] QUESTIONING CIRCUMCISION: $17.95
    A JEWISH PERSPECTIVE
    Ronald Goldman, Ph.D.

Like the American cultural practice of circumcision, Jewish circumcision is dependent on the acceptance of cultural myths. Endorsed by five rabbis, this revealing book examines the intellectual, emotional, and ethical conflicts surrounding Jewish circumcision, as well as the religious and historical background of the practice. The appendix includes sample alternative rituals.

> "Thorough, moving, convincing, and of staggering importance.
> I think this book will change Judaism for the better."
> —Michael Koran, Jewish educator

[ ] CIRCUMCISION: THE HIDDEN TRAUMA $26.95
    Ronald Goldman, Ph.D.

Call toll-free 1-888-445-5199 for credit card orders.
For mail orders, please print clearly.

Send me copies of the above titles. (Indicate quantities in brackets.)

Name _____

Address _____ _____

City _____State _____ Zip _____

Daytime Phone _____

Shipping and handling is $4.00 for first copy, $1.00 for each additional copy. Massachusetts residents add 5% sales tax.

Total enclosed $ _____ (US dollars only)

Make checks payable to and send to:

    Vanguard Publications
    P.O. Box 8055
    Boston, MA 02114   (Bulk discounts available.)

If you want us to send information to a friend or colleague, please include his or her name and address.

Prices subject to change without notice. Allow 2–4 weeks for delivery.

5